THE
ST. VALENTINE'S DAY
MASSACRE

but caused me to look a second time, and I saw George Goetz, garbed in a perfectly fitting police uniform.

Goetz enjoyed his costume, and strutted about the house imitating a policeman making a raid. He lowered his voice, talked out of one corner of his mouth, and impersonated several officers he knew, much to Gus' amusement. Goetz had such a good time Gus insisted on trying on the uniform, and since it was too small for him and made him look ridiculous, he took the role of a Keystone cop. Some of the boys came in later in the evening, and George and Gus repeated their show.

Gus rarely came home after that until February 14, 1929 when he and Bob Carey came in about noon. They had little to say, but in a short time sent me out after papers.

Before I got back to the house I ~~knew what had~~ knew what had happened. The sheets were devoted to the massacre that morning.

The papers said the killers wore police uniforms and more than one hinted the police actually had engineered the slaying.

Six of Moran's gang had been wiped out, in addition to a friend of theirs who was not a member of the gang. The killing had occurred at a garage at 2122 North Clark Street.

When I got to the house I threw the papers in Gus' face and ran into my own room. I was too sick with horror to shed tears.

Gus and Carey spent most of the afternoon sitting in front of the windows. They said very little that would give me an inkling of how the mass killing was executed, but naturally in time I got the complete story from hearing Gus, Carey, and Goetz discuss the mistakes that were made.

Bryan Bolton and Jimmie "Swede" Moran had been assigned to watch the garage from a room Swede had rented across the street. The syndicate was well aware that the Moran gang held meetings there, and had instructed the spies to give the "high ball" when Moran and his gang had gathered.

Gus, Carey, and other American boys in the Italian syndicate were staying nearby in the home of Rocco de ~~Grace~~ GRAZIA, who still is in the employ of the syndicate.

While the Italians could plan a "job" with criminal skill,

THE ST. VALENTINE'S DAY MASSACRE

The Untold Story of the Gangland Bloodbath That Brought Down Al Capone

WILLIAM J. HELMER & ARTHUR J. BILEK

Cumberland House
Nashville, Tennessee

Published by
Cumberland House Publishing, Inc.
431 Harding Industrial Drive
Nashville, TN 37211-3160

Cover design: Gore Studio, Inc., Nashville, Tennessee
Text design: John Mitchell

Library of Congress Cataloging-in-Publication Data
Helmer, William J.
    The St. Valentine's Day massacre : the untold story of the gangland bloodbath that brought down Al Capone / William J. Helmer, Arthur J. Bilek.
        p. cm.
    Includes bibliographical references and index.
    ISBN-13: 978-1-58182-329-0 (hardcover, alk. paper)
    ISBN-10: 1-58182-329-0 (hardcover, alk. paper)
    ISBN-13: 978-1-58182-549-7 (paperback, alk. paper)
    ISBN-10: 1-58182-549-8 (paperback, alk. paper)
    1. Organized crime—Illinois—Chicago—History. 2. Mass murder—Illinois—Chicago—History. 3. Mass murder investigation—Illinois—Chicago—History. 4. Prohibition—Illinois—Chicago. 5. Capone, Al, 1899-1947. I. Bilek, Arthur J., 1929- II. Title.
    HV6452.I3H45 2003
    364.1'06077311—dc21

                                                                                          2003013993

Printed in Canada

1 2 3 4 5 6 7—12 11 10 09 08 07 06

CONTENTS

ACKNOWLEDGMENTS

Thanks, first of all, to Georgette Winkeler, whose memoirs helped inspire this project; to J. Edgar Hoover, who kept them buried out of sight in FBI files; and to contemporary newspapers, although they invariably spelled the name Winkler, as used in this book.

Present-day thanks to Ed Baumann, Dan Behnke, Thomas Bohling, Mark Buslik, Janette Calloway, Marian K. Caporusso, Roger Carlson, Mars Eghigian, Marlene Golden (daughter of Jeanette Landesman), George Hagenauer, Dr. Mark Haller, Gordon Herigstad, Fred Inbau, Wayne Johnson, Nathan Kantrowitz, Jeffery King, Richard Lindberg, Robert Lombardo, Mathew Luzi, Lee Lyons, Jeff Maycroft, Abe Marovitz (attorney for the Winklers), Rick Mattix, David Miller, Paul Newey, Jack O'Rourke, Lawrence Raeder, Robert Reader, Chuck Schauer, Paul Siler, Brad Smith, Walter Spirko, Dr. Loyal Tacker, Jeff Thurston, Neal Trickel, Walter Trohan, and Mike Webb, for their generosity in granting interviews or supplying research; with special gratitude to Mario Gomes, Rose Keefe, and Michael Schiltz.

Editor John Mitchell took it from there, for which we thank him and Cumberland House.

MEMORANDUM FOR MR. JOSEPH B. KEENAN,
ACTING ATTORNEY GENERAL

          With reference to your inquiry as to information furnished
by Bryan Bolton concerning the identity of the persons perpetrating the
St. Valentine's Day Massacre in Chicago, Illinois in 1929, you are
advised that Bolton was questioned concerning this offense. Bolton
stated that the persons who actually perpetrated this massacre were
Fred Goetz, Gus Winkler, Fred Burke, Ray Nugent and Bob Carey. Bolton
stated that he personally purchased the Cadillac touring car which was
used in this massacre, having been furnished with the money to make this
purchase by Louis Lipschults. Bolton claims that he purchased this car
from the Cadillac Company on Michigan Avenue in Chicago sometime before
the massacre happened and assumed at the time that he purchased the car
that it was to be used in hauling alcohol. Bolton believes that he used
the name James Martin in purchasing the car. The object of this massacre,
according to Bolton, which was planned by members of the Capone organi-
sation, was for the purpose of eliminating "Bugs" Moran from the bootlegging racket in Chicago. Bolton claims that the plot to perpetrate
this killing was initially developed at a place on Cranberry Lake, six
miles north of Couderay, Wisconsin, where one George operated a resort.
Al Capone, Gus Winkler, George Zeigler, Louis Campagna, Fred Burke, Bill
Pacelli (reported to be an Illinois State Senator) and Dan Saratella are
reported to have been at the resort operated by George on Cranberry Lake
at the time the killing was first planned, this being in October or
November of 1928. Bolton states that Jimmy McCrussen and Jimmy "The Swede"
Moran were selected to watch "Bugs" Moran's garage, since they both knew
Moran by sight, in order to learn his movements.

                              when the killing took place the persons
actually perpetrating therein did not know the identity of each of their
victims but rather than risk the possibility of missing Moran, killed
all of the persons found in the garage.
          RECORDED & INDEXED
          As indicated above, Bolton states that Fred Goetz, Gus Winkler,
Fred Burke, Ray Nugent and Bob Carey were the actual perpetrators of the
Massacre. According to Bolton, Claude Maddox of St. Louis, Tony Capesia
of Chicago and a man known as "Shocker" also of St. Louis, burned the
Cadillac car after the Massacre.

          In discussing this matter, Bolton has informed Special Agents
of this Bureau that at the time of the St. Valentine's Day Massacre,
Chief of Detectives Stege of the Chicago Police Department was on the
payroll of the Capone Syndicate, receiving $5,000 per week, and kept
the members of the syndicate informed as to the whereabouts of Bugs Moran.

          Respectfully,

          John Edgar Hoover,
          Director.

INTRODUCTION

D URING PROHIBITION, CHICAGO'S BEER WARS turned the city into a battleground, secured its reputation as "gangster capital of the world," and laid the foundation for nationally organized crime. The bootlegger bloodshed was greater there than anywhere else, and Americans followed the fighting like an Underworld Series until 1929, when Al Capone, the "Babe Ruth of American gangsters," knocked one out of the ballpark with the St. Valentine's Day Massacre.

The machine-gun murder of seven men by killers dressed as cops became the gangland "crime of the century," and despite the largest reward offered until that time—one hundred thousand dollars in an era when newspapers cost three cents—it defied a police solution. It also long defied a journalistic solution, but after enough evidence pointed to Capone, his guilt was accepted and later embellished in countless histories, biographies, movies, and television specials derived from the same few facts, not all of them correct.

This is the first book to examine the massacre itself, based on new information that revises and often contradicts the popular accounts. The killers' ingenuity was a trademark of Capone's South

Side gang, and because it destroyed his most troublesome North Side rivals, writers have long surmised that the gangster known as "Scarface" ordered the execution-style slayings to gain supremacy in Chicago's underworld.

Evidence now suggests that it was not Capone's intention to exterminate his enemies wholesale, or to order a slaughter that would make him the country's first "Public Enemy Number One," cost his empire countless millions in crackdowns by police, and hasten the repeal of Prohibition. Instead, it was a case of bad timing and worse judgment by a secret crew known to Capone's mostly Italian mob as the "American Boys."

Some of this new information emerged shortly after the massacre but was deftly ignored by law enforcement officials. It began resurfacing in 1935, first in a manuscript written by one gunman's widow and then in a lookout's confession, both long interred by the FBI. J. Edgar Hoover wanted no part of Chicago's political corruption, of organized crime, or of an unsolved mass murder which might distract public attention from the federal government's first "War on Crime" against bank robbers and kidnappers that was making Hoover a national celebrity.

So the director withheld the bureau's information from local and state authorities until a Cook County prosecutor went over his head to the U.S. Justice Department, which "advised" Hoover to share it. He grudgingly did so, in a capsulized version that implicated two important politicians and a high police official, at which point the prosecutor and Chicago police quickly resealed the can of worms before reporters could peek inside. With George "Bugs" Moran's North Side mob dismantled and Capone in Alcatraz for nothing more exciting than income tax evasion, the original accounts would petrify into permanence, as far as history was concerned.

Events surrounding the massacre survive in police department files as the brief statements of officers on the scene, their canvassing of the block, witness accounts of the arrival and departure of the killers, listings of the vehicles in the garage, reports of evidence long since lost, and little else. Investigative work by detectives and the state's attorney's office seems to have vanished. Most of the coroner's inquest that survives sheds light mainly on the then-new science of ballistics and the machine-gun trade in general, but missing are those sessions in which the main witnesses are questioned.

These pages can be partly reconstructed from Chicago newspaper accounts, which otherwise document the dragnet search for other local mobsters and a dozen different police theories, few of which named Capone (who was conveniently living in Florida with an airtight alibi) until no one else was left. Events preceding and following the massacre are included as speculation by the police and newspapers, but their connection with the murders is either tenuous or the product of hindsight.

Besides revising the account of the massacre itself, this book examines the misguided political reform movement that helped Al Capone rise to power as well as the invention of the Thompson submachine gun, its discovery by Chicago's gangsters in 1925, and its introduction to New York in 1928 by the same American Boys who would later use the weapon in the St. Valentine's Day Massacre. Their fate and that of Bugs Moran are also covered, along with the two-year manhunt for Fred "Killer" Burke and the tribulations of "Machine Gun" Jack McGurn, who beat his indictment for the massacre only to be convicted of white slavery under a federal law that was stretched to include interstate sex with his girlfriend, whom the press dubbed his "Blond Alibi."

The investigation launched by Chicago's district police was joined by the city's detective bureau, the Cook County coroner, and investigators and prosecutors from the state's attorney's office. For reasons that are finally becoming apparent, it's difficult to say which agency tried harder *not* to solve the crime. Still, the massacre set the stage for future racketeering and helped revive the Chicago Crime Commission, whose members personally financed the country's first crime laboratory that introduced forensic ballistics to American law enforcement.

Looking back, the machine-gun bullets fired on the morning of February 14, 1929, marked the beginning of the end of Al Capone, for after that bloodbath the sinister power he had learned to wield so expertly by 1928, after newspapers had been calling him "Al Brown" or "Tony Caponi," soon dissipated like the gun smoke in the North Clark Street garage. It took the massacre to make Capone a household name as the world's most notorious gangster, who learned the hard way that the power to tax also could be the power to destroy.

Gus Winkler   *Georgette Winkler*

THE
ST. VALENTINE'S DAY
MASSACRE

I

ST. VALENTINE'S DAY, 1929

T HE TEMPERATURE HOVERED AROUND EIGHTEEN degrees and an icy wind was keeping the pavement slippery with blowing snow as Elmer Lewis wrestled his Nelson-LeMoon delivery van through the Thursday morning traffic on Chicago's Near North Side.

Lewis worked for the Beaver Paper Company downtown in the Loop, and he may have wished that St. Valentine's Day was a legal instead of sentimental holiday so he could still be home in bed, or doing almost anything besides shivering his way up North Clark Street in the unheated cab of a truck whose rock-hard suspension jarred every bone in his body. He kept a tight grip on the massive steering wheel, trying to avoid the slick trolley rails while craning his head to find the shop where he needed to drop off a package. And that could be why he didn't notice the black Cadillac until he was nearly on top of it. The touring car had darted out of Webster Street on his right and was turning left in front of him when he saw it and jammed on the stiff mechanical brakes. Too late. His left front bumper struck the rear fender on the driver's side of the expensive machine, which pulled over to the opposite curb and stopped.

Just what Elmer didn't need—a collision with a Cadillac. And, worse, a police Cadillac, judging from the bell on the driver's-side running board. Chicago detectives used such cars, meaning there probably would be hell to pay for failure-to-yield, or damage-to-city-property, or whatever the cops might cook up to cover their own bad driving. So he was both surprised and relieved when the Cadillac's driver, looking spiffy in chinchilla topcoat and gray fedora, only glanced at the dent and waved at him to keep going.

Elmer jerked the truck into low and headed north again, sufficiently rattled that he overshot the address he was looking for and had to walk back half a block to deliver the package to number 2129. Going in, he noticed that the Cadillac was still across the street but had moved a little farther south on Clark and now was stopped in front of number 2122, a nondescript brick garage about thirty feet wide with its front window blacked out by paint and a sign that read, S-M-C CARTAGE CO.

After Elmer dropped off the package and was heading back to his truck he heard popping sounds coming from the garage across the street. He assumed these were backfires, a common traffic noise with the hand-adjusted ignition systems of the day. Climbing into the cab he noticed the Cadillac pull away from the curb, pass a streetcar with a quick howl from a siren he hadn't noticed, and continue south on Clark toward the Chicago Academy of Sciences at Armitage before other traffic blocked his view.

A few others heard the same popping and saw what looked like two uniformed police officers with guns marching two or three men in topcoats, hands raised as though under arrest, out to the waiting Cadillac. One who thought this suspicious was Jeanette Landesman, a thirty-four-year-old housewife who lived with her husband, Max; son, Robert; and mother, Pauline; over Sam Schneider's tailor shop at 2124 North Clark. It was a little after 10:30, breakfast dishes had been put away, and now she was in the kitchen ironing clothes when rapid knocking sounds came through the wall from the adjoining brick garage.

She had never heard a machine gun, but from frequent newspaper accounts of gang shootings she could imagine what one must sound like. And while she didn't know exactly what kind of moving and shipping was done by the SMC Cartage Company, she and others in the middle-class German-Irish neighborhood assumed that it probably involved booze. Chicago's thousands of speakeasies had to be steadily supplied from beer and liquor depots all over the city, and after nine years of Prohibition, unobtrusive "moving" and "packing" and "storage" firms had become part of the local landscape.

Thus, the vagueness of the business next door plus the constant warfare between rival bootlegging gangs caused Mrs. Landesman to wonder if the racket she heard might be the muffled sounds of gunfire. When the noise stopped, she went to the living-room window and looked down in time to see men scramble into what appeared to be a detective car, which then sped south on Clark toward downtown, passing a streetcar on the wrong side before losing itself in traffic somewhere around Armitage. Her elderly mother, who had been gazing out the window from her favorite front-room chair, observed the same thing and remarked that a few minutes earlier she had seen what looked like a second detective squad stopping briefly at the garage.

Now even more curious, Jeanette Landesman hurried down two long flights of stairs, heard a dog howling, and tried to peer through the building's front window. She couldn't see inside so she tried the door, but it was stuck. She went back upstairs to find Clair McAllister, a self-employed sign painter who rented the rooms below hers, and asked him to find out if anything was wrong in the garage.

McAllister could also hear the dog, and as he forced open the front door he was hit by the strong odor of burned gunpowder. The small front office space to his left was empty, so he cautiously approached a doorway in the direction of the howling and found himself a dimly lit garage area filled with trucks, cars, and smoke. He picked his way between two of the vehicles and soon encountered a bleeding man on the dirty concrete floor, trying to crawl. And beyond him, along the north wall, was a scene that belonged in a slaughterhouse. There were bodies everywhere, in blood-soaked suits and topcoats and coveralls, flesh and fabric ripped by bullets, some with their heads blown apart.

McAllister must have gasped or made some exclamation, for the wounded man looked up and managed to utter three words that were not exactly germane to the situation:

"Who is it?"

That nearly unhinged McAllister, who could only think to say, "I just come to help you out." Then he ran from the garage and up the stairs, yelling to Mrs. Landesman to call the police and a doctor because there were a whole bunch of men in the garage, all shot up.

Meanwhile, looking out the second-floor window of her flat at 2125 North Clark, almost directly across the street, Josephine Morin was also thinking there was some kind of trouble in the garage. When she saw the men in civilian clothes enter the touring car at gunpoint, she assumed that the place had been raided and some bootleggers arrested. "After a while, I went downstairs to see what all the commotion was about," she later told police, and that's when someone said that the garage was full of dead men.

After McAllister had rushed from the building to call for help, a curious tradesman poked his head inside. James Wilcox had been delivering coal on North Clark and was trying to sort out a mix-up in addresses. Marie Benson, who ran a rooming house across the street and a few doors north, at 2135, was telling him he had the wrong place; she hadn't ordered any coal. About that time he also heard what he thought was the sound of backfiring.

Before returning to his truck Wilcox saw the same thing witnessed by Josephine Morin: men with guns climbing into a black touring car and speeding away. So after making sure the action was over, he, too, decided to investigate and had just encountered the wounded man when the first policeman arrived. He stayed around long enough to learn what had happened, then excitedly telephoned his employer to tell him about the "shooting on Clark Street, near where I was supposed to be delivering coal. . . . I heard that six men were killed, and I saw one of them!"

At that time, six were dead; the mortally wounded man would soon bring the total to seven.

The call made by Mrs. Landesman around 10:30 or so in the morning went to the Thirty-sixth District station house at 1501 North Hudson Avenue, about half a mile away. A district desk sergeant named Harrity answered the telephone, and his conversation drew the attention of Sergeant Thomas J. Loftus, who was working the eight-to-four day shift and was the only patrol officer in the station on that otherwise slow Thursday morning. He had been chatting with Bill Rudd, a young cop-buff who lived nearby on Seminary Avenue and liked to pal around with police, but from the tone of Harrity's voice, Loftus sensed that something was up; a highly agitated citizen was trying to convince a dubious desk sergeant that the building next door was full of death and destruction. Harrity hung up the phone and asked Loftus to see if anything serious was going on at 2122 North Clark—in a garage, a report of a shooting, and see the complainant, a Mrs. Landesman at 2124.

To Loftus's annoyance, the station's two Model A Fords were out on patrol and Bill Rudd didn't have a car, so he asked a telephone repairman named Corrigan who was working in the building to give him a ride to the scene. He invited Rudd to come along if he wanted to. As the three were leaving, officers George Love and Thomas Christie drove up in one of the police Fords, and Loftus told them to follow, in case there was anything to the report.

When the two cars arrived at SMC Cartage around 10:45 A.M., Loftus saw a woman leaning out an upstairs window over the tailor's shop and excitedly pointing to the building next door. Loftus went in first and shooed out the coal-truck driver, who was wide-eyed, jabbering, and pointing toward the back, where the dog was still howling. He first encountered the man on the floor, and near him lay a snubnose .38-caliber Colt Detective Special. Then, by the light of a single two-hundred-watt bulb hanging from the ceiling, he saw the gruesome tangle of bodies. One was draped over a chair; the others were lying at different angles to one another, some face up and others face down in pools of blood, two with their heads blown apart and brains splattered everywhere. In his thirty-eight years of police work, Loftus had never seen anything approaching such carnage. He shouted to Bill Rudd to lock the front door, call the station, and "have them notify Deputy Commissioner [Thomas] Wolfe, the Bureau of Investigation, the switchboard, and everybody concerned."

He saw that the first man was still alive, trying to speak, and recognized him as a young bootlegger and police character named Frank Gusenberg, who had an older brother, Pete. He leaned down and asked: "Do you know me, Frank?"

Gusenberg could barely speak. "Yes, you're Tom Loftus," he muttered.

Loftus, who had known Gusenberg since he was a paperboy, asked him what had happened, and Gusenberg whispered, "I won't talk." Then he added, "Cops did it."

That didn't register, and Loftus tried again, without much luck. Finally he said, "You're in bad shape," but Gusenberg only replied, "For God's sake, get me to a hospital." Loftus assured him that a wagon was on its way.

"I asked him if they had all been lined up against the wall, and he again repeated, 'I won't talk,'" the veteran officer wrote in his initial report of the incident. "Then the wagon came and I told them to hustle him over to the Alexian Brothers Hospital. That was done. I then walked back and felt Pete's pulse and I then told the wagonmen to get a doctor. They got Dr. Frederick M. Doyle, 2314 North Clark Street, and he tried all six men and stated they were all dead."

In his excitement, Bill Rudd had called the main police number, POL-1313, instead of the Thirty-sixth District, leaving the Hudson Avenue station in the dark regarding events on Clark Street and causing some grief for an eighteen-year-old cub reporter named Walter Spirko, who worked for the City News Bureau that served all six Chicago dailies, had the police beat and was supposed to check with the coroner's office at least once an hour for any newsworthy violence or criminal activity. But he also had been warned by his boss, Isaac Gershman, that cops liked to pull practical jokes on young reporters, so he was suspicious when he was told that several people had been shot in a garage on North Clark Street. Still, he called his office, only to have "Gersh" assure him that the boys in blue were having a joke at his expense. When Spirko saw the coroner himself put on a Chesterfield topcoat and derby hat and hurry out the door, he called his office again, but Gersh still wouldn't believe him.

Finally Gershman agreed to telephone the Thirty-sixth District police station, which only confirmed his suspicion that the whole thing was a hoax, for Harrity at the Thirty-sixth had his own doubts about Mrs. Landesman's call, had heard nothing from Loftus, and would only tell Gershman that the North Clark Street trouble involved some men "hurt in a brawl." It was almost half an hour before anyone at headquarters informed the district police station about the mass killing, and it was longer than that before Spirko could convince Gershman to send a reporter. Later, Gershman gave Spirko a stern lecture on the importance of sounding convincing.

At the hospital at 1200 Belden Avenue, Officer James Mikes was assigned to stay with the barely conscious Gusenberg, and he tried to question him, with no success. "Who shot you?," he would ask, and Gusenberg would answer, "Nobody shot me." The badly wounded man was fading fast, and Mikes asked him if he wanted a priest. He said no in a whisper that was barely audible. At 1:30 P.M., he died.

That same afternoon most newspapers rushed into print "extras" with banner headlines but few facts, many of them wrong, and Friday's papers devoted their front pages and picture sections almost entirely to the murders. Even the relatively restrained *Chicago Daily News* gave the story its full eight-column banner and tried to capture the horror of the crime in a melodramatic sidebar:

KILLING SCENE
TOO GRUESOME
FOR ONLOOKERS

View of Carnage Proves a
Strain on Their
Nerves

IS LIKE A SHAMBLES

It's too much to tell. You go into the door marked "S-M-C Cartage company." You see a bunch of big men talking with restrained excitement in the cigarette smoke. You go through another door back of the front office. You go between two close-parked trucks in the garage.

Then you almost stumble over the head of the first man, with a clean gray felt hat still placed at the precise angle of gangster toughness.

The dull yellow light of a lamp shows dark rivulets of blood heading down to the drain that was meant for water from washed cars. There are six of the red streams from six heads. Bodies—four of them well dressed in civilian clothes—two of them with their legs crossed as they whirled to fall.

It's too much, so you crowd on past the roadster with the bullet holes in it to the truck behind.

TOO MUCH FOR THE DOG

You look at the truck. It is something to look at because the men were fixing it. It's jacked up, with one wheel off. You look and the big man called "Commissioner" looks and a crowd gathers, and then it gets too much for the police dog you had failed to notice lying under the truck, tied to it by a cheap yellow rope.

It gets too much for the big brown and gray police dog
and he goes crazy. He barks, he howls, he snarls, showing
wicked white teeth in bright red gums.

The crowd backs away. The dog yowls once more and
subsides.

Your thoughts snap with a crack back to the circle of yellow lamplight, where six things that were men are sprawled.

It's still too much. You push out into the fresh air. . . .

But it was the *Herald and Examiner* that came up with the most
memorable lead sentence of all: "Chicago gangsters yesterday graduated from murder to massacre."

The cold-blooded killing of seven men certified Chicago as gangster
capital of the world, if anyone still had doubts; it would soon make
Al Capone a national household name, the most notorious mobster
in history; and the use of submachine guns confirmed that weapon
as the gangster equivalent of the cowboy's six-shooter.

In the absence of solid information, both the police and the press
rushed to fill in the gaps with speculation and guesswork, which
after countless retellings in magazines, books, and movies are now
accepted as gospel. Except for the long-standing enmity between
Capone and Moran, and the St. Valentine's Day deaths, not many of
these claims stand up to careful examination.

Contrary to widely held belief, it now seems unlikely that Capone
ordered the wholesale slaughter so he could "take over" Chicago.
The mistaken killing of a public official in 1926 had sent him into
hiding for three months until the city calmed down, so he knew the
price of fame. The mass murder made headlines around the world,
throwing police into a year's enforcement frenzy that cost the
Capone empire possibly a hundred million in 1929 dollars.

A hijacked shipment of Old Log Cabin whiskey is supposed to
have been the bait used to lure the Moran mob to the garage, but
this story may have originated with a Prohibition official who told
reporters that a truckload had been stolen on Indianapolis Boulevard two weeks earlier, or with police who had heard of two more
recent thefts. Another theory had the Moran gang driving trucks to
Detroit to buy smuggled Canadian booze from the Purple Gang
directly instead of through the Capone "Syndicate."

A relative of Moran recently revealed the actual reason for the meeting. A month earlier, Bugs had been winged by a bullet fired from a passing car as he and a friend left a nightclub on Ontario Street, and Moran wanted to retaliate. The now-elderly man told Moran biographer Rose Keefe:

> I can tell you one thing—there was no meeting with out-of-town gangsters or any plans to unload bootleg. They were there to meet George because he'd been shot and they were losing their territory to Capone. George was always thinking his [phone] lines were tapped and they were waiting for their chance to find out where he'd be and finish him off.

How far other crime historians are off target should have been apparent from the fact that Moran was assembling his top lieutenants and gunmen. Except for the unlucky mechanic, none of the victims were dressed for the manual labor of unloading crates or planning an all-day drive to Detroit and back. They were dressed in pricey suits and ties, fine scarves, street shoes, and expensive fedoras. One was even sporting a carnation.

The story still persists that the lookouts were the Purple Gang's Keywell brothers. That came from a witness who "partially" identified one of the Keywells from police photographs, and it earned her a prominent mention in the next day's newspapers, but most of them failed to report that she later changed her mind.

Another witness, a youngster named George Arthur Brichet (Brichetti in some accounts) reported that a second phony detective car had parked in the alley behind the garage. This was probably the one seen by Jeanette Landesman's mother and later found destroyed in suburban Maywood, but which is omitted from most chronicles of the massacre.

Most accounts do not identify the actual shooters, or mistakenly list Capone mobsters whose names had become familiar to the police and the press. Nor did the hit team involve only the four or five men seen by witnesses; it probably included as many as a dozen, counting the lookouts and the men in the second "detective" squad. The lookouts probably did mistake another North Sider for their primary target, Bugs Moran, who literally dodged a bullet. Moran lived only a block away, at the Parkway Hotel, 2100 Lincoln Park West, and when he reached the corner of Griffin and Clark, he spotted the phony police car in time to either retreat or (some believe) duck into a coffee shop. In any case, he was not among the victims, and only early news reports suggested that he'd been kidnapped by the gunmen.

How the actual triggermen, backups, and lookouts were recruited by Capone is a story in its own right. They were mostly from the St. Louis area, veterans of the Egan's Rats gang, and they introduced the Tommygun to New York that same year. Capone's largely Italian mob referred to them resentfully as the "American Boys," and when unpaid taxes landed Capone in prison in 1932, his successor, Frank Nitti, disbanded the last of them with bullets.

What did Al Capone think at his Miami estate when his hired gunmen managed to create international outrage by their execution-style murder of seven people, including a visiting optician, and still miss Bugs Moran? Nobody knows. But it may have been something like, *If you want anything done right, you got to do it yourself.*

II

PROHIBITION, CHICAGO STYLE

A T LEAST FIVE HUNDRED UNSOLVED gangland murders since the start of Prohibition had inured the average Chicagoan to the idea of bootleggers killing each other, and some even enjoyed hobnobbing with celebrity mobsters. That one of the St. Valentine's Day Massacre victims was an unlucky optician may have troubled some gangster buffs who enjoyed danger's proximity without weighing the risks, but most patrons of the city's speakeasies, nightclubs, and gambling joints trusted local gunmen to avoid shooting noncombatants. This moved a Nebraska newspaper to comment: "Outsiders, apparently, do more worrying about the plight of Chicago than the residents themselves."

Not that the residents had much choice, but many did take a perverse pride in their city's reputation for toughness. Those who visited friends in another town or country were expected to have at least one blood-curdling tale to tell, even if they had to make it up.

But in everybody's book, the St. Valentine's Day Massacre exceeded the murder limit even for gangsters, disturbing the city's complacency and doing more than any other single event to advance the movement for Prohibition's repeal. Whether in or out of office, Chicago's Clown Mayor "Big Bill the Builder" Thompson made no bones about his contempt for dry laws, but Police Commissioner William F. Russell, as an ostensible enforcer of them, dismayed temperance leaders by calling the massacre "one of the fruits of Prohibition":

> Prohibition is the root of these gang killings, and despite the most vigorous efforts to stop them, they probably will continue as long as the Volstead Act is a law. . . . Take away the incentive by legalizing the sale of wholesome beer and you eliminate the bootlegger.

In the same Milwaukee paper that headlined the massacre and blamed it on rogue cops, an unrelated story reported more arrests for drunkenness in the year just ended than before Prohibition. That was followed two days later by the *Chicago Tribune*'s banner headline, DRY LAW DOOMED, SAYS REED, reporting a U.S. senator's threat to "name the hypocrites in Congress who vote dry and drink wet." Improved automobiles, paved highways, the telephone, and "flaming youth" all contributed to Prohibition's failure, as did a system of law enforcement that was antiquated, unprofessional, and becoming more corrupt every day. By this time, many advocates of moderation were concluding that the "noble experiment" had blown up in the country's face, and Chicago was the poster city for Prohibition's problems.

While the Eighteenth Amendment was marching slowly but surely through thirty-six state legislatures and into the Constitution, national Prohibition looked like a victory of traditional village values over modern urban depravity. What it did instead was destroy what respect citizens had for the rule of law, afford rural and small-town people their best opportunity since Reconstruction or the western range wars to corrupt their own police and politicians, and become a source of such enormous profits that crime had no choice but to get "organized." Distribution systems for beer and liquor already were in place, and as these were taken over by the criminal community, bootleggers in one city had to forge alliances with the bootleggers in others, or the booze would not get through. Soon a national network existed, providing avenues for other criminal endeavors from prostitution to gambling to loansharking to labor racketeering.

These offenses fell into the legal category of what are now called "consensual" crimes, as opposed to violent crimes committed by armed robbers. Both types of criminals tended to patronize the same lawyers, bondsmen, gun sellers, doctors, and car dealers who constituted an underworld support group. Capone might hire robbers because they were lawbreakers by nature and profession, but he could truthfully claim that "I never stuck up a man in my life. Neither did any of my agents ever rob anybody or burglarize any homes while they worked for me. They might have pulled plenty of jobs before they came with me or after they left me, but not while they were in my Outfit."[1]

That was the difference between the organized gangs for whom bootlegging was a "racket" and the bandit or outlaw gangs who were armed robbers operating as raiding parties. Some lawbreakers abandoned violent crime when Prohibition promised better money and fewer risks, some returned to robbery following its repeal, and others found their true calling as racketeers. A few ex-robbers might still answer the call of old friends who needed their expertise for a really big-time heist, like a six-figure payroll, but for the most part racketeers and robbers were different breeds of criminals who collaborated when convenient or would sell the other out if the stakes were high enough.

Every large city already had gangs, the successors to Nineteenth-Century neighborhood and ethnic groups that originally had banded together for social, benevolent, or defensive reasons but later found profitable ways to employ themselves collectively. They offered neighborhood shopkeepers "protection" (mainly from themselves) or worked as "muscle" for politicians, competing taxi companies, and even newspapers. Such crime was "organized" only to the extent that illegal operations required payoffs to the police, who were ruled by politicians, who were financed by prostitution and gambling interests and kept in office by gangs, who were subsidized by the politicians, ad infinitum. Cities like Chicago and New York especially were good examples of how well local government and local vice could complement each other when everyone cooperated.

By the turn of the Twentieth Century, New York had become justly famous for its "fighting gangs," which battled one another over turf and toughness before discovering they could do it for money at polling places on orders from Tammany Hall. The value of Chicago's street gangs had been discovered early on by such powerful (and colorful) aldermen as Michael "Hinky Dink" Kenna and "Bathhouse John" Coughlin, who protected vice lords (and ladies) like "Big Jim" Colosimo and the Everleigh Sisters. If Chicago's Everleigh Club had been the Taj Mahal of bawdyhouses in the days of the legal saloon, Big Jim's places were one-stop shopping centers of drinking, gambling, and the more proletarian forms of prostitution—at least until the eve of Prohibition, when the older Colosimo fell in love with Dale Winter, a young and exceptionally pretty out-of-work actress who had taken a job singing at his popular cabaret on South Wabash Avenue. With Dale returning his affection, Big Jim decided he had too much money and not enough time. To free up more of it for his songbird, he divorced the frumpy wife who had financed much of his vice empire and turned its management over to his nephew, Johnny Torrio, imported from New York.

Torrio had made a name for himself in Brooklyn, where by 1909, at age twenty-seven, he was a graduate of the Five Points Gang, had operated a brothel, owned a saloon, and worked election wonders for the Tammany political machine. That year he was summoned to Chicago to help his Uncle Jim deal with some Black Hand extortionists, whom he met in a South Side railroad underpass ostensibly to pay them off but instead simply killed them. That sent the desired message to other extortionists, and Torrio had stayed on as Colosimo's bodyguard, political fixer, and man of vision. It was Torrio who acted as liaison with the city's other local gangs and ward politicians, and who foresaw, as Colosimo would not, the enormous profit potential in the Eighteenth Amendment.

Torrio understood that, through the alchemy of Prohibition, alcohol could be transmuted into gold, but with Big Jim's head in the clouds of true love, he needed an apprentice, preferably one with muscle. As luck would have it, Torrio's former business partner Frankie Yale (also spelled Uale), was needing a safe harbor for a promising employee at his Harvard Inn dancehall near Coney

Island. Alphonse Capone was a beefy young fellow with a lot of presence and a generally winning personality, except on occasion. Two years previously, his cheek had been carved by an inebriated patron, but Scarface Al's immediate problem was the police, who were hounding him about some murders and attempts not covered under the insurance premiums Yale paid to local civic officials.

Al Brown, as Capone would call himself upon moving to Chicago, knew how to get things done. It's generally believed that one thing he did was to help Torrio arrange the murder of Colosimo, shortly after Big Jim's marriage to Dale, in the vestibule of his restaurant on May 11, 1920. The shooter probably was Frankie Yale, who (he would explain to police when detained at a railroad station) just happened to be in Chicago that day, "visiting."

Prohibition was only four months old when a bullet in the head sent Colosimo to the big brothel in the sky, leaving Torrio free to organize the illegal manufacture and importation of booze. With every brewery either closing or converting to tepid "near beer" (called "horse piss" by Chicagoans), he masterminded the purchase of many of these plants, often in collusion with their former owners and usually in partnership with other gang leaders. This created a pax Torrio of interlocking financial interests as everyone worked hard to develop his allocated territory. It was Prohibition that reversed the order of things in the hierarchy of urban crime, for soon the more ambitious gangs grew into major business operations that now could buy the politicians they previously had worked for.

Ironically, Prohibition also tended to reduce a city's crime rate, especially for property crime. The huge profits in illegal alcohol afforded a less hazardous occupation for burglars, thieves, safecrackers, and even robbers, as well as for gunmen who became personal bodyguards or the underworld's policemen. Now they provided security against hijackers, often with the help of off-duty cops who could earn a few weeks' police pay just for protecting one load of beer or liquor in unfriendly territory, or paying off brother officers working the streets. The low-key Torrio quickly emerged as leader of a fairly orderly syndicate that included at least a dozen neighborhood gangs, the best aldermen money could buy, enough of the city's police force to minimize dry-law enforcement, and as many state and federal Prohibition agents as needed to avoid prolonged disruptions of service.

For a time, bootlegging had expanded in a more or less peaceful manner. Not only were there plenty of profits for all, but Prohibition's unexpected windfall of easy wealth and Torrio's bland charm encouraged some of the city's gang leaders to divide up Cook County equitably among themselves in order to forestall competition. By 1923, however, bootlegging had become so popular in the criminal community that it gave rise to territorial disputes. Lacking legal means to resolve their differences, rival gangs and independents began resorting to murder as an instrument of underworld policy.

Torrio's job as Chicago's leading crime boss had its share of headaches, but his real problems began with Dean O'Banion, a bellicose Irish lad who had risen from punk to mugger to safecracker to labor goon to political fixer to killer (although legend has him regularly attending Mass) in wards that included the ritzy Gold Coast and the Near North Side. At the start of Prohibition, O'Banion was content to distribute Torrio beer and buy into Torrio breweries, and had he been more tolerant of "greaseballs" (as he commonly called his South Side colleagues), his own political connections combined with Torrio's business sense might have produced an operation of true criminal greatness.

Unfortunately, O'Banion hungered for greater independence and could not resist hijacking the occasional Torrio booze truck or humiliating the South Siders in other ways that kept their friendship strained. Following a period of generally increasing violence and deteriorating relations, Torrio's patience ran out when O'Banion refused to forgive a large gambling debt owed by one of Little Italy's Genna brothers to the Ship (a Cicero, Illinois, casino in which they both held an interest) and also conned him into buying his share of the large Sieben Brewery in the 1400 block of North Larrabee Street, just in time for the plant to be raided by a handpicked crew of cops under Chief Morgan Collins while Torrio was inspecting the premises.

The bust meant jail time for Torrio, because of a prior bootlegging conviction, and that was the last straw. It was time to call

Frankie Yale. At noon on November 10, 1924, three men fitting the descriptions of Yale and two members of the Genna gang entered O'Banion's flower shop at 738 North State Street, ostensibly to pick up a floral arrangement for a dear departed friend. When they walked out, O'Banion was ready for a funeral of his own. Chicago newspapers marveled at the novel technique employed: After a few minutes of friendly chatting, two of the gunmen pumped O'Banion's hands in a farewell gesture and then held on so he couldn't reach for a gun while the third pumped him full of bullets. (Most Chicago papers reported that O'Banion was killed while greeting his customers, so they could call it a "handshake murder.")

O'Banion was Chicago's only celebrity gangster at the time, and with his slaying the lid came off. "Little Hymie" Weiss (who was not Jewish but actually a Polish Catholic born Earl Wojciechowski) assumed leadership of the North Siders and swore vengeance against Torrio, who had made the papers because of the Sieben arrest, and Capone, known to Weiss but few reporters before January 10, 1925. That night his limousine was ambushed at Fifty-fifth and State and his chauffeur wounded, which caused a minor commotion and prompted the Big Fellow to order a thirty-thousand-dollar armor-plated Cadillac with bulletproof glass.

Ten days later, on January 20, the trio of Hymie Weiss, George Moran (identified as "George Gage"), and Vincent Drucci shot Torrio in front of his apartment building in the city's pleasantly quiet South Shore neighborhood. The "thinking man's gangster" survived, and after serving his term for the Sieben conviction he and his wife sailed to Italy for a much-needed vacation before he returned to the relative safety of New York as gangster emeritus, leaving his Chicago affairs in the hands of Al Capone.

Over the next five years Capone, now identified with Cicero, would create the greatest illicit liquor combine in history, in spite of his gangland enemies—or over their dead bodies. The North Siders were Irish in temperament if not in nationality and had no great fondness for the "dagos" now dominating the business; they also felt obliged to avenge the death of O'Banion. The year 1925 marked the beginning of the Beer Wars, or the "Battle of Chicago," and the bootleggers fighting it would unveil a new and remarkable weapon—this country's first "submachine" gun, which sprayed .45-caliber pistol bullets at a rate of eight hundred rounds per minute.

Interestingly, the first gangster to bring one to Chicago had been Dean O'Banion himself. He discovered it in Colorado, where copper company guards were using the novel weapon to intimidate striking miners, and where his friend "Two-Gun" Louie Alterie owned a ranch, the Diamond D, at which hard-working hoodlums could kick back for a little R & R. Alterie put on a rodeo to entertain O'Banion, who took a thousand feet of home movies, and in return "Deanie" awed local visitors by showing off his car's bullet holes, telling how each was acquired. On his way back to Chicago, O'Banion was in such a good mood that he bought three of the "baby machine guns" (as newspapers called them) in Denver, only to be murdered before he could issue them to his troops.

III

THE GUN THAT MADE THE TWENTIES ROAR

THE SAME YEAR THE VOLSTEAD Act became the law of the land, an obscure New York City arms firm contracted with the venerable Colt's Patent Firearms Manufacturing Company of Hartford, Connecticut, to build fifteen thousand Thompson submachine guns. At that time the public had never heard of a "submachine" gun, much less a "Tommygun," nor had the military or the police or the country's lawmakers. To most people, the term *machine gun* referred to the big German Maxim or British Vickers or American Browning weapons of World War I—belt-fed, water-cooled, fifty-pound contraptions that required two or three men to carry, set up, and fire. Lack of portability made them strictly defensive weapons, and from sandbagged "nests" or other fortified emplacements they could blanket No Man's Land with a blizzard of bullets that made infantry charges practically suicidal, a few Sergeant Yorks notwithstanding.

Consequently, the idea of a hand-held machine gun that was smaller than a rifle seemed pretty far fetched, and this represented a major marketing problem for the fledgling Auto-Ordnance Corporation. Indeed, it was a problem the original company never did solve, so the gun languished in a Colt's warehouse virtually unknown for nearly five years and might have joined the scrap heap of ideas whose time had not yet come but for Chicago's rowdy bootleggers, who rescued it from obscurity. In a big way. By the time the Thompson was used in the St. Valentine's Day Massacre, it already had become the firearm that most symbolized Prohibition violence. The press and the public alike were calling it the "Tommygun," the "chopper," and the "Chicago Typewriter," much to the dismay of its inventor.

Intended originally for the army, the Thompson gun was developed by Brigadier General John Taliaferro (pronounced Tolliver) Thompson, a retired ordnance officer with an inventive streak who believed that, in an age of heavy machine guns, allied infantrymen desperately needed more firepower. Financed by robber baron Thomas Fortune Ryan, who may have had ulterior motives, Thompson formed the Auto-Ordnance Corporation of New York in August 1916, hoping to replace the Army's bolt-action 1903 Springfield with a semi-automatic rifle that utilized a simple and novel breach-locking mechanism. Some experimental models would successfully chamber and fire standard .30-'06 ammunition, as the Army required, but ejected the empty shells with nearly as much force as the bullets. And no amount of tinkering would correct the problem.

In 1917, Thompson's chief engineer, Theodore Eickhoff, announced this unhappy situation to the general, who had returned to the Ordnance Department when the United States entered the war. Eickhoff also had to report that the only U.S. service cartridge suited to the special breach-locking mechanism was the one least desirable—the relatively low-powered .45-caliber pistol cartridge used in the Army's Model 1911 Colt automatics.

Thompson pondered this, asked some technical questions, and then brightened. He told Eickhoff to forget the rifle; instead they would build a revolutionary one-man, hand-held, fully automatic weapon chambered for pistol ammunition. It would be a "trench broom," he declared, and to distinguish it from the large and bulky automatic weapons that fired rifle ammunition, he would call it a "sub-machine" gun. As Eickhoff recalls, Thompson then rose from his chair and sprayed the room with imaginary bullets, fired from the hip, like a Chicago gangster of the not-too-distant future.

A few of the guns were sold to private detective agencies and the security offices of large mining and manufacturing companies in the South and West to deal with "labor riots," and a few went to Cuba and South America. Otherwise, sales figures were so low that Auto-Ordnance laid off most of its employees, and the gun drifted out of the picture except as a novelty item in the catalogs of large firearm distributors and sporting goods houses, such as that of Chicago's Peter Von Frantzius, where its retail price was knocked down from $225 to $175.

That's what the Thompson was selling for when things began boiling over in Chicago's bootlegging community. It could be hidden "under a coat for instant use," just like Auto-Ordnance said, and the fact that one could buy a submachine gun easier than a handgun did not lessen its appeal. The knowledgeable customer was aware that a gunman with a pistol had to move in dangerously close to his target, and if the first bullets failed to do their work, the target usually shot back. When the intended victim had bodyguards, a pistol was out of the question. The knowledgeable customer would also know that a gunman with a sawed-off shotgun lacked nothing for deadliness but still had to work at fairly close range, and that buckshot sometimes failed to penetrate the doors or other bodywork of automobiles. Finally, he would know that a competent gunman with a Thompson could get a kill (maybe several) at any reasonable range, or from the safety and anonymity of a speeding car; and that a machine gun had the bonus feature of deterring counterfire from bodyguards. They either went down with their employer or dove for the nearest cover.

Chicago gangsters had not yet discovered this wonderfully murderous weapon when bootlegging began changing from a sport to a hazardous occupation. An increasing number of gangland shootings in 1923 and 1924, combined with increasingly obvious political corruption, stirred voters to replace flamboyant Mayor Big Bill Thompson with William E. Dever, a reform candidate who ran for office on a law-and-order platform.

While not a Prohibitionist himself, Dever promised to enforce the law, purge the police of rotten apples, and generally clean up municipal government. What he really did was upset the existing and orderly system of graft, which threw the criminal community into confusion just when gangland alliances already were breaking down. Police raids closed the most popular cabarets and vice dens in the Levee district, causing Torrio to lay low and Capone to move his headquarters a few miles west to the Hawthorne Hotel in the suburb of Cicero, a town which he quickly took over. This move roughly coincided with the Sieben Brewery raid, the murder of O'Banion, the retaliation shooting of Torrio, and the killing of Frank Capone, Al's older brother, by deputized Chicago police sent by Mayor Dever to restore order in Cicero polling places during that city's primaries in April 1924. With Greater Chicago fast becoming a shooting gallery, to the bemusement of the country and especially New York, local newspapers reported the Cicero action quite matter-of-factly. For example:

> One man was killed and two were wounded, one probably fatally, during election disturbances yesterday.
> Voters and precinct workers in some sections of the city were slugged, intimidated and even kidnapped. There were narrow escapes from death as rival gunmen in fast automobiles fired volleys while near polling places.

The above points up a major difference between hoodlums in the country's two largest cities. While New York's Jimmy Walker would soon become its handsome, debonair, and acceptably corrupt mayor, that city liked to project a cosmopolitan image as the nation's center of culture and sophistication, and its five-borough geography with two dividing rivers helped maintain gangland boundaries. Moreover, Mayor Walker and crime boss Arnold Rothstein were both "refined" and considered street violence bad for tourism, conventions, speakeasies, and any other business; head-bashing was reserved for the city police.

Chicago, although a showcase of post-fire architecture and world-class museums, was better known as Carl Sandburg's "City of

Broad Shoulders" and "Hog Butcher to the World," and had been ruled eccentrically if not insanely by Mayor Big Bill Thompson, who was anything but dapper. Once a cowboy, at least in mentality, he reluctantly had withdrawn from the 1923 election because of scandals in his administration. But he would return like a P. T. Barnum four years later—staging Wild-West-style campaign parades complete with bucking horses and tumbling clowns—and declare himself "wetter than the middle of the Atlantic Ocean."

Thompson's style, before Dever and after, was to bluster about anything that would get out the vote and otherwise deny or shrug off Chicago's legacy of lawlessness, crooked cops and politicians, ballot-box stuffing and polling-place shootings, and the tossing of bombs, which popped like firecrackers in a private war between unions and construction contractors. Not counting despondent "drys," about the only soreheads who found no glamour in the city's tough-guy reputation (the term "hard-boiled" was coming into popular usage) were businessmen represented by the Association of Commerce and the Chicago Crime Commission, the first in the country and not yet fully awake.

Thus, after 1923 Mayor Dever had the dubious privilege of presiding over four years of bloody bootlegging battles that rocked Chicago, while the Torrio crime syndicate took over some of the smaller southern and western suburbs and restored order in Cicero, once the Chicago cops had pulled out. Now Chicago's South Siders— at least those still part of the original Torrio cartel—were described in the press as the "Cicero mob," and virtually all of their favored candidates would be elected officially in 1924 and succeeding years.

IV

THE CHICAGO BEER WARS

HISTORY HAS NOT GIVEN DEAN O'Banion proper credit for discovering the submachine gun in Colorado and bringing three of them to Chicago in late 1924. For one thing, he hardly had time to unpack them before Frankie Yale arrived from New York and led a shooting party to Schofield's flower shop at 738 North State Street, of which O'Banion was part owner. The business was directly across he street from the Holy Name Cathedral at Superior and State, where O'Banion may have attended Mass, may have been an altar boy, and may have sung in the choir—activities that are short on substantiation but long on the kind of irony reporters like when a wild, wealthy, and ostensibly Catholic bootlegger bites the dust.

Dion, as he's often called, was actually his baptismal name—received late in life for a Catholic, at age twelve. He was born Charles Dean O'Banion in the northern Illinois town of Maroa (not Aurora, as usually reported), and he usually went by Dean or Deanie rather than Dion, a name that appears in many books. He seemed to relish breaking laws and no doubt would have set some kind of record for criminal conduct if the future hadn't caught up with him on November 10, 1924, at the age of thirty-two. Whether he even had time to test his Thompsons, nobody knows.

What had saved O'Banion from a life of prison terms or worse was Prohibition, which quickly made him a wealthy benefactor of Chicago aldermen on the city's North Side, which in turn made him a protected species. At the time he was killed, O'Banion was far better known and more greatly feared than the Torrio Syndicate or Capone, who was still unknown to most reporters. Like other bootleggers, O'Banion paid off the right authorities, but most of the protection he had needed since his teenage days came from himself. He and his original gang were longtime buddies notorious for their impulsive behavior, and until his marriage to a girl named Viola, his partnership in Schofield's, and his increasing political influence made him too prominent for pranks, he and his cronies resembled a young gangster version of the Keystone Kops. They had performed well enough breaking heads in the city's newspaper and taxi wars and rolling the occasional drunk, but their free time was spent at such sports as happily terrorizing pedestrians by driving their car on the sidewalk. Once, after a pointless earlier dispute, Dean felt obliged to shoot a rival, Hershie Miller, in the midst of a crowd leaving a downtown theater, but he dodged the courtroom bullet by pleading self-defense.

And meanwhile, having learned the art of safecracking from a local master named Charles "Ox" Reiser, Dean had added that crime to his repertoire. On one occasion he managed to blow the walls out of a building without opening the safe; as late as 1922 it cost him thirty thousand dollars to secure an acquittal after police caught him at a blasted safe covered with plaster dust. Citing what must be one of the world's lamest alibis, he explained that he was simply a good citizen who'd heard a terrible explosion in a nearby building, saw the "petemen" (safecrackers) scrambling out an upstairs window, and rushed in hoping to capture the rascals. The judge must have had to gavel his bench repeatedly to quell the courtroom laughter, but Deanie walked.

O'Banion's murder amidst his flowers was a declaration of total war between the original booze cartel headed up by Torrio and the North Siders who were forming enough alliances with other gangs to constitute a syndicate themselves. The South Siders had taken over Cicero on the West and were still numerically superior, while the North Siders were smaller in number but steadily expanding their control from the wealthy Gold Coast on the Near North Side all the way to Chicago's northern city limits and beyond. While both outfits were equal opportunity employers, the South Siders had annexed Little Italy on the Near West Side and were otherwise dominated by Italians. O'Banion's North Side successors would find themselves working with the Sicilians on their west flank, especially the Aiello brothers, who had their own beef with Capone over control of the Unione Siciliana, or Sicilian Union,[2] which became a war of its own.

Little Sicily was an especially impoverished neighborhood also known locally as "Little Hell" because the burn-off fires at the city's gas works adjoining the nearby Chicago River gave the eastern nighttime sky an ominous reddish glow. The area included "Death Corner" across from St. Benizi's Catholic Church at Oak and Cambridge, where bodies were dumped from cars. What made it useful to the Irish, besides the murderous reputations of certain residents, was the very absence of conventional "law and order" (the Sicilian Union was an enforcement and judicial system combined) and the fact that so many families supported themselves, as they did in Little Italy, by cooking homemade alcohol in small kitchen stills. This wicked product could be used for "needling" barrels of the legally manufactured near-beer back up to proof, or cut with tap water and variously flavored to pass for bathtub gin[3] or aged-in-the-bottle whiskey in the city's grubbier speakeasies, which numbered in the thousands.

That was not yet a major consideration, as plenty of the "Real McCoy" (so-named for an early and honest East Coast rum-runner) was still being trucked or freighted cross-country courtesy of Brooklyn's Frankie Yale, a major supplier to Chicago and the Midwest, or coming down from Canada via Detroit. Yale was national chief (if there even was such an office on paper) of the Unione, and so long as Torrio's booze monopoly was functional he could service most of the city with quality liquor from the large "rum fleet" anchored off New York's Long Island. The Genna brothers in Little Italy and the Aiello brothers in Little Sicily had plenty of household "alky-cookers" in their respective neighborhoods to provide the urban version of moonshine.

The local Unione chief, Mike Merlo, enjoyed the respect of both Torrio and O'Banion and had helped keep peace between those two, so Merlo's death from natural causes on November 8, 1924, sealed O'Banion's fate. During the overnight journey it took Frankie Yale to reach Chicago by train, the three-gun florist (as newspapers liked to describe him) no doubt had put his best efforts into Merlo's elaborate funeral arrangement when the grief-stricken Yale and two gunmen-in-mourning dropped him into his roses, or whatever flower suited a reporter on the scene. The next morning's *Tribune* banner blared in the declarative style of the day: KILL O'BANION, GANG LEADER.

The unfortunate departure of Mike Merlo invited payback by Torrio for the Sieben Brewery swindle and arrest. Under Mayor Thompson, Torrio might have beaten the rap, but the mayor's office now was occupied by reformer William Dever, the police were nervous as to the proper handling of bribes, and judges and politicians were still testing the waters of corruption. This meant that the Lord High Bootlegger would soon spend a short stretch in the cooler, leaving his wobbly empire in the hands of Al Capone. Al Brown, as he was still generally known, had observed that Dever's raid on the brewery involved no district police; they were already there, guarding the beer trucks for the boys. Dever and his chief had brought in strangers from other police districts who didn't know any better than to follow orders. That unnerving situation, plus the padlocking of Colosimo's and the Four Deuces, had led Capone to move his headquarters to the Hawthorne Hotel in Cicero, where he camped next door in the Anton Hotel until his new offices and home away from home were brought up to code, Capone style.

Meanwhile, Dean O'Banion had gone to meet his maker in a ten-thousand-dollar casket followed by dozens of carloads of flowers from every political stooge in town, the most garish displays coming from his bootlegging buddies and adversaries. The funerals of many heads of state involved smaller turnouts, because O'Banion was much beloved for his generosity and buoyant personality, at least in public, and because Schofield's was good window dressing for his gang's board meetings.

With O'Banion's death, some long-established gangs and newer groups rebelled against Torrio's leadership and declared their independence, while others openly or secretly allied themselves with the North Siders, usually on the basis of culture. For example, most Irish were Catholics who objected to prostitution, promiscuity, abortion, and bad booze, which to them included wine. The Italians made a bigger thing out of their Catholicism, with religious festivals and public displays of holiness, but they didn't blink at brothels or rotgut liquor that could blind or cripple people if insufficiently "rectified," for wine was their principal drink. Finally, Italians and Sicilians were lumped together as foreigners, even to an Irishman barely off the boat.

Skirmishing among various neighborhood gangs was nothing new and even had subsided with territorial allocations, but once Dever became mayor an increase in police crackdowns upset the tidy distribution system that Torrio had engineered. The cops were unclear as to which politician was calling the shots and who was or wasn't protected, and the Sieben deal had seemed like a good time for O'Banion to stick it to Torrio, who was losing control of city government. The death of peacekeeper Mike Merlo and O'Banion's noontime murder in his own flower shop on State Street, "That Great Street," in the shadow of the Chicago Tribune Tower, abruptly ended any mutual tolerance between O'Banion's North Side "Irish" and Torrio's "dagos."

What was not foreseen by Torrio were the anger and loyalty of O'Banion's inner circle of friends and their determination to avenge their fallen leader. Any place, any time, by any means. The battles that broke out were not called wars for nothing, and the new commander of the North Side forces, Hymie Weiss, made other gangland hotheads look like pansies by comparison.

Why Polish Catholic Earl Wojciechowski took such a Jewish-sounding name as Hymie Weiss is anybody's guess. It's possible that he fancied it would improve his relations with the city's Jewish gangsters, but more likely he understood that Wojciechowski was just too tough to pronounce and "Weiss" was close enough, and his friends may have dubbed him Hymie partly as a joke. In any case, Weiss must have been much stronger in personality than in intellect, didn't much care what he was called, and vowed death to the South Siders connected with the Syndicate with a fearlessness that verged on foolishness.

Unlike the general public, he knew that Capone was Torrio's muscle and may have decided to go after him first. On the morning of January 12, 1925, at the corner of State Street and Fifty-fifth, a carload of

North Siders riddled Capone's automobile with bullets, badly wounding his chauffeur, Sylvester Barton. On the other hand, the shooters were far out of their territory, the target car was a Cadillac (a Syndicate trademark, the way another gang might favor Lincolns), and Torrio and Capone both lived on the Far South Side (at 7011 South Clyde and 7240 South Prairie, respectively), so it's conceivable the attackers thought they were shooting at Capone's boss—not that it mattered. It turned out the Cadillac's passengers were Capone's cousin and a restaurant employee, but the sight of his shot-up car inspired Capone to order a virtual tank of a Caddy that was armored until it could hardly move.

A week later Weiss didn't miss, but he didn't get a kill, either. On the unusually balmy Saturday afternoon of January 25, the temperature was nearly forty when Torrio dropped off his wife to do some downtown shopping while he conducted business with First Ward Committeeman Michael "Hinky Dink" Kenna, whose political clout had not been diminished by the nervousness and uncertainties in other areas of city government. Kenna and his crony Bathhouse John Coughlin, the First Ward Alderman who, despite his nickname, was the sartorial envy of city hall, were to Chicago graft what the U.S. Bureau of Standards is to weights and measures. They might well have been Carl Sandburg's inspiration when that famous chronicler of the city's dark side penned a verse entitled "Cahoots":

> Play it across the table.
> What if we steal this city blind?
> If they want any thing let 'em nail it down
> Harness bulls, dicks, front office men,
> And the high goats up on the bench,
> Ain't they all in cahoots?
> Ain't it fifty-fifty all down the line,
> Petemen, dips, boosters, stick-ups and guns—what's to hinder?
> Go fifty-fifty.
> If they nail you call in a mouthpiece.
> Fix it, you gazump, you slant-head, fix it. . . .

Chicagoans defined an honest politician as one who, when he was bought, stayed bought. But at this time it still wasn't clear who had the most clout and to whom one should sell out.

His business with Hinky Dink concluded, Torrio, who disdained diamond stickpins, pinky rings, and bodyguards, and easily passed for a prosperous, well-mannered executive—who in fact tried to conduct bootlegging like any other business—helped his wife load packages into the car that would take them back to their fashionable South Shore apartment building, where the two were known to neighbors as a pleasant couple named Langley who owned a brokerage, or something.

What happened then was enough to lower neighborhood property values. Anna Torrio, her arms loaded with packages, was backing through the foyer door, intending to hold it open for her similarly loaded-down husband, when two of O'Banion's closest friends emerged with guns from an idling automobile parked at the nearby corner on Seventieth Street. Weiss had a shotgun and Moran a .45 automatic, and with their usual poor judgment they expended their first barrage on the bodywork of the car, missing Torrio, who was protected by its heavy doors, but wounding the chauffeur in the leg. In his dash to reach the building, Torrio gave Weiss and Moran the clear shots they needed, and he was hit by projectiles from both the .45 and the shotgun. Moran ran over to put a slug through Torrio's head, only to discover that his pistol was empty. At that moment, Vincent Drucci, at the wheel of their car, saw a van turn onto Clyde Avenue and began honking the horn. Weiss and Moran, believing Torrio to be a goner, ran to their vehicle and escaped.

A woman neighbor who witnessed the shooting frantically called the Woodlawn police station, which dispatched two officers and an ambulance. And when Torrio's identity became known, the response was more lively, both at the scene and at the Jackson Park Hospital where he was rushed. In spite of bullet and buckshot wounds to his jaw, neck, chest, stomach, and right arm, Torrio pulled through; in spite of eyewitness identifications of Weiss, Moran, and Drucci, the badly battered Torrio only shook his head. Over the next few days so many suspects were prodded into Torrio's room and then released that his doctors began to object on medical grounds, so in an effort to look as if they were doing something useful, the police arrested Al Capone.

After the shooting the limping chauffeur, Bobby Barton, brother of Sylvester who had been wounded in Capone's car a week earlier, had made it to a pay phone a few blocks away to call Capone at the Hawthorne Hotel. "Mr. Brown" was one of the first to reach the hospital, didn't keep his names straight, and after checking on the condition of "Mr. Langley," who also didn't keep his names straight, told skeptical police that the shooting couldn't have been the work of the North Siders' three top musketeers because Torrio and the late O'Banion had always been "best friends." Anna Torrio had a ringside view of the attack, but when asked by police to describe the gunmen she brushed them off with, "What's the use?"

While Capone was entertaining the cops at the station, two or three carloads of hard-looking men arrived at the hospital claiming to be Torrio's good buddies. The duty nurse advised their spokesman that visiting hours did not extend to two A.M. but indicated that she could summon one of the police guards from the room if they wanted to discuss the matter. The would-be visitors decided they could come back at a more convenient hour. Upon learning of this clumsy attempt, Capone moved into an adjoining room. Meanwhile, the wounded Barton brothers were probably wondering if driving cars for Chicago mobsters had been a good career move after all. Three weeks later, on February 9, Capone helped his still-wobbly mentor down the hospital's back fire escape to a touring sedan that whisked him to safety.

In this case the safest place was in the town of Waukegan, some thirty miles north of Chicago, behind the bars of the Lake County Jail where Torrio could do his time for the Sieben bust. The building looked properly forbidding, but like a medieval castle its purpose now, with Torrio in residence, was more to keep danger out while its most important prisoner enjoyed the amenities of a mini-resort inside. In fact, Torrio, despite the extra time granted by the court for his recovery, had checked in early, received his wife and trusted visitors at his convenience, and otherwise tried to conduct business as usual. If anything discouraged him, it was a sense of failure to organize Chicago's bootlegging and related activities into a peaceful kingdom over which he could preside like a benevolent despot, counseling gang members to forgo their rough and rowdy ways (robbery, burglary, safecracking, shooting) and authorizing violence only in rare cases of betrayal or recidivism.

Keeping gang violence to a minimum was how New York had managed to avoid the spotlight of national notoriety. It helped that the city was about to elect Jimmy Walker as mayor. The amiable Walker knew just how much law to enforce without seriously inconveniencing his boodlers, bootleggers, barkeeps, or the average New Yorker who found Prohibition had made for safer streets, thanks to the closing of raucous saloons with their reeling drunks and pestering harlots. Without meaning to, Walker had turned drinking into an exciting indoor sport, attractive to flappers and floozies at a propitious time when the new women's equality movement was earning them the right to vote. And also without meaning to, he invented the call girl.

New York's wild days began in 1928 with the killing of gambler Arnold Rothstein, reputed fixer of the 1919 World Series, and the spectacular machine-gun murder of Brooklyn gang lord Frankie Yale. The city's first response to such broad-daylight violence was to blame it on an influx of uncivilized gangsters from Chicago. That was the town where the West began, at least to New Yorkers, some of whom weren't entirely sure that it didn't start in western New Jersey. While cooling his heels in the Waukegan jail on his Sieben conviction, Torrio himself had sadly concluded that the Second City was unwilling to be tamed, and in abandoning Chicago he bequeathed his problems to Al Capone, who probably did not say (several famous-quotation books notwithstanding), "You can get much farther with a smile, a kind word, and a gun than you can with a smile and a kind word."

Capone took over the Torrio operation without fanfare, and newspapers were slow to recognize him as Torrio's singular successor. Some spelled his name Alfred Caponi, Tony Caponi, or Alfonso Capone, while others got his name right part of the time but also referred to Cicero's "Torrio–Brown" gang, using Capone's alias. Nor did Capone assume his new position without a genuine fear for his life, not only from the North Siders still bent on killing him but also from disgruntled gunmen in several other gangs which had formerly belonged to the Torrio cartel. O'Banion's funeral had been quietly attended by South Siders Frank McErlane and "Polack Joe" Saltis, signaling their defection to the North Siders, whom they hoped would help protect their territory from the South Side O'Donnells, led by brother Spike, who had been slow to take up bootlegging owing to his imprisonment for an armed robbery.

The O'Banionites needed a period for mourning—or for plotting revenge—but after some conferences (and probably a few shootings) convinced them of Saltis and McErlane's sincerity, they evidently loaned their new South Side allies one or more of Deanie's brand-new submachine guns as a goodwill gesture. Exactly when the more demented McErlane acquired the gun and why it didn't see action until the fall of 1925 might have been the result of the police and political confusion that prevailed during Mayor William Dever's first full year in office, when city government and city bootlegging were in equal disarray.

Since taking office with a vow to clean up city politics, Dever had been padlocking dives, joints, beer flats, clubs, and speakeasies without so much as consulting the local aldermen—at least not in Republican wards. How many reopened the next day or the next week has never been calculated, but by the summer of 1925 things looked bleak, and a sense of panic prevailed not only among the working-class beer-drinkers but also among those of the wealthy who had neglected to fill their basements and coal bins with enough pre-Volstead booze to survive what now was beginning to look like a prolonged drought. Colosimo's and the Four Deuces both had been ceremoniously shuttered for the benefit of the press, as if to make Dever's point, and the gang's leadership accommodated him by moving to the adjoining suburb of Cicero.

Little Italy occupied the territory roughly bounded by Taylor Street up to Congress and from the Chicago River west to Ashland, and there the home-cooked alcohol industry was ruled by the Genna family, which retained an uneasy relationship with Capone. So, with the failed attacks on both Capone and Torrio, the O'Banions settled for knocking off as many of the several brothers as the occasion permitted. Meanwhile, the Saltis–McErlane Gang on the Far South Side had been largely ignored by Dever's troops—or were sufficiently Irish, or Democrats, or rogue Republicans, or considered too crazy—and they felt confident enough to retake territory lost to the South Side O'Donnells now that Brother Spike was back on the street. And they had their O'Banion submachine gun to give them an edge in firepower.

The corner of Western Avenue and Sixty-third Street was practically a city in its own right, with its wide four-lane intersection surrounded by such consumer businesses as a large Walgreens drug store on the northwest corner, and it was there that Spike O'Donnell often could be found. A forest of street lights made the intersection nearly as bright as day, and Spike was at his post in front of the drugstore on the Friday evening of September 25 when he heard his name shouted from a touring car that had passed through the intersection heading east to west.

If the shout was to identify O'Donnell among the other pedestrians, it probably wasn't necessary, because he was a distinctively tall, lean, and well-dressed fellow in his middle twenties who stood out in any crowd. It was also a mistake. Spike instantly dove to the sidewalk as a barrage of machine-gun bullets passed over him and took out the plate glass windows of the drugstore. Everyone nearby did the same thing, and as the car vanished into the darkness beyond Western Avenue, O'Donnell got back to his feet, surveyed the damage, and walked casually into the drugstore, where a wide-eyed clerk emerged from behind the soda fountain to give him a drink of water.

What the cops couldn't figure out, and what Spike didn't tell them, was how so many men with .45 automatics could squeeze into one automobile, even a touring car.

Barely a week later, on the evening of October 3, the Tommygun struck again. Someone in a traditional black touring car emptied most of a drum into the headquarters of the Ralph Sheldon gang, killing one Charles Kelly—presumably the Thompson's first victim—who was standing in front of the building, and fatally wounding a Thomas Hart, who died later without even making it into the Chicago Crime Commission's gangland body count, or Tommygun history.

But at least the police had figured out what all the bullet holes meant. According to *The Chicago Daily News*:

> A machine gun, a new note of efficiency in gangland assassination, was used to fire the volley from the black touring car, killing one man and wounding another in front of the Ragen Athletic Club . . . at 5142 South Halsted St. last Saturday night.

Captain John Enright of the stockyards police said today his investigation satisfied him that a machine gun had been used, and that the same gun had been used in an attack on Spike O'Donnell at 63rd St. and South Western Ave. . . .

"The bullets were fired from a machine gun," Captain Enright said, "because we find that more than twenty bullets were fired into the clubhouse. Witnesses say they came in too rapid succession to be revolver shots. However, we are basing our theory on something more than that. . . .

"So far as their being bullets as were fired at 'Spike' O'Donnell, I compared them with bullets which Englewood police picked up at the time and they are identical."

The eyeball test was good enough for police at the time, and despite the machine gun, most newspapers buried the story on an inside page. The wire services picked it up as a short human-interest item—the latest wrinkle in Chicago gangland warfare. But that was it. The papers paid even less attention two weeks later when the persevering McErlane shotgunned Spike O'Donnell's car, wounding his brother, Tommy.

If McErlane's first attacks were poorly reviewed by both the police and the press, he finally attracted notice as Chicago's Tommygun pioneer on February 9, 1926. That shooting, in spite of the usual poor marksmanship, earned the *Chicago Tribune*'s banner headline the following morning and started the Thompson on its road to ill fame:

MACHINE GUN GANG SHOOTS TWO

Thirty-seven bullets from a light automatic machine gun were poured into the saloon of Martin (Buff) Costello, 4127 South Halsted street, last night, by gangsters striving to assassinate two rivals for the highly profitable south side traffic in good beer.

Both men were wounded. William Wilson, 329 South Leavitt street, was shot in the head and probably fatally wounded. John (Mitters) Foley, 2838 Wallace street, vice president of the Ice Cream Wagon Drivers union, beer runner, and onetime stick-up man, was struck in the forehead but not seriously injured.

The same day that story appeared, Al Capone, as though fearful of lagging behind in the underworld arms race, sent two of his men to the hardware and sporting goods store of Alex V. Korecek to place a rush order for three Thompson guns. Korecek, whose otherwise modest shop on Eighteenth Street bordered the tough South Side neighborhood known as the Valley, had no desire to become an underworld arms dealer. However, from the looks of both customers he decided this was an order he could not refuse. Soon enough he'd regret having inherited his departed father's business.

At this time Capone wasn't overly concerned about the North Siders, who hadn't shot at him lately and seemed content to chip away at the Genna family tree. His immediate problem was with the West Side O'Donnells, led by brother Klondike and no relation to the South Side O'Donnells, led by brother Spike. The West Siders were loosely allied with the O'Banions and amounted to Irish potatoes in the growing vineyards of eastern Cicero. While their removal was more preemptive than counteroffensive, it would turn out to have serious repercussions that Torrio's heir did not anticipate. The Korecek weapons made their debut on April 23, 1926, when Capone gangsters poured ninety-two bullets into the beauty shop of Pearl Hruby at 2208 South Austin Boulevard in Cicero, wounding Pearl's gangster-boyfriend, James "Fur" Sammons of the West Side O'Donnells. But that hardly rated a police call compared to the mini-massacre four days later.

About 8:30 on Tuesday evening, April 27, 1926, Ed Maschek was in no particular hurry to get to his home in Berwyn and had decided to stop for a beer at the Pony Inn at 5613 West Twelfth Street (now Roosevelt Road), a thoroughfare that becomes the northern city limits of Cicero on its way to Oak Park and Berwyn. His Model T was chugging west a few car lengths behind an expensive green Lincoln with several passengers who evidently had the same idea, for the word was out that the Pony had upgraded its brew from the Capone product served in nearly all the speakeasies in that area to a better brand supplied by some other bootleggers. This was a chancy move by owners Harry Madigan and Mike Wendell, and what Maschek didn't know was that the Lincoln's passengers included members of the Klondike O'Donnell gang, which was expanding its operations to the point of encroaching on enemy territory. Both cars were moving at a leisurely pace when a black touring car containing four men pulled out of a side street and began tailing the Lincoln, forcing Maschek to drop back.

The Lincoln pulled up to the curb in front of the Pony Inn and three men had started getting out when the touring car pulled alongside, coming almost to a stop. Maschek was about to pull up behind the Lincoln when all hell broke loose. The touring car's driver floored the accelerator while his passengers poked guns out of the side curtains and nearly shot the Lincoln and the tavern to pieces. One man from the Lincoln staggered to the vacant lot next door, trying to get out of bullet range; another collapsed on the sidewalk; and a third, glasses dangling from one ear, managed to crawl a few steps toward the speakeasy's entrance before he collapsed.

Maschek had jammed on his brakes and didn't see how anyone could have survived, but two men protected by luck and the Lincoln's bodywork scrambled out, pulled two of their companions back into the car, and sped off. Maschek jumped from his Ford and reached the tavern at about the same time that Madigan, Wendell, and two patrons, after making sure the attackers were gone, came running outside. The victim who had made it as far as the lot groaned curses that his friends had left him to "die like a dog," which he did shortly after being rushed to Western Suburban Hospital. Some two hundred bullets and shotgun slugs had peppered the two-story building, causing the owners and patrons to hit the floor in the belief that they were the targets. Afterward, with gun smoke still in the air, they recognized the mortally wounded man as Thomas "Red" Duffy, one of their new bootleggers.

An elderly woman who lived above the tavern, and who happened to be looking out her window, later described the scene to police and reporters: "It was daylight still and I saw a closed car speeding away with what looked like a telephone receiver sticking out the rear window and spitting fire." The Thompson gun doesn't resemble a telephone receiver, but it hardly seemed a point worth questioning in the excitement of the occasion.

Meanwhile, the Lincoln's panic-stricken driver and his one uninjured passenger, Myles O'Donnell, headed straight for the house of Klondike O'Donnell at 122 South Parkside, near Columbus Park, with two bodies cooling in the back. The rattled Klondike told them to keep going and to dump the blood-soaked Lincoln and the stiffs anywhere but in Chicago, preferably somewhere they wouldn't be tripped over.

Some time later the Oak Park police found the bullet-riddled Lincoln, still containing five fedoras. And the next morning Berwyn police found two corpses stretched out in a field at Sixteenth Street and Wisconsin Avenue, each shot seven times. One, which officials identified as bootlegger James Doherty was taken to a funeral home, but the other, with all the identifying labels cut from his clothing, had been left at the scene for Chicago police to examine. Easily recognizable from pictures in the newspapers, which had lavishly praised his success at getting death penalties in seven of ten well-publicized murder cases, the corpse was that of twenty-seven-year-old William H. McSwiggin, assistant state's attorney, popularly known as Cook County's "hanging prosecutor."

The newspapers trumpeted the story on page one under the headline STATE'S ATTORNEY MURDERED BY GANGSTERS! or whatever words fit their particular format. The three additional bodies qualified the hit as a mini-massacre, and for the first time in years Chicagoans were truly alarmed. Gangsters killing gangsters was page-three news, unless the victim was well known or stray bullets took out a pedestrian. But killing a public official, especially a well-known prosecutor, compelled the state's attorney, the mayor, the police commissioner, the chief of detectives, and other public figures to declare war on the city's gunmen, round up hundreds of suspects, padlock speakeasies and whorehouses all over Greater Chicago, and otherwise proclaim that this time the criminals had gone too far.

Known gangster hangouts were suddenly empty, and even Al Capone had gone into hiding. One of his refuges was the home of Dominic Roberto, whose attractive young wife, Rio,[4] was a nightclub singer domestic enough to provide a safe harbor for a man whose hold on Cicero was finally making him known to the police as Torrio's successor.

The crime was so shocking that it rated the lead article in *Collier's Weekly* under the catchy title, "Machine Gun Madness," in which the writer pulled out all the stops:

> This Thompson submachine gun is nothing less than a diabolical engine of death . . . the paramount example of

peace-time barbarism . . . the diabolical acme of human ingenuity in man's effort to devise a mechanical contrivance with which to murder his neighbor.

The nationwide publicity surrounding the killing of a public official acquainted the entire country with the submachine gun, turning it into the "Tommygun"—the Chicago gangster's weapon of choice.

When the smoke cleared, all the police really had were a dead prosecutor, three dead bootleggers who would not be missed, and a Thompson submachine gun which the shooters had thrown from their car. The weapon's serial number had been ground off, but Auto-Ordnance Sales Manager Marcellus Thompson, son of the inventor, knew where to look for the gun's secret serial number (stamped on the receiver under the foregrip mount) and caught the next train to Chicago to volunteer his services.

It would soon become apparent that his services were not particularly welcome, but Thompson's comments in *Collier's*, at the time one of the country's most popular magazines, acquainted millions of Americans with the wild side of Chicago:

> "I trailed this gun down by its number, and found that it had gone, through a prominent sporting-goods store in Chicago [presumably Von Lengerke and Antoine's, by way of a wholesaler in Valparaiso, Indiana], to a foreigner who owns a sporting-goods store in 'The Valley.' . . .
>
> "That 'Valley' is a tough place. It's a hangout of some of the worse of the Chicago gangs.
>
> "As soon as I got the address I got into a car and hurried out to the store. I felt I was taking my life in my hands because I was sure that the gangsters knew I was in town and was trying to trace down the gun. One automobile loaded with gangsters hovered around my car and passed us several times. I haven't the slightest doubt that the men in this car were armed. . . .
>
> "I went to the state's attorney's office too with the facts. William McSwiggin was an assistant state's attorney, and I wanted to be sure that the facts about the selling of the gun

would get into the hands of State's Attorney Crowe. It was pretty hard for me to get to Mr. Crowe. I practically had to force my way in to him, and I told him what I had discovered about the dealer in arms.

"I had done all I could do, and so I went back to New York."

The city police immediately picked up Korecek and during three days of interrogation treated him so roughly that even Marcellus Thompson was moved to pity. At one point the cops brought in a suspect whose appearance before the frightened and battered Korecek caused him to pass out. When revived with cold water, still shaking and barely able to talk, he assured police he'd never seen the fellow before. On May 1, out of nowhere, a writ of habeas corpus was filed for Korecek's release. Asked by reporters who his unknown friend was, he said he didn't know. "But I know he isn't any friend of mine!" he added and begged to remain in jail.

Korecek somehow managed to survive both the cops and Capone, and Capone, of course, survived the police investigation.

Capone had gone to ground at Dominic Roberto's until McSwiggin had been laid to rest with a funeral as grand as that of any gang leader's, possibly cursing his bad luck at wasting a perfectly good assistant state's attorney who was on the take and whose death had generated enormous negative publicity. Over the next few weeks, however, it began to look like McSwiggin simply had been in the wrong place at the wrong time and with the wrong people.

What was he doing entering a speakeasy with a group of bootleggers, two of whom he had failed to convict for murder the previous year? Al Dunlap, editor of *The Detective*, a magazine for law enforcement personnel, and incidentally a sales rep for the company that made Thompson guns, lamely claimed that McSwiggin had gone to the speakeasy for him, trying to retrieve some bulletproof vests for which he hadn't been paid. A police official claimed that McSwiggin was doing undercover work, which naturally required him to fraternize with hoodlums. The most interesting theory was that the West Side O'Donnells had appointed themselves the official beer suppliers to the northeastern part of Cicero, and to establish credibility they had brought along the unsuspecting McSwiggin, who would not have knowingly crossed Capone.

These and other theories were tried and found wanting, except that the last seemed entirely plausible. But after a blue-ribbon coroner's jury, five special grand juries, and a federal grand jury started uncovering McSwiggin's underworld connections, even his police-sergeant father, who had vowed to avenge his son's death, decided that the wisest course of action was to back off and hope the press would do the same. Since reporters had their own connections to preserve, in both the underworld and the state's attorney's office, they tried not to let unproven speculations disturb the public's original belief that gangsters were becoming so fearless they could murder public officials.

When the dust settled, it was clear that McSwiggin's extracurricular activities should remain with his remains, and Capone had learned that killing even a crooked public figure, even by accident, would cause an uproar. Unlike an entertainer for whom "there's no such thing as bad publicity," criminals prefer to work in the dark.

Capone already had learned that it did not pay to stir up the police. During the summer of 1922, when he was twenty-three, he partied himself into such a state that he crashed his car into a taxicab parked near the corner of Randolph and Wabash in downtown Chicago, injuring the cab driver. He climbed out waving a gun and a special deputy sheriff's badge (almost everybody had one), threatening to shoot first the injured cabbie and then a nosy streetcar conductor who had witnessed the accident. The police arrived before more blood was spilled, but "Alfred Caponi" was charged with drunk driving, assault with a motor vehicle, and carrying a concealed weapon.

After the prisoner calmed down and proper discussions could take place with the proper authorities, all charges were dropped before Capone was further inconvenienced. Then on May 8, 1923, in Heinie Jacob's tavern only half a block from the Four Deuces, a punk named Joe Howard roughed up Torrio's whoremaster Jake Guzik, who went straight to Capone, who in turn stormed down to the speakeasy and sobered other patrons by firing six bullets into Howard. Nobody saw the shooting because everything "happened so quickly," but Capone decided he should lay low for a week and practice anger management. When he was sure no drunk had suffered pangs of conscience and tattled to police, he appeared at the state's attorney's office, asked if anyone wanted to talk to him, and was told no by an ambitious young prosecutor named William McSwiggin.

Three years later, when McSwiggin met the West Side O'Donnells and then his Maker, State's Attorney Robert Crowe, who was not given to understatement, called it "the most brazen and dastardly murder ever committed in Chicago" and started shuffling through all the different theories, favoring those which did not disgrace McSwiggin. However, Chicago police Captain John Stege declared from the start that the slaughter was the work of the "Brown–Torrio gang of Cicero." Fearing that the competing police agencies would declare the murder and the mystery "solved" simply by shooting him on sight (and there was in fact just such a plot involving several Chicago detectives), Capone remained in hiding at Dominic Roberto's and in northern Indiana for three months before arranging to surrender secretly to federal agents on July 28 at the Illinois state line.

Two and a half years later the murder was still "unsolved," Big Bill Thompson was back in the mayor's office, business and bloodshed were back to normal, and Capone had tried to exonerate himself once and for all by testifying before the federal grand jury which had earlier indicted him. "Just ten days before he was killed I talked with McSwiggin," Capone stated. "There were friends of mine with me. If we had wanted to kill him, we could have done it then and nobody would have known. But we didn't want to; we never wanted to."

To a reporter who continued pestering him, Capone was even more forthcoming: "Of course, I didn't kill him. Why would I? I liked the kid. Only the day before he got killed he was up to my place and when he went home I gave him a bottle of Scotch for his old man. I paid McSwiggin and I paid him plenty, and I got what I was paying for."

This was not what Chicagoans wanted to hear, even if it was true. But it took the McSwiggin murder to expose the degree of anarchy to which the city had descended during the well-intentioned Dever administration, and in a perverse way it invited the return of Big Bill Thompson to the mayor's office on his promise to run a wide-open town. The adage "Better the devil you know than the devil you don't know" seemed to appeal to voters, much to the dismay of reformers. But the McSwiggin case also marked the beginning of intense public interest in political corruption and locally organized crime.

V

"DEVER AND DECENCY"

IF MAYOR WILLIAM DEVER'S EFFORTS at reform were frustrated at every turn, they also were no picnic for Al Capone. Dever's crackdowns in Chicago had sent Capone into exile in Cicero, where Chicago police had killed his older brother Frank during the election violence of 1924. The Sieben Brewery swindle that same year led to O'Banion's murder and set off one beer battle after another, including counterattacks on Torrio and Capone in 1925, when the submachine gun made its inaugural appearance.

Torrio had turned over his position to Capone, who made both the city and the Tommygun synonymous with Prohibition crime by killing McSwiggin the following April. After the death of that assistant state's attorney, Capone barely escaped Dever's raiders, who were deputized by a county judge and hit Cicero with a blitzkrieg of axes, sledgehammers, and padlocks while Mayor Joseph Klenha and his own police force stood by helplessly.

Since abandoning Chicago, Capone had turned that nearly moribund suburb into a night-and-day carnival of bars, nightclubs, gambling joints, whorehouses, and combinations of all three, which

Klenha could not have prevented even if he'd tried. Much of the consumer spending that had been keeping Chicago wet and wild was now bringing prosperity to Cicero, whose main industry had been the giant Western Electric plant a block east of the Hawthorne Hotel. With Mayor Klenha and virtually everyone else in city government on the gangland payroll, Capone's gunmen, unhampered by legalities, had then kept the peace with only a few killings of political or underworld opponents in what amounted to a pruning process, and street crime was practically eliminated.

Nor was it necessary for Capone's men to round up Chicagoans at gunpoint and force them to engage in Cicero's wide-open revelry. Harness bulls (street cops) and Syndicate gunmen fraternized on the sidewalks, ready to deal with the occasional problem patron ejected by a club's "security" personnel, who could barely fit into their size XXL tuxedos, tailored to accommodate shoulder holsters. With McSwiggin's death Chicago's deputized police found the suburb's liveliest places closed for repairs, but they still laid waste to much of the town whose city hall basement was suspected to be the sampling room for various kinds of beer.

After his three-month absence, Capone was just getting Cicero back on its feet when the restless North Siders resumed their efforts to kill him. The attack took place at about noon on September 20, 1926, while Capone was eating lunch at the Hawthorne's Italian restaurant, and while it made the front page of every Chicago paper, the event was not judged important enough for banner headlines. Several automobiles full of North Side gunmen, presumably including Hymie Weiss, cruised slowly past Capone's headquarters from west to east on Twenty-second Street (Cicero's main thoroughfare) and poured three hundred to one thousand rounds of buckshot and machine-gun bullets into the front of the Hawthorne and the Anton Hotels, hitting the three businesses in between, some parked cars, and wounding three or four people, one seriously.

As usual, every newspaper published its own version of the event, and nearly every crime writer since then has added cars to the motorcade, which differed as to where Capone was eating and how he escaped injury, and agreed only on the one thing that probably wasn't true.

Virtually every book describes a lead car coming down the street firing blanks to disperse pedestrians and draw Capone to the window.

However, Thompson guns won't work with blanks unless the muzzle has a constricting device to build up enough barrel pressure to work the blow-back action. If sound effects are desired, just shoot high.

The number of cars in the motorcade has grown from three or five to eight or a dozen, as later writers embellished the event. In most accounts one machine-gunner gets out of his car and stands or kneels in the street, hosing down the area like a fireman, and several witnesses do confirm this. (In a 1967 movie that includes the event, it's George Segal.) But Capone, either shoved to the floor by a bodyguard or scampering out the back door, was infuriated. The Hawthorne was supposed to be off-limits. He received unwanted publicity because of the attack but did get some mileage out of it by paying for the damage to the stores and parked cars, spending five thousand dollars to save the eyesight of a woman injured by flying glass on the sidewalk, and establishing that other gangsters also had Tommyguns.

The attack on the Hawthorne occurred barely two months after Capone had emerged from hiding, had eluded incrimination in the McSwiggin matter, and was trying to rebuild Cicero into a vice mecca he could be proud of. But to this day the siege of Cicero is regarded as the mother of all drive-by shootings, and regardless of how many cars were involved, it was a vivid reminder that Capone would never be safe as long as Hymie Weiss was alive. For recklessness and audaciousness it was Weiss's finest hour, as befitting his valedictory.

Three weeks later, on October 11, Weiss, his bodyguard Patrick (called "Paddy") Murray, and two others arrived in front of the Holy Name Cathedral and started across the street to Schofield's Flower Shop when a machine gun and a shotgun opened up. Weiss fell with ten slugs in him and Murray with fifteen. The others were not primary targets and survived their lesser wounds.

The guns were fired from an upstairs window in a rooming house next door to Schofield's, but the Thompson had jammed after thirty-five rounds because a bullet lodged in its barrel. Some of the slugs strayed into the cornerstone of the cathedral, knocking out a chunk of the limestone, and while later writers have made it sound as if the hits had rewritten the pious inscription, most photographers at the scene didn't think it merited a picture. Nor did the shot-up cornerstone become a Chicago tourist attraction, as might have been expected, and since then most of it has been covered by wide concrete steps.

Police naturally failed to catch the shooters but did come away with the jammed Tommygun, which had been tossed onto the roof of a doghouse in an alley. A week later they found that a second machine-gun nest had occupied a third-floor corner room in a building at State Street and Superior. Apparently its purpose was to nail anyone who ran south or had made it into the flower shop thinking they could escape out the back. This was a typical of Capone; the window was diagonally across from the cathedral and commanded the entire intersection, leaving nothing to chance. The range was greater, but so was the view. The machine-gun bullets that killed Weiss and his bodyguard were fired at a shorter range and nearly head-on. The other victims, who arrived in a second car and were a few feet behind, received less serious wounds, probably from shotgun pellets, and either made their way to a nearby doctor's office or otherwise vanished.

The fact that no gunfire came from the second nest may indicate that the shooters displayed discipline, since many slugs fired from there would have ricocheted up State Street, possibly hitting bystanders. State Street wasn't as peaceful then as it is now, for two blocks away was McGovern's Liberty Inn (and bawdyhouse) where Dean O'Banion had once been a singing waiter, and other dives were plentiful. Washington Park, known as Bughouse Square, was in the same neighborhood fronting the Newberry Library.

The main thing was that after the attack on the Hawthorne, Capone needed to strike back quickly to make his point, and the North Siders still were headquartered above Schofield's.

Capone probably didn't know, but Weiss's bodyguard, Paddy Murray, had a brother-in-law with the same last name, James Murray,[5] who was serving time at Leavenworth for masterminding in 1924 what is considered the greatest train robbery in American history, at Rondout, some thirty miles north of Chicago. "Motorized bandits" led by the Newton Brothers of Texas, who had already robbed some eighty banks with very little gunplay, made off with between two and three million dollars in cash, securities, and jewelry. An unintentional shooting had caused that caper to unravel, and Murray ended up in the pokey. But as a North Sider more by geography and politics than by loyalty to the O'Banions, news of Paddy's death would not have endeared him to Al Capone.

By this time the gangland body count had reached about three hundred since the start of Prohibition, and if there was an element of irony in the war between Capone and the North Siders, it was that the O'Banions initiated the attacks but usually missed, while Capone, retaliating, usually did not. This was making Capone look bad, since it was the number of dead bodies that mattered. Chicagoans would have needed a scorecard to keep track of the carnage, but Capone, whose name was cropping up more often, seemed to be winning.

This was not to Capone's liking for several reasons. If his reputation for ruthlessness had once been an asset, now every mysterious murder was being laid at his doorstep, and that was bad for business. He also had to consider his wife, an aging mother, and a growing boy, Albert Francis, or "Sonny," who was going on ten and was being teased and tormented by schoolmates because of his father's line of work.

Torrio's departure not only made Capone the target of North Sider bullets, it also burdened him with what amounted to a giant corporation whose often unruly distributors and retailers required an army of gunmen to maintain some semblance of order and quality control. Management couldn't exactly fire subordinates, but it could shoot them—or at least make it clear that bullets spoke louder than words.

Until O'Banion rebelled in 1924, the pax Torrio had allowed bootlegging to evolve from competing one-man bands into a citywide orchestra composed of a string section here, woodwinds there, and other instrumentalists working together harmoniously under a director who had tried to sleight no one and still keep his patrons happy. It's unclear who coined the expression originally, but under Torrio, Chicago was the "city that worked," albeit in its own special way.

It worked at a price, but the price was affordable to Chicagoans who might otherwise have had to wend their way through a maze of honest but passive-aggressive bureaucrats instead of tipping a fixer who could get things done. It also kept them in beer and booze. The city's best hotels hired permanent "guests" to send chatty, hand-written notes to prospective visitors extolling the beauty of the city, the hotel's luxuries, and concluding with a cute reference to the bell boys' eagerness to respond to any "whispered" request, adding, "Who said this country's dry!"

O'Banion's murder ended the bootleggers' relatively peaceful coex-istence about the same time that Dever's Democrats wrecked Chicago's perfected system of graft, which followed the Chinese model of the day. A *Harper's* writer tried to explain to American readers (who were developing a fascination with the mysterious Orient) why Chinese culture had always accepted a practice that best translated as "squeeze," so long as it did not violate their sense of *li*, or that which is right and reasonable. This, he suggested, derived from the Confucian ideal of the superior man so disciplined in virtue that he lives not by laws but by grace. Chicagoans, he could have pointed out, might be engaging in bribery, graft, grease, payoffs, skimming, rackets, the fix, and the pass—all contrary to statutory laws based on Christian teachings—but they should not exceed what was accepted as right and reasonable.

Torrio and later Capone were hardly Confucians, but they instinctively understood the principle of *li*, as did their favored politicians and civic officials, down to the cop on the beat. In retro-spect, Prohibition was an unreasonable law and Chicagoans had overwhelmingly opposed it, so while the bootlegger technically might be a lawbreaker, he was obeying a higher calling, unless greed blinded him to *li* and he had to be—well, machine-gunned, the Chicago equivalent of righteous Confucians putting a persistent wrong-doer to the sword.

When Capone eventually became a celebrity gangster, he would denounce the graft associated with Prohibition as well as the law's fundamental hypocrisy. "When I sell liquor," he said, "they call it bootlegging; when my patrons serve it on silver trays on Lake Shore Drive, they call it hospitality."

Chicago did in fact have several honest politicians, usually in wards that included a university. They were articulate enough to be newsworthy and harmless enough to be a protected species, like the whooping crane. Fifth Ward Alderman Robert Merriam, the son of a reform mayoral candidate a few years earlier, was one who recognized his own unique status in such matters and would declare, with what sounded like a touch of pride: "Chicago is unique. It is the only completely corrupt city in America." (When someone claimed another city was equally corrupt, he'd answer, "But it isn't nearly so big!")

This ambivalence was reflected in the press. *The London Daily News* stewed that in Chicago, "Three thousand hooligan gangs are carrying on a campaign of brigandage and murder." The paper went on to describe death lists, machine-gun fire, bullet-swept streets, and the Illinois governor's threat to place the city under martial law.

In its "Terrifying Chicagoan" editorial, the *Tribune*'s sardonic sense of humor would not have amused Capone, who had come out of hiding only to remain a prisoner of his own need for protection. His first effort to arrange a truce with the North Siders was answered by their motorcade of machine-gunners who shot up his Cicero headquarters. So he killed Hymie Weiss and tried again, hoping that Weiss's successor, Vincent Drucci, would call off the attacks. Drucci agreed to a conference at the Morrison Hotel on October 21, 1926, and it was attended by the leaders or emissaries of all the city's major gangs. (It probably helped that Joe Saltis and Frank McErlane were both locked up at the time.) Territories from the Torrio days were reconfirmed or reallocated, and the truce seemed to hold, at least among the gang leaders.

This didn't stop the troops from settling some old scores, but at least no spectacular gun battles took place, and Dever's police, with payoffs still in disarray, took pleasure in potting individual gunmen when given the chance. One victim was North Side gang leader Drucci, picked up by the cops on April 4, a primary election day, and killed by his arresting officer when the two began trading insults. Accounts of the shooting differed—the officer claiming Drucci had tried to grab his gun, a witness saying the cop simply lost his temper and plugged Drucci with four bullets. Drucci's lawyer cried "murder," but no charges were filed and the police chief said his shooter should be given a medal.

With the demise of Drucci, the North Side torch passed to George "Bugs" Moran, who was less cerebral than "Schemer" Drucci but no less ambitious, given several new developments. One was racketeering, in which the control of labor unions could be extended to such trade groups as the laundry associations. Another was the courtship initiated by the Sicilian Aiello brothers, who had no great fondness for Little Italy's Genna clan, whom the North Siders had been knocking off for their suspected role in O'Banion's death and were presumably allied with Capone, who was trying, at least, to control the Unione Siciliana by proxy. Believing that Prohibition could not last forever, both Moran and Capone had begun to develop gambling operations, starting with highly profitable dog tracks in the western suburbs and bigger and better casinos in the city itself.

This is where Big Bill Thompson came in. He had shaken off the scandals that precluded his running for a third term in 1923, and the prospect of his return to the mayor's office would mean a revival of institutionalized corruption. His 1927 campaign against Dever was one of the most bizarre in the annals of American politics—and the counterfeit-cowboy-turned-showman mayor squeaked past the incumbent, who could not come up with a campaign slogan any better than "Dever for Decency."

VI

BACK IN THE SADDLE

BIG BILL THOMPSON HAD NOT been idle during his four years out of office. Among other endeavors he commissioned the construction of an impressive yawl on which he intended to sail to South America in search of the elusive (and perhaps imaginary) "tree-climbing fish," but the vessel foundered on a reef of cash-flow problems about the time it reached New Orleans. He returned to Chicago to make continuing news with his one-man war against Britain's King George, demanding that statements favorable to the British be purged from local school books. He added that if King George came to Chicago, he would "punch him in the snoot."

Thompson had his defenders, in a way. Many believed that, unlike other politicians, Thompson grafted for the "common man," rather than for special interests, which was relatively true. Cowboy humorist Will Rogers decided that, "They were trying to beat Bill with the better-element vote; the trouble with Chicago was that there ain't much better element." And while Thompson was pilloried in most newspapers, a more tolerant opinion was offered by pundit Elmer Davis writing in *Harper's*, who called him "an artist, living by inspiration and not by reason . . . riding an inspiration until it gives out, because he can always get a new one, just as good. . . ." A less kindly opponent declared Thompson to have the "carcass of a rhinoceros and the brain of a baboon."

The Chicago Crime Commission estimated that gangsters (mainly Capone) had sunk $260,000 into Thompson's Republican campaign. The police were out in force with rifles and now machine guns of their own to deal with gangland violence at the polling places, but because the gangs were likewise patrolling to prevent Dever forces from "stealing" the election, the voting was nearly peaceful. Two Democratic precinct clubs on the North Side were bombed, two election judges were kidnapped and beaten, and several shots were fired into a West Side polling place, but only a handful of voters said they were driven off by gun-waving hoods. The only newsworthy fatality was Vincent Drucci, who likely would have voted for Thompson had he not been killed by police the previous day.

Thompson's political antics may have been embarrassing, but some of his public works had turned Chicago into a showcase city, an industrial and shopping center for the American heartland, a land of legend for visitors to and from. His instincts were widely shared by a population that blamed the city's "gangster problem" and pandemic corruption on the monumental failure of Prohibition.

Efforts by Dever and his ivory-tower reformers to enforce that law had backfired to the extent that even many "drys" were having second thoughts. A debate was raging over just what percentage of alcohol in beer made it "intoxicating." The traditional saloon had been shuttered, but the speakeasy and the beer flat were thriving, doctors were prescribing alcohol for nearly any malady, and the wholesale counterfeiting of prescription blanks and liquor seals had turned drug stores into "package" stores. Nightclubs and cabarets that enjoyed even moderate protection were serving ice or setups for the hip-flask crowd, along with "highballs," "fizzes," "rickies," and "special drinks not listed." What had once been taverns now were called "soft-drink parlors" in telephone directories. Both the "wets" and the "bone-dry" Prohibitionists could cite statistics showing that Americans were drinking more booze than ever or less booze than ever, so little notice was paid to the data from either side.

What was actually alarming was the amount of poisonous alcohol being consumed, everything from "canned heat" uselessly squeezed through layers of fabric to poorly rectified "rotgut" and a concoction called Jamaican Ginger that would get the drinker looped but often contained enough wood alcohol to destroy eyesight and damage the nervous system, resulting in an awkward gait known as "jake leg." It could also kill. In a desperate effort to continue producing the alcohol needed by legitimate industry, government chemists kept coming up with different ways to add poisons that did not destroy its chemical properties but made it undrinkable if not deadly and could not readily be "cooked" out.

The number of bootleggers killed by armed but untrained, politically sponsored, and often inept enforcement agents looked good initially, but a closer examination of the body count disclosed that most victims were small-time neighborhood operators, and some were ordinary citizens who'd had a bottle under the front seat, panicked at being stopped by a cop, and tried to make a run for it. The toll among the enforcers was likewise climbing, giving the press two sets of fatalities to combine into a death list that could be blamed on Prohibition, one way or the other. By the late 1920s a back-window "bumper sticker" appeared pleading, DON'T SHOOT—I AM NOT A BOOTLEGGER.

On the legal front, some states introduced and some even passed "life for a pint" laws that could permanently imprison an habitual offender for mere possession, but the public outcry against such draconian punishment stopped most such legislation in its tracks. Meanwhile, it had become a bad joke the way some plainclothes agents flashed their badges at "protected" speakeasies and then wracked up large food and booze bills "on the house."

Big Bill Thompson had a remedy for all this. When reelected he proclaimed that henceforth no policeman could violate the sanctity of a business or a private home without a warrant, which practically eliminated enforcement of the Volstead Act in Chicago—especially since the city had allocated no funds for that purpose. His victory declaration that he was "wetter than the middle of the Atlantic ocean" spared Chicagoans the inconvenience of traveling to the suburbs and was a policy, he said, that would rid the city of the gunmen who were shooting up the place. His victory was widely celebrated by drinkers, bootleggers, and even the police, who despised dry-law enforcers.

After Thompson's 1927 victory his well-wishers turned the Loop into something resembling a carnival. Even the Police Department

Quartet, which frequently accompanied him on his travels, expanded its repertoire to include a ditty composed for the occasion:

> *Happy days are here again,*
> *The gang is feeling swell again,*
> *The mayor's coming back again . . .*
> *He was out for a while,*
> *But he's back with a smile,*
> *And he'll shove the others all about,*
> *Just like they took his appendix out!*

With Big Bill back in office, officialdom relaxed, and some hard-nosed cops found themselves exiled to places or positions where they could not seriously obstruct the city's return to "normalcy," to borrow a term coined by a former U.S. president. Moreover, it seemed that Thompson's revolt against Prohibition was paying off in diminished gangland violence, at least for a few months.

What Chicago didn't recognize, or had mistakenly attributed to battling bootleggers, was the new game in town—actually an old game that was attracting greater gangland interest, and another one that was not only reviving but thriving, because there was a definite sense that the "wets" were winning the national war of words that favored relaxation of the Volstead Act. These were racketeering and gambling, the foundations of nationally organized crime.

But at the time, attention remained focused on Prohibition, which was a much more visible issue because it concerned a much more tangible product in a "free country" that was paradoxically notorious for its efforts to outlaw sin. Enforcement proposals differed greatly, as some of the most ardent anti-Prohibitionists believed that the Eighteenth Amendment, however modified by statutory law, would remain part of the U.S. Constitution. No amendment had ever been repealed, but the way things were going, the bootlegging gangs saw Prohibition weakening and profits falling.

Truckloads of barrels and bottles involved large vehicles, manpower, and payoffs to local authorities, and more and more bootleggers were discovering that the more hazardous business of hijacking loads of booze still eliminated the grief connected with purchasing it from less-than-reliable wholesalers. Those had their own problems dealing with rum-runners whose vessels were targeted by the Coast Guard, which itself was proving corruptible, and with ship-to-shore "go-through" guys who might instead be hijackers, or whose speed-boats had limited cargo space and risky landing arrangements.

Just constructing a tunnel system that permitted cases and barrels to be delivered to one address and then conveyed under eight or ten shops (whose owners expected a cut) to a speakeasy down the block, which itself might be shuttered at the whim of the police or the federal "hooch hounds," had added substantially to the start-up costs when Prohibition looked permanent. Now prices also were dropping as large breweries, turning out near-beer for the sake of appearance, diverted much of their extracted alcohol to bogus companies which changed names every week. The breweries also stocked grocery shelves and "cordial shops" with "malt" products that preserved their trade name and might be used in the family kitchen, but which also provided the syrup or extracts that turned many homes into micro-breweries and mini-distilleries.

Even wineries had figured out a means of producing "bricks" of processed grapes which, if not carefully watched, would ferment into homemade wine. So while the rest of the country agonized over how to deal with the Eighteenth Amendment, the increasingly organized criminal operations which bootlegging had spawned began looking for easier ways to enrich themselves.

There had always been profits in sports betting, from horse and dog tracks to boxing matches, and from the entertainment business in all its forms, including casino gambling. And there was money to be made from labor unions and trade associations, especially when mismanaged, as many already were. But there was as yet no common or generic name for these diverse activities, particularly the illegal ones.

How about . . .

VII

RACKETEERING

ONTROL OF LABOR UNIONS WAS an old tradition and more or less legal if a labor leader did more for the membership than just collect dues. When a strike could be averted only by paying off a union leader, members still might benefit if their wages increased even a little or they obtained medical and other benefits. But when union dues mainly lined the pockets of a union's leaders, and any construction project was mainly an opportunity to shake down the businessman, "collective bargaining" could be called racketeering.

The word *racket* supposedly originated in New York to describe wooden noise-making devices, but it quickly evolved into a reference to any rowdy entertainment activity requiring admission tickets which neighborhood youths might force upon unhappy shopkeepers who had no use for them. By the Twenties it had become a euphemism for extortion, and eventually referred loosely to any criminal or easy-money enterprise.

One Prohibition-era racket was opening "nightclubs"—a term also coined in New York to describe a lavishly decorated ballroom with tables for dining, a dance floor, a stage for floor shows, and sometimes a connected casino operation—which could not easily be closed by a few cops with a padlock. These usually had greeters, ranging from a scantily clad Texas Guinan, whose customers liked to be called "suckers" (and who also spent time at Chicago's Green Mill Ballroom, 4802 North Broadway) to a jabbering shill in festive garb pointing the way to perdition. Inside would be cloak rooms, foyers, cigarette counters, cigarette and "26"[6] girls, usually a balcony, an expensively paneled manager's office that probably had a concealed door to the regular office for middle management and an exit leading to an alley.

If one knew where else to look—usually behind a huge fellow squeezed uncomfortably into a tuxedo, guarding a velvet curtain drawn across another door in an alcove, behind which was a comparatively skinny fellow whose well-tailored tux allowed for a shoulder holster. He likely had a gun permit as chief of security, but his main job was to supervise the legally separate casino, whose whopping profits made "nightclubbing" quite affordable, as implied by newspaper ads that promised NO COVER CHARGE for the often extravagantly produced shows and big-name entertainers.

Racketeer was supposedly a Chicago term derived from New York's *racket*, although the practice itself pre-dated New York, the Greeks, the Romans, and probably Moses and Noah. In the Roaring Twenties, newspapers began applying the term to gangsters who insinuated themselves into industrial, union, and trade associations. The granddaddy of Chicago rackets was the cleaners and dyers business, which included laundries, tailors, and suppliers of everything from hotel bed sheets to restaurant napkins and tablecloths, as well as the neighborhood shops that handled household washing and dry-cleaning. The common element in this process was an independent or a unionized truck and driver, the first of which could be terrorized and the second told whose establishment to tend.

Chicago's premier racketeer was "Big Tim" Murphy who, after a stint in the state legislature and then one in state prison for robbery, had the field much to himself until challenged by Moran's North Siders, who made their debut by way of the laundry racket. This encompassed everything from dry cleaning to "wet wash" laundries to tailors and various unions servicing them. Recalcitrant owners and drivers were beaten or had their laundry trucks burned, and if that failed to do the job the gang resorted to bombs, quaintly referred to as "calling cards" if no great damage was desired. The upshot of this was a consumer revolt, as Chicagoans who objected to the substantial cost increases actually started sending their laundry to he suburbs.

The laundry business was absurdly complex, involving more than half a dozen unions in one capacity or another as well as "open shops," and a similar number of "associations" controlling every aspect of the industry. It was a wheels-within-wheels operation baffling to customers and the press alike, with the different associations so similarly named that no outsider could tell one from another. That changed when the owner of a chain of laundries with his own cleaning plant tired of knocking on the door of State's Attorney Robert Crowe, who was supposed to regulate such businesses.

After nearly three years of futile efforts to interest the authorities, the owner, Morris Becker, said the hell with it and released a long letter he had written earlier to Crowe in which he politely lamented the inability of the law to protect him or his employees. The letter did not ask for any further action on the part of the state's attorney's office, and at a press conference Morris explained quite matter-of-factly that he had solved his problems by taking them to Al Capone.

He told reporters that he no longer had "any need of the police, of the courts, of the law. I have no need of the Employers Association of Chicago. With Al Capone as my partner, I have the best protection in the world." This gave newspapers an amazing story to run under a headline like AL CAPONE FIGHTS RACKETEERS. Such stories usually were not given the prominence that invited readers to take them too seriously, but they should have.

Instead, they were treated as short items with novelty appeal, such as Capone's unsuccessful efforts to introduce turtle racing at his speakeasies. He supposedly had seen this action while visiting Little Rock, Arkansas, bought five thousand turtles that for one reason or another refused to perform, and finally had his men release them in the city's parks. Given their long life expectancy, any very old turtles still found in Chicago's inland lakes or lagoons could be Capone originals.

While the turtle racing failed, the laundry stunt didn't, and the benefit to Capone was that he could honestly list "laundry business" as his Chicago occupation when hassled by the police in one city or another. He was a business partner of record, and many other shop owners became eager to rent their premises to Becker as a "manager-owned store." This inspired the co-authors of a book on racketeering to remark that "a standing army of hoodlums, handy with sub-machine guns and easily mobilized in high-powered motor cars, can upon occasion bring a sense of security that statutory laws no longer convey!"

The letter to Crowe had been written in December 1927. The partnership with Capone was formalized in April, 1928. On the night of June 26, 1928, Big Tim Murphy opened the front door of his home at 2525 West Morse Avenue to see who was ringing the bell at such a late hour—and was greeted by a barrage of machine-gun bullets. Either side may have taken out Big Tim, for he was in everybody's way, but with his demise and the diminishing profits from their speakeasies, the North Siders plunged more deeply into racketeering.

So did Capone, although he was credited with knocking the city's laundry prices back down to normal and in later years was complimented by Becker as being the most honest partner he could have asked for. In fact, that was one of Capone's paradoxical if not redeeming qualities: He placed great importance on loyalty, which was not always reciprocated, as he would later discover, and on being a man of his word.

By now Big Bill the Builder was becoming a mayor in name only, neglecting the corruption he had once so adroitly supervised as he ambled in and out of town, often on crackpot missions, and began showing signs of mental and political deterioration. Since the defeat of Dever, Capone had moved his headquarters back to Chicago, setting up shop first in the Metropole Hotel and then in the Lexington, a block apart on South Michigan Avenue at Twenty-third and Twenty-second Streets, respectively. He might have taken up the reigns of local government himself except that he had his hands full trying to stay alive. He was spending as much time as possible in the safety of his Florida estate, summoning his generals as needed and otherwise coming back to the city for funerals and political emergencies.

By 1928 the enormous opportunity presented by Prohibition was no longer the deciding factor in gangland leadership. "Organized crime" in Chicago was becoming disorganized, fragmenting into warring factions engaged in bootlegging, racketeering, gambling, and prostitution that even the underworld's recognized leaders could not control. And with Big Bill Thompson on mental sabbatical, there was nobody at the helm.

VIII

THE WAR OF SICILIAN SUCCESSION

BROOKLYN'S FRANKIE YALE WAS GENERALLY regarded as national president of the Unione Siciliana and had employed Al Capone as a waiter and bouncer at a scruffy dive called the Harvard Inn, no relation to the university. While attending that Harvard, Capone acquired his conspicuous facial scars in 1917, about two years before New York homicide detectives came looking for him in connection with other work he'd done for Yale. Yale packed him off to Chicago where he joined Johnny Torrio and Big Jim Colosimo, whose heart had gotten in the way of his head, blinding him to the opportunities presented by Prohibition—which, as it happened, took effect the day Capone turned twenty-one, in most places the previously legal drinking age.

Yale came to Chicago to visit his three old friends and left one of them dead before returning to Brooklyn. It was strictly business, and Torrio, with the help of Capone, soon organized a dozen other gangs into a bootlegging cartel whose scope rivaled anything put together by the country's oil tycoons since the proliferation of the motor car—the main difference being that gasoline wasn't illegal.

When the booze cartel created by Torrio started to unravel in 1923, and when O'Banion's major North Side gang openly rebelled, it was Yale who returned to Chicago, ostensibly to attend the funeral of local Unione Siciliana President Mike Merlo. While in town, he did Torrio and Capone another favor by killing Dean O'Banion. This was considered the beginning of the Chicago beer wars, and the North Siders quickly attacked Torrio and Capone. Although the South Side and West Side beer wars pitted Capone and his allies against the North Siders and theirs, Yale was spared mainly because Brooklyn was out of range.

Because of his Italian heritage, Capone had not been eligible for membership in the Sicilian Union, but he should have had enough influence to dictate who would follow Mike Merlo as president— and it wasn't Tony Lombardo, the man Capone thought had earned the position. It was Angelo Genna of the "Terrible Gennas," whose warehouse-size bottling plant in Little Italy had a working relationship with Capone's Outfit and operated so openly that police congregated at one door for payoffs while trucks picked up booze at another. But the Gennas were also expanding their control in Capone territory as they made their moves on the Unione Siciliana in Little Sicily, which then neighbored Moran territory and was otherwise controlled by the equally fierce Aiellos.

The killing of Angelo Genna took place on May 26, 1925, as he drove down Ogden Avenue and was generally attributed to the North Siders with whom the brothers had been feuding, for they were suspects in the killing of Dean O'Banion. But Capone's resentment over Angelo's Unione coup and the power struggle with the Sicilians in Little Italy made his own gunmen suspects as well.

Angelo's brother Mike was slain on June 13 in a gun battle with police whom he mistook for North Siders. With him at the time were the Sicilian "murder twins" Albert Anselmi and John Scalise, who killed two of the cops in the wild shootout. (Their first trial ended in a hung jury, but they both got off on a plea of self-defense in their second trial, incredibly enough, because the police had given chase without "probable cause." Whenever cops found the bodies of Italians and Sicilians who had no criminal record, it was believed they were killed for not contributing to the Anselmi-Scalise defense fund.) Less than a month later, on July 8, brother Anthony "Tony the Gent" Genna received the O'Banion "handshake" treatment on Grand

Avenue near Curtis Street, and his surviving brothers, Sam and Pete, wisely joined yet another brother, James, in Sicily.

Sam "Samoots" Amatuna, who was supervising the Gennas' operation on behalf of the Syndicate, tried to take over the Unione, but his term in office was cut short by two gunmen who tracked him to his favorite barbershop on March 10, 1925. Several shots were fired, and Samoots passed away in a hospital three days later.

At last, with most of the competition dead or fled, Capone's man Tony Lombardo became president of the Unione Siciliana. He changed the Chicago chapter's name to the Italo-American National Union, moved its main office from Little Sicily down to the Hartford Building at 8 South Dearborn, and opened membership to Italians. He also tried to polish up the tarnished image the organization had acquired in the old Black Hand days, when it moved from a hands-off policy to opposing them, negotiating for the lives of potential victims or for their safe return.

Capone believed Lombardo had the makings of a Mike Merlo and could quell the violence between the Unione, his mob, and maybe the North Siders, who favored Tony Aiello for geographic and business reasons. At Capone's urging, Lombardo sought to placate everybody by accepting Aiello as a co-president, in name but with little authority. Lombardo set up shop next door in the offices of the Italo-American Loan Plan Bank, which dominated the Unione and its other new co-president, Bernard Barasa, a sometimes judge also favored by Capone.

The Aiello clan of brothers and other relatives were particularly put out by this arrangement because they had virtually sponsored Lombardo when he first came to America. When brother Joe was finally elevated to share the leadership, he found the position mostly ceremonial and deeply resented what he considered yet another snub by Capone. Thus, he set aside ethnic favoritism and hooked up with the North Siders on the principle that an enemy of my enemy is my friend.

Joe Aiello was one of a large family of brothers, cousins, and uncles from "Little Sicily." Instead of going through channels, he took his grievance straight to Yale, who believed Joe was more properly in line for the Unione job and could be counted on to give him a slice of the ever-expanding Chicago pie. Yale's interest in Chicago derived partly from Torrio's return to New York and partly from loss of face when his personal favorite, Aiello, was relegated to second or even third place in the Sicilian Union. It also derived from jealousy of Capone, who had managed to achieve dominance in nearly all phases of the Chicago and suburban underworld without attracting serious attention, and from simple greed. After all, Capone was raking in enormous profits from bootlegging and a dog track as well as other enterprises, ranging from protected gambling casinos in several parts of the city and its western suburbs to prostitution in the seedier hotels in those areas of Cook County where gambling also flourished.

Racketeering and extortion knew no geographic boundaries, but there were places west of Chicago where the dog tracks, though technically illegal, were also thriving, thanks to a series of restraining orders from judges owned by Capone. None of this income was finding its way back to Frankie Yale or, for that matter, to either the national or local Unione Siciliana, although its members remained an important source of home-cooked alcohol for the lower class of speakeasies that served needled beer and synthetic whiskies, gin, and rum.

Capone grew suspicious of Yale when Chicago's supplies of "the Real McCoy" from the East Coast rum fleet became sporadic and a spy he sent to New York managed to feed back rumors of Yale's perfidy before getting himself killed. This is standard crime-history lore which may or may not have tipped Yale's hand, but Yale's interest in Capone's dog track already was well known and raised Capone's suspicions even further.

Thus, by the middle of 1927 Capone was ducking bullets from both the North Siders, now captained by Bugs Moran, as well as the Aiello brothers. About this time Joe Aiello also placed a fifty-thousand-dollar price on Capone's head, but Capone's vast intelligence network kept his main marksman, Machine Gun Jack McGurn, busy knocking off both local and out-of-town bounty hunters.

What the press could not quite fathom at the time was the four-way war between the Chicago Syndicate (which was mostly Italian), the Unione Siciliana (under whatever name, and which now accepted Italians), the North Siders, and the Sicilian Aiellos, who had formed a marriage of convenience with the Moran forces.

Capone began spending as much time as possible out of the city, usually in Florida, but also in California, Wisconsin, Michigan, Indiana, and even Iowa, where he owned part of the Julian Hotel in Dubuque. He reputedly protected small counterfeiting and distilling operations around the eastern Iowa town of Maquoketa, which was then a convenient stopover on the main road about halfway between Dubuque and Davenport.

When business or bullets dictated a brief absence from Chicago, he camped comfortably at the Miami Gardens, a roadhouse now operating peacefully on northern Indiana's main route to Florida. It still has rooms once used by prostitutes at one end of the second floor, and at the other end a well-furnished room that was Capone's closest out-of-state office, complete with an expensive multi-nozzle bath and shower (still in good working order) constructed with the same costly Nile-green tile that made his Lexington Hotel bathroom so distinctive.

IX

CHICAGO'S "PINEAPPLE PRIMARY"

T HE WARFARE AMONG THE DIFFERENT criminal factions was going full blast at the end of 1927, and on more than one front. The beer wars had continued despite the efforts of Capone to call a truce after the killing of Hymie Weiss; the Syndicate had been drawn into racketeering by North Sider efforts to take over the Master Cleaners and Dyers Association and its subsidiaries and unions; both sides had competing dog tracks; and both sides had taken full advantage of Mayor Thompson's mental and physical deterioration to expand their betting parlors into casino-style gambling at several clubs in the city.

The downside to these increasingly open clubs and bars and less obvious brothels was a citizens' rebellion against the escalating violence and open defiance of the law in general. Outfit gunmen and North Siders were engaging in daylight shootouts in respectable parts of the city, including at least one by the big Standard Oil Building on Michigan Avenue.

The Chicago business community, worried by the city's reputation for violence, had virtually bypassed the mayor's office and his cronies to work with what few competent civic leaders might still impose some control. Voters were less subtle, and while patronage still continued to give Thompson considerable influence in too many wards, the Thompson-Crowe machine itself was weak enough that many believed it could be dismantled by means of a rebellion against the office holders who had less underworld support. The Republican and Democratic Parties both had factions which had crossed party lines to campaign for individuals regardless of their political affiliation. The result was a Republican primary election on April 10, 1928, that was certifiably the wildest in the city's history.

The "Pineapple Primary," so named for the army's fragmentation hand grenades (although black powder and dynamite remained the underworld favorites), turned into a prolonged Fourth of July, with gangland fireworks exploding at the rate of one every other day. Reporters came to Chicago from every major city and several foreign countries, like war correspondents, and if they tended to exaggerate, it was not by much. A newspaper columnist's parody of the National Anthem has appeared in so many books on the subject that it has become a doggerel classic:

> *The rockets' red glare,*
> *The bombs bursting in air,*
> *Gave proof through the night*
> *That Chicago's still there.*

The election amounted to a war among gang leaders supporting different candidates who stood to control thousands of patronage jobs that would directly or indirectly benefit some criminal faction, usually at the expense of another. But despite the chilly Tuesday morning weather, more than half a million hearty Chicagoans lined up to participate in a spectacle that gave literal meaning to the expression "Vote early and vote often."

It was a day when the graveyards gave up their dead, men with thick rolls of dollar bills kicked life into the residents of alleys sleeping off their hangovers, gangland hoods trained machine guns on the crowds at polling places, and in at least one ward a policemen showed voters which name to check with the barrel of his service revolver. Ballot boxes were stuffed in some wards and lost in others. In a futile effort later to make sense of the day's anarchy, investigators found many addresses to be vacant lots or a stable where "every horse voted."

All of the daily newspapers covered the election in detail, expressing varying degrees of horror and amazement at Chicago's expense. However, the *Columbus Evening Dispatch* probably won the prize for its concise front-page banner:

CHICAGO VOTES IN TERROR
CHICAGO, APRIL 10—(INS)—In the first four hours of Chicago's voting in the primary election today the following disorders were reported to police:

One alderman was released after he was said to have been kidnapped.

One political worker was shot.

Four election workers were kidnapped.

Three election workers were badly beaten.

Seven reports were received of ballot-box stuffing.

Eleven polling places reported invaded by hoodlums.

The entire election board, officials and clerks of the precinct polling place on the West side reported kidnapped by gangsters today and the ballot boxes wrecked. . . .

Detective squads in touring cars and precinct cops in Ford flivvers raced from one disturbance to another with gongs clanging, to either quell violence or control it according to the orders of the precinct captains. They typically arrived too late to prevent the beating or kidnapping of a poll watcher, election supervisor, or precinct worker, but of those two fates the officials who counted themselves lucky were the kidnap victims, who usually suffered no broken bones before their release after the polls had closed.

No one will ever know, based on the official ballot count, whether the excesses of one side offset the excesses of the other. However, to nearly everyone's amazement, most of the candidates supported by Big Bill Thompson were soundly defeated, putting an end to rumors that he might run for president. This didn't greatly matter to Capone, since the Democrats were as corruptible as the Republicans, and Thompson still had three years in office.

If the entire country marveled at Chicago's madness, New York in particular looked down its nose at the plight of the Second City. Mayor Jimmy Walker would eventually go down in scandal, but so far he and a more tightly controlled police department had kept the lid on gangland violence without depriving citizens of their booze in speakeasies and clubs whose operators were by nature more discreet. Every neighborhood had its "speaks," including some of the classiest around and north of Broadway's fabled theater district, where some residents of well-tended brownstones on the numbered side streets had to post notices that their building was *not* a speakeasy.

While Walker nimbly dodged the issue of Prohibition, Thompson had virtually outlawed its enforcement in his widely publicized speeches and his edicts on warrants. New York, Illinois, and nearly every other state had originally passed laws similar to the Eighteenth Amendment, and under the Volstead Act the states were supposed to enforce the law concurrently with the federal Prohibition Unit, or Prohibition Bureau, as it came to be known.

Most states, however, allocated only limited funds for that purpose, and by 1928 some had opted out entirely to "Let Sam do it," referring to the federal government. Worse, some states and localities had practically turned the law around, allowing it to become a convenient source of revenue that spared taxpayers the cost of raising police salaries. The idea then became, "Let bootleggers do it."

The shambles this made of Chicago's political and judicial system was reflected in the election violence of 1928's Pineapple Primary, which chagrined even Al Capone, whose mob had done its share to enliven the event. His name had finally found prominent mention as a Cicero gang lord in the national magazine *Forum* the previous October, giving him a taste of things to come. It also was cropping up more often in local newspaper articles, if not yet making headlines.

Word of mouth was ahead of the press in that respect, so Capone was predictably suspicious when approached by an emissary of seventy-six-year-old Frank Loesch, the newly appointed president of the Chicago Crime Commission. Loesch wanted to meet with him privately, even secretly, at the Lexington. Capone could see no harm in that and was curious, even flattered.

He had to admit that Chicago's reputation as the country's gangster capital was not serving anyone's interest. The years since 1923 had been the most murderous ones since the city began keeping count, ranging from fifty-two to more than seventy gangland killings annually, not counting gangsters killed by cops and Prohibition agents killed by bootleggers. In 1927 Capone had been visited by a group of New York mobsters, including Lucky Luciano, who supposedly remarked, "Chicago's a goddam crazy place. Nobody's safe on the streets."

That was a bit of an overstatement, since the average Chicagoan who had no underworld connections was not in real danger and didn't mind the awe he inspired when traveling out of town. But the city's legitimate businessmen were dismayed that tourists were staying away, and out-of-town business visitors feared for their lives. What's more, the city was preparing to celebrate its one hundredth anniversary in 1933 with the Century of Progress World's Fair that would include a replica of the original Fort Dearborn, which had figured in an Indian massacre about that time. What commercial interests wanted to avoid was a gangster massacre, for conditions in that quarter had only been going from bad to worse.

The meeting between Loesch and Capone went well. Loesch later admitted that he felt uneasy walking into a hotel whose patrons seemed to be mostly young Italian men in suits and fedoras who had nothing better to do than sit in the comfortable chairs and study him suspiciously over newspapers they were pretending to read, or who stood chatting with desk clerks, bell boys, and other employees near elevators, watching him out of the corners of their eyes.

After a few preliminaries Loesch was ushered into Capone's fourth-floor corner office with its novel parquet flooring, heavy drapes over horrific wallpaper that sported a tropical (as in Florida) motif, massive ornate desk, and large portraits of George Washington, Abraham Lincoln, and Big Bill Thompson. When he was welcomed warmly by Capone himself, Loesch was hard put to maintain the stern, businesslike manner he had been practicing in his mind, for Scarface Al Capone proved to be gracious and soft-spoken, and except for the scars looked like anything but a movie-version gangster.

Capone listened politely to Loesch's lecture on how the anarchy and bloodshed of the April primary had made Chicago a national spectacle, and how a repeat performance could not be tolerated during the national election in November. There are varying accounts of the actual conversation and whether the World's Fair was discussed, but both men believed they had prevailed. For Capone, a visit initiated by the head of the Chicago Crime Commission was evidence enough that civic leaders recognized his underworld stature and also the influence he wielded in the political community. He agreed with Loesch that the violence surrounding the election had been shameful, and without conceding that his mob was a party to it, assured Loesch that the national election would be peaceful. Loesch later made it sound as if he'd really put the mobster on the spot: "Now look here, Capone, will you help me by keeping your damned cutthroats and hoodlums from interfering with the polling booths?"

Other accounts have Loesch appealing to Capone's patriotism, which was something the gang boss took pains to emphasize, politely correcting people who called him an Italian instead of an American. In any case, Capone displayed a sense of responsibility and good citizenship. "Sure," he said. "I can handle all the dagos . . . but what about the Saltis gang? They have to be handled different. Do you want me to give them the works, too?" Loesch could imagine what Capone meant by "give them the works," so he probably waffled on that point. Capone continued: "All right. I'll have the cops send out squads the night before the election and jug all the hoodlums and keep them in the cooler until the polls close."

Loesch and Capone shook hands, and on election eve in November 1928, seventy police cars scoured the city, picking up every known hood who appeared on the streets. Loesch later told an audience, "It was the squarest and most successful election day in forty years. There was not one complaint, not one election fraud, and not one threat of trouble all day. . . ." In a perverse sort of way, both Capone and Loesch capitalized on their respective ability to get things done, or not done, as the case may be.

X

THE AMERICAN BOYS

O NE REASON CAPONE BELIEVED HE could deliver a tame election is because he had a new weapon he believed would end the conflict between himself and the North Siders and between his mob and the Sicilian Union—but not without bloodshed, to be sure. His new gunmen came as a surprise to Capone in more ways than one, for they were the last remnants of the Egan's Rats mob from St. Louis and would soon become known to Capone's Italians as the American Boys.

The Capone organization was large enough geographically and in manpower that it had to be an equal opportunity employer, but its members were still predominantly Italian and Sicilian, as dictated more by neighborhoods than nationalities. The group that eventually would become the American Boys was a motley assortment of hoodlums who routinely engaged in bootlegging when there was nothing worse to do—like robbing, stealing, shooting, or kidnapping.

This last crime was a variation on the Black Hand extortion threats to life or property that rarely occurred outside the Sicilian immigrant community. Thus, even the wealthy did not feel particularly threatened when kidnapping was revived during Prohibition, because the victims typically were bootleggers abducted by rivals and released unharmed upon payment of only a few thousand dollars (although the price kept climbing). Such kidnappings were considered to be on a par with hijackings, and neither crime was considered a police matter. The risk increased only when the hijacker or kidnapper could be identified, for gangland justice did not bog itself down in matters of due process.

The criminal generally credited with turning the "snatch" into a full-blown racket was Fred Burke, one of several Egan's Rats members who'd had to flee St. Louis following a series of robberies and shootings in the mid-1920s, and after the gang locked horns with the Birgers in southern Illinois. He had set up shop in Detroit, where he worked as an independent gunman for the Purple Gang, or anyone else, while developing his own snatch racket with some St. Louis fugitives in other cities.

His most trusted colleague in Chicago was Gus Winkeler, spelled Winkler in the press,[7] whose wife had a sister living there and who knew, personally or by reputation, Claude Maddox, born John E. Moore, whose Circus Gang had the beer and booze concession at the western edge of Dean O'Banion's "Gold Coast" on the Near North Side. Winkler had arrived in the city on May 20, 1927, and soon was joined by two other St. Louis expatriates, Ray "Crane-Neck" Nugent, known to Mrs. Winkler as "Gander," and Robert Carey, otherwise called Bob Conroy or Bob Newberry (not to be confused with North Sider Ted Newberry).

Al Capone, having ventured back into Chicago with the implicit blessing of Mayor Big Bill Thompson, now controlled what was left of the House of Genna in Little Italy. But with Joe Aiello's designs on the Unione Siciliana and the Aiello clan becoming a major threat in its own right, the last thing the Big Fellow needed was the news that one of his men had been kidnapped.

And the last thing Winkler, Nugent, and Carey needed was to receive, instead of their anticipated ransom payment, an invitation to meet personally with Al Capone.

The summons may have been linked to a poor choice of hotels by Winkler. Upon arriving in Chicago, he had checked into the Alcazar at 3000 West Washington, just a few blocks from Machine Gun Jack McGurn's Guyon Hotel on the same thoroughfare leading into Oak Park, which touched the northwest corner of Cicero. When his wife, Georgette, arrived a short time later, they moved into the Leland Hotel on the Far North Side, near a rented flat on Grace Street where he already had stashed a Detroit kidnap victim named Henry Wertheimer, a gambler, probably as a favor to Burke. When one of Capone's lieutenants was snatched, it didn't strain his vast intelligence network to link Winkler and his friends to the racket operating in Detroit, since St. Louis was a common denominator and Claude Maddox had known one or more of them before moving to Chicago.

To Nugent and Carey, the worrisome thing about a personal invitation from Capone was that if he knew their names, they already should be dead. Both were packing their bags when Winkler shook his head, and they nervously accepted his suggestion that they might as well meet with the gang lord and face the music. Georgette Winkler, whose memoirs have her continually worrying and praying (but that's about all) for her Gus to give up his life of crime, readied herself to flee to yet another city, or to the Cook County Morgue.

Capone's emergence as Chicago's "crime czar" was due in large part to the comeback victory of Big Bill the Builder in his campaign against "Dever and Decency," which had moved one politician to remark, "Who's attracted by decency?" Dever's frequent reminders that Thompson was widely supported by the criminal community had won Dever praise in the media, which applauded his four-year fight against corruption and gained him the backing of intellectuals and the business community, but Thompson still had the cleverness to turn Dever's accusations of underworld connections into a joke. He evoked titters and chuckles by addressing crowds, including groups of society women, as "My fellow hoodlums!"

Thompson's campaign addressed some issues of genuine civic importance, but what made him a national nut-case were such stunts as naming pet rats after his political opponents and courting the Irish vote by ranting against pro-British references in the city's school texts. The latter inspired a *New Yorker* cartoon depicting a Chicago cop waving through a convoy of booze trucks with an apology for thinking they were loaded with history books.

Of greater interest to Capone was Thompson's proclamation that he would thumb his nose at Prohibition. This was a signal to Capone that under a reform-proof mayor, life in the city would return to normal. By the end of the year, the lid was off gambling, speakeasies, prostitution, racketeering, and killings—and the worst was yet to come.

Newspapers were sufficiently preoccupied with the chaos in city government, the failings of Prohibition, and gangland violence in general that Capone's move back to the city went virtually unnoticed. That he was Torrio's successor, trying to rebuild the Syndicate and expand its operations, had put him back at the top of the underworld pyramid, but this was still a work in progress. Those retained in or returned to public office with Thompson's election figured this out in the subtle ways politicians do: though hirings, firings, promotions, retirements, and (in Chicago) killings that altered the money flow, that is, who took over the payoffs and who expected them.

Changes in police officials were determined not by a chief of police or even the police commissioner but by ward aldermen and committeemen who privately dictated enforcement policies that filtered down to the street through district captains. Left out of this complex system was the average Chicagoan, who might know how to dodge certain taxes if he knew the right "fixer" but who learned little about the underworld hierarchy because police reporters themselves were caught in the middle. A few, like Jake Lingle, were actually on the payroll, but most newsmen simply knew they could not alienate the police department sources without being "scooped," and they profited one way or another to the extent they were "trusted" in mob circles. When a major crime rocked the city, both sources dried up, speculation became dangerous, and all six daily newspapers were left to quote what little police and political leaders had to say at press conferences.

Civic officials and the criminal community both understood that Al Capone had achieved underworld supremacy, and so Gus Winkler had good reason to be surprised when he and his friends were summoned by Capone to discuss the kidnapping of one of his gang. When his initial alarm subsided, the source of worry shifted to his two apprehensive friends, who were sorely lacking in the social graces and needed to be presentable enough to avoid embarrassing him in front of Chicago's crime kingpin.

Georgette Winkler's account in her memoirs describes the crash program her husband undertook to polish up the beer-flat manners of his partners in crime. She was hardly a professional writer, but her clichés were in style at the time:

> "I'm going to talk turkey to you guys," he addressed Nugent and Carey when they had gathered in our rooms a few hours before their appointment with Capone.
>
> "This guy Capone is a big shot," he continued. "He's bigger than the police in this man's town, and that's something. Now you guys act like gentlemen."
>
> For over a half hour he drilled them like a school teacher. He told them how to hold their hands, their hats, and their tempers. He told them how to answer the questions he thought Capone would ask, and had them repeat the answers until he was convinced they had memorized them. . . .
>
> In an agony of suspense I paced the floor all night, clasping and unclasping my sweat soaked palms. About five o'clock in the morning I heard Gus' key rattle in the door, and he walked in as unconcernedly as if he had been at a night club. He looked at me in surprise.
>
> "Say, what're you doing up?" he said. "You look like hell. . . .
>
> "Capone," I said in a strangled voice. "What did he say, what's he going to do?"
>
> Gus' face lighted. "You've got him all wrong," he said. "Al Capone is a swell fellow. He didn't even get rough. He talked to us like a Dutch uncle trying to show us we were in the wrong racket and couldn't last long at it. He told us to quit. Then he set up the drinks and took us to a swell feed."
>
> Then his face darkened. "Do you know what those dirty bums of mine did? They got drunk—and after that

preaching I gave them. There I was, trying to act like a gentleman crook, and those damn fools had their feet on Al's desk. I was ashamed for a big shot like Capone to see what kind of company I was in. Then he offered us some money, and I refused in a hurry so Bob and Ray would take the tip. But can you beat it—both those monkeys took what he offered them.

Gus said after they got to the door Capone called him back and took his hand, saying, "Cut it out, Gus. If money is so hard to get you have to go in a bum racket like the one you're in now, drop in and see me.". . .

Presumably, the Capone man held by Gus and his friends was released with profuse apologies all around, and Winkler quit the snatch racket. His decision probably was prompted by news from Detroit that their earlier victim, released for thirty-five thousand dollars, was connected with the Purple Gang, and that one of the local kidnappers had since been shot.

Winkler and his wife then moved to an apartment building at Twenty-sixth and Fifty-second Avenues in Cicero, and Gus began hanging out at the Greyhound (later Montmartre) tavern in the Hawthorne Hotel, where Capone still had offices. It was there that he met Fred Goetz, a high school athlete and college dropout otherwise known as "Shotgun George" Zeigler (also spelled Ziegler), and Byron "Monty" Bolton, alias O. B. Carter, both of whom worked for Capone in some capacity. Winkler introduced them to Fred Burke, who had worn out his welcome in Detroit.

Burke's snatch racket had expanded to include gamblers and was beginning to inspire imitators from New York to California, where good candidates were provided by nearby Tijuana's betting parlors and gambling barges anchored just outside U.S. territorial waters. Soon the Hollywood movie colony began to feel at risk, creating a market for bodyguards.

What probably sent Burke to Chicago, where he looked up his old St. Louis friends, including Egan's Rats veteran Claude Maddox (the favored alias of John E. Moore), was the prospect of his arrest by the Detroit police on suspicion of machine-gunning three Chicago gamblers in the Milaflores Apartments the previous March on behalf of whichever underworld faction they had managed to antagonize. So, with the addition of an experienced armed robber and former kidnapper turned professional killer, Capone found himself befriending a group of outsiders, mostly unknown to Chicago cops and even to crime historians, who soon would constitute a special-assignment crew: the American Boys.

This assortment of multitalented hoodlums came together between the fall of 1927 and the spring of 1928. Winkler and his St. Louis friends were not yet on Capone's payroll, and they induced Fred Goetz and Byron Bolton to join them in Toledo, where Nugent's family was then living. Toledo had a thriving crime community without a crime lord (Yonnie Licavoli, also from St. Louis, would not become the top hood there until 1930), but some underworld character had tipped off Nugent to a safecracking job at the American Express Company. Despite some major missteps, the Chicago crew pulled off the caper on April 16, 1928, netting two hundred thousand dollars and killing a policeman in the process. This kind of crime was not condoned by Capone and earned them a tongue-lashing. To discourage such freebooting, Capone put Winkler and his friends on salary, Gus for the then-princely sum of two hundred dollars a week.

They still hung out at the Hawthorne (which remained a mobster watering hole even after it changed its name to the Western and later to the Towne Hotel) and soon got to know Louis "Little New York Louie" Campagna, Machine Gun Jack McGurn, Tony Capezio (a partner with Claude Maddox in the Circus Café), and Rocco de Grazia, among others. This group included some of Capone's top lieutenants and was one reason why he could assure Chicago Crime Commission President Frank Loesch that the violence that had marked April's Pineapple Primary would not be repeated in November.

Meanwhile, Mayor Thompson had all but abdicated his throne, leaving civic authority largely in the hands of Corporation Counsel Sam Ettelson. He also replaced thoroughly incompetent Police Commissioner Michael Hughes with William F. Russell, who was honest (by Chicago standards) and had a gift for candor. As deputy commissioner four months earlier, he had told a *Daily News* reporter, "Mayor Thompson was elected on the 'open town' platform. I assume the people knew what they wanted when they voted for him. . . ." With city politics back in a state of confusion, those like Loesch who fathomed the new underworld hierarchy could rightly think of Capone as the city's unofficial "crime commissioner."

Capone's name had acquired greater familiarity during the pre-election campaigning, and his favorite mayor had to treat him as a liability. The decision by Calvin Coolidge not to run for a second term as U.S. president raised the specter of Thompson seeking the Republican nomination for the office, which scared the national party speechless. With Capone now back in the city at the Metropole Hotel (newspaper readers were finding out) and taking over the nearby Lexington, voters were being asked if they wanted their city run by gangsters. This forced Thompson to reinstate Hughes as police commissioner as a gesture of reform, and Hughes soon declared, for public consumption, that he had run Capone out of town.

In truth, Capone was leaving anyway, to finalize his purchase of an estate on Miami's Palm Island, but in a exercise of misdirection he went to California first. His reputation preceded him, and an unwelcoming committee of cops sent him back to Chicago. Hughes supposedly had bet a reporter the price of a new hat that the gangster was just a bad memory, although Capone, after detraining at Joliet to dodge Chicago police, managed to slip quietly back to his home on South Prairie Avenue by car that same evening. The hoops he had to go through in the days before Christmas 1927 did not improve the Big Fellow's mood, even when Thompson decided that his presidential chances had been nullified by the April defeat of virtually every candidate supported by the Thompson–Crowe machine.

Capone had returned to Chicago to participate in the Pineapple Primary and, accepting Thompson's flip-flop as a political necessity, had done his unsuccessful best to support the Thompson-Crowe candidates. It hadn't particularly mattered which faction won; nothing of great importance was riding on the outcome, and Capone still had the Aiello-North Sider alliance to contend with. In the summer of 1928, before his visit from Frank Loesch, he had taken over several floors of the Lexington Hotel. He soon moved his private office from the second floor to a fourth-floor corner room (out of rifle range of any nearby buildings), installed his own movie theater, and even leased the ballroom as a gymnasium for his men.

As for the hazards presented by the North Siders and the Aiello faction of Sicilians, Capone had quietly secured a beachhead in enemy territory through his American Boys. Claude Maddox had been in the fray as an independent contractor at least since 1924, when he and a crony were shot (presumably by rival gangsters over union matters) about the time that police killed Capone's older brother Frank during polling-place disturbances in Cicero. Some three years later Maddox was definitely in the Capone camp and was opening a place on North Avenue called the Circus Café, a hang-out for a group that called themselves the Circus Gang.

The Italians, other loose cannons, and the American Boys who were gravitating to the Circus Café from St. Louis would become Capone's avenging angels, though they didn't know it at the time. In 1928 they were busy defending their bootlegging territory by bomb-ing any speakeasies and distilleries on the southern boundary of Little Sicily and contesting the efforts of Moran's North Siders in the racketeering field. The extent to which they shot up Sicilian and North Sider operations west of Division and North Avenue has never been established, but those streets were in their territory and they probably did their part.

Before and after the Pineapple Primary, at least four out-of-town gunmen had come to Chicago to collect the fifty-thousand-dollar bounty that Joe Aiello thought would gain him control of the Unione Siciliana. Each hoodlum who made a bid for it went home in a box, their murders unsolved. Twice Capone's staff machine-gunners had tried to discourage this bounty hunting by laying waste to the Aiello Bros. Bakery and headquarters at 473 West Divi-sion Street, in Little Sicily.

What the Aiello assassins failed to do, Capone nearly accom-plished on his own. On the third weekend of September 1928, after a game of golf with suburban Burnham's "boy mayor," Johnny Pat-ton, Capone was squeezing himself into a car when the pistol he sometimes carried went off accidentally, causing a flesh wound in his leg. One or two Chicago papers ran short items speculating that the victim was Capone and let it go at that, but the incident made *The New York Times* and many years later Capone's caddy that day told the story in an issue of *Sports Illustrated*. After treatment under an assumed name in a closely guarded suburban hospital, he limped back to the Lexington and then returned to Fortress Capone in Florida.

Scarface Al had successfully thwarted the Moran gang's takeover of the cleaning and dyeing industry, acquiring notoriety in the process, and continued competing with Bugs Moran's dog track, the Fairview Kennel Club, much to Moran's annoyance.

The previous November, police searching an Aiello mobster had found the address of an apartment facing 4442 West Washington, the home of Tony Lombardo, and a key to a room in the Atlantic Hotel. The room's windows looked down on the cigar store of Hinky Dink Kenna, whom Capone often visited, and was empty except for two rifles and two pairs of binoculars. When the detectives used their powers of persuasion on the suspect, they came up with the name of Aiello, but his arrest and interrogation yielded nothing they didn't already know.

Aiello was about to be released until an officer noticed some suspicious-looking men sitting in parked cars, arriving by cab, or idling about outside the building. Having a major gang leader shot as he left detective bureau headquarters would have been more than a little embarrassing, so officers nabbed the most obvious gunmen and locked them up on weapons charges.

Among those incarcerated was Little New York Louie Campagna, a well-known member of the Capone team, and it could be that descending on the detective bureau was an audacious stunt to get Aiello's attention. A police eavesdropper in the guise of a prisoner in an adjoining cell heard Campagna tell Aiello that his days were numbered. The next day, when Aiello was being released, he demanded police protection and was given an armed escort as far as the curb, where his lawyer, wife, and young son picked him up in a taxi. He then disappeared for eighteen months, taking some of his brothers with him.

But with the North Siders now cozy with the Sicilians, the Capone–Aiello war showed no signs of ending, and Capone decided it was time to put his American Boys to work. They were assigned to take out the man whose power and profits had diminished as Capone's expanded, and who had made the Aiellos his Chicago representatives in matters of the Cicero dog track and the Sicilian Union that Capone now controlled. And if Aiello had yet to surface, at least they knew where to find Frankie Yale.

XI

THE MURDER OF FRANKIE YALE

T HE MEETING AT WHICH FRANKIE Yale's fate was decided may well have taken place at Capone's Palm Island estate in Florida in June 1928. Among those believed to be in attendance were Charles Fischetti, Dan Seritella, Jake (or Jack) Guzik, Jack McGurn, Albert Anselmi, and John Scalise. Crime historians often come up with different names, usually including McGurn, because he grew up in Brooklyn, and the Scalise-Anselmi murder team, because both were professional killers and not much else. But information that surfaced a few years later, from Georgette Winkler and Byron Bolton and references in FBI documents, call much of this into question. What's certain is that some of the guns came from Miami and some Chicagoans purchased a used Buick at a Nash agency in Tennessee around the end of June. And on the afternoon of July 1, 1928, the submachine gun made its first appearance in New York City.

The killers were not McGurn, Anselmi, and Scalise. They were Fred Burke, Gus Winkler, Fred Goetz, and Little New York Louie Campagna, whose mother lived near Yale and who knew the city better than McGurn. Gus had told his wife, Georgette, only that

Capone had ordered him to take Campagna and Goetz to New York "on a job." He added, "I can't tell you what it's about, and don't expect to hear from me until I get back. Capone has given strict orders no one of us communicate with Chicago."

So Georgette Winkler was surprised when Campagna's girlfriend and wife-to-be told her she'd been talking with Louie in New York, calling from his mother's house, and she should come over if she wanted to "say hello to the boys." From Irene (as Georgette knew Goetz's girlfriend, Irene Dorsey) she learned that Goetz also had been calling home, and one morning when she was visiting, Campagna's girl called to say the boys would be home soon. "When I asked her how she knew, her answer was, 'Read the papers.'"

Irene hurried out to get a morning newspaper, which carried the murder of Frankie Yale on its front page, complete with a picture of his body stretched on the sidewalk next to his expensive Lincoln coupe, which had crashed into the front steps of a tidy brick bungalow in the Homewood section of Brooklyn. The most likely version of events has Yale receiving a telephone call at a coffee shop he owned, or perhaps a speakeasy, and then hurriedly leaving to go home. All Winkler told his wife was that he and his companions had scouted Yale's home, hangouts, and likely routes of travel, and partly by luck had recognized his distinctive tan car at a busy intersection.

Goetz and Campagna had wanted to start shooting immediately, but Gus, who was driving, yelled at them to hold off because traffic congestion would have created problems (and probably more casualties) and complicated their escape. So they followed Yale until he turned onto a residential street, then pulled alongside and blazed away. The hit team abandoned their car near the Brooklyn ferry landing and headed back to Chicago.

New York's first murder by Tommygun caused such a commotion that the local police immediately declared the killers to be Chicagoans. That would later be proven when slugs removed from some of the St. Valentine's Day Massacre victims were found to match those taken from Yale. But even before that was established, *The Literary Digest* published an editorial cartoon depicting a giant gunman extending himself from Chicago to Manhattan.

The phone calls made from New York to Chicago by Campagna and Goetz had Capone fuming. These had been traced by New York City police, who also found calls had been made from Campagna's Chicago home to Winkler's when their wives talked. All three were called on the carpet by Capone himself, and Winkler was infuriated to learn (if he didn't already know) that Campagna and Goetz had violated orders. So the cops in both cities had a pretty good idea who had murdered Yale, even if they couldn't prove it.

The man who had bought some of the guns left in the abandoned Buick was the manager of Miami's Ponce de Leon Hotel who had been wined and dined by Capone, enjoyed consorting with an important gangster, and had left the weapons in a room of his hotel as requested. No crime in that. A machine gun left in the Buick was traced to the gun shop of Peter Von Frantzius, the principle armorer for Chicago gangs who brought Thompsons discreetly but could own them legally, as the city's gun law did not hold them to be "concealable." The car dealer in Tennessee who had sold the automobile could say only that it was purchased for cash by a "Charles Cox" and he had never seen the vehicle again.

The death of Yale ended his meddling in Chicago affairs but not the war between Capone and the Aiellos, who were laying low and being represented by Bugs Moran's North Siders. Their main source of grain alcohol remained Little Sicily and the local Sicilian Union still controlled by their enemy. On September 7, 1928, a week after Yale's death, Tony Lombardo and two bodyguards left what now was called the Italo-American Union in the Hartford Building at Dearborn and Madison and after crossing the street were distracted by the sight of workmen using block and tackle to hoist a real airplane to the top of the big Boston Store as a customer attraction.

The spectacle had already drawn a crowd in the Loop's busy shopping district, and as the three men made their way past other sightseers, two gunmen stepped from the doorway of the Raklios restaurant and killed Lombardo with two shots to the head and mortally wounded a bodyguard. The other bodyguard pulled a gun and began chasing one of the shooters, only to be grabbed and disarmed by a cop.

The noontime murder of Lombardo on a crowded downtown street made national headlines, and Gus Winkler remarked to his wife, Georgette, without elaborating, "Looks like somebody's getting back at Capone because of Yale."

A week after that, on September 14, the Union's new president took office. He was Pasqualino "Patsy" Lolordo, brother of the uninjured bodyguard, and he survived less than five months. About 2:30 on the afternoon of January 8, Lolordo and his wife, Aleina, returned from shopping to their home at 1921 West North Avenue, where two men were waiting to drink and talk. After half an hour the two left, and a few minutes later three more men dropped by for an even more convivial meeting that lasted until four o'clock or so before the group joined in a toast. The toast included some eighteen shots fired at or into Patsy Lolordo. Joe Aiello was back in town.

The murders of Lombardo and then Lolordo generated not only the usual headlines but also much speculation as to who was betraying and shooting whom. One or both of the Lombardo killers resembled one or both of the North Side's Gusenberg brothers. One of the visitors to the Lolordo home was supposedly identified by Patsy's grief-stricken wife as Joe Aiello (police Captain John Stege would later deny this), before she lapsed into the customary silence of a Sicilian widow.

The shooters may have been the Gusenbergs and Albert Kachellek (who went by the name Clark), but one writer suggested that Tony Lolordo had shot Lombardo to obtain the Union presidency for his brother Pasqualino. Another writer heard that a Capone gunman had shot Lombardo because he was leaving the fold. In some stories the cop who disarmed the pursuing bodyguard was on the sidewalk, while others placed him in a store. Just keeping Lombardo and two Lolordos straight has placed a strain on crime historians of the period.

The War of Sicilian Succession had taken the lives of a dozen or more Union presidents or candidates since 1921, not counting Mike Merlo, who died of natural causes in 1924. Now Joey Aiello was in line for he post, but his tenure would likewise be short, even though he took great precautions. Aiello was at the top of Capone's hit parade but harder to reach than Bugs Moran. Lolordo was slain on January 8, 1929, and St. Valentine's Day was just around the corner.

XII

Blood and Guts

GETTING BACK TO THE MESS at 2122 North Clark Street: Police Sergeant Tom Loftus,[8] after discovering that Frank Gusenberg was still alive, called for the police wagon, which doubled as an ambulance. He was trying to talk to the wounded man when Officers Christie and Love came in, looked at the bodies, checked some for signs of life, and then tried to do what policemen at a crime scene are supposed to do: keep people out of the garage.

Bill Rudd was stationed at the door at this point, at least until more police arrived, because everyone who entered the building and saw the carnage had to step outside to catch his breath. The still-warm corpses were not just dead, they were riddled with bullet holes, and one had his head blown apart, which had sprayed blood and brain matter everywhere. Cops at most murder scenes where only one or two victims are found, especially if the slaying appears gang-related, dispel their own tension by cracking a few bad jokes to one another. But this clutter of corpses left observers nearly speechless. The silence was broken only by muttered expletives, a few comments and questions spoken solemnly, and the howling and barking of the dog, which was tied to the axle under a truck bed and snapping at anyone who approached.

The delivery man who had seen the departing killers and after some hesitation decided to investigate had been chased out when Loftus arrived. His excitement was obvious to anyone on the street, and a crowd soon gathered, trying to find out what had happened. The police wagon sent to pick up the mortally wounded Gusenberg reached the garage about the same time as the first detective squad from headquarters. By now, Sergeant Harrity at the Hudson District Station had received more calls about the shooting and realized that Mrs. Landesman's frantic voice was not simply that of some overwrought woman, and he sent the district's other Ford racing to the scene.

Communications were entirely by telephone. The police stations were linked by teletype machines, but these were used mainly for routine messages and administrative announcements. Ironically, several ranking police officials were in Detroit that same morning examining this country's first two-way police radio system. They returned in a hurry and in light of the North Clark Street slaughter wrote reports favoring adoption of the new technology. Captain John Stege, the department's gangbusting chief of detectives, cut short his vacation in Miami, where he could have gone fishing with Al Capone.

Although it's not mentioned in any police report, the activity at the garage also attracted the attention of a *Chicago Daily News* delivery van driver who was dropping off papers at a nearby shop. He didn't know what the commotion was all about, except that it involved a shooting, and called his newspaper. City Editor John Craig collared photographer Russell Hamm, who jumped into his car and sped to the scene at about the same time that Hack Miller of the *Chicago American* was running red lights on Ogden Avenue, which angled northeast across the city to intersect Clark at Armitage, about a block south of the garage.

The first photographer to arrive may never be known, but Hamm recalls that once he had entered the front office, his path was blocked by two or three cops who were reluctant to open the door to the garage area behind. The dog was still barking hysterically, and the police, not yet knowing who or what awaited them, had pulled their revolvers before giving the door a hard kick. Hamm, armed only with his early Speed Graphic camera, followed them in and saw that the dog was secured. He also saw other cops, looking up in surprise, and he saw the bodies.

By now *Chicago Tribune* photographer Mike Fish had joined the group, along with Tony Berardi from the *American*. Other photographers soon arrived, including David Mann of the *Herald and Examiner*, John Steger of the *Tribune*, Fred Eckhardt of the *Daily News*, and Al Madsen from the Underwood & Underwood wire service.

The first reporter on the scene was a cub named Walter Trohan, who, like Walter Spirko, was also beginning his journalism career by way of the City News Bureau. Gershman was his boss, too, and Gersh was finally hearing enough police sirens and bells to give some credence to Spirko's excited phone calls. If there was a mass murder on North Clark Street, City News would look pretty foolish missing it, so he told Trohan to check it out. Trohan thought this should justify cab fare, but Gersh said no, and although the young newsman grumbled about having to take a streetcar, he was still the first writer at the scene.

More reporters arrived within minutes, including Willis O'Rourke of the *American*, Ray Quisno of the *Herald and Examiner*, and Frank Honeywell and John Dougherty of the *Tribune*.

Meanwhile, Miller and Fish had teamed up to get overviews of the slaughter. One steadied a tripod-mounted camera on the rib-and-fabric roof of a Modal A Ford parked next to the office door overhang where Hamm was perched, while the other held the flash-powder tray. The garage began to fill with smoke from the picture-taking, and the police were losing patience with the press. According to Miller, a "big fat copper" told Fish to stop, and Miller responded with a rude noise. The cop, thinking it had come from Fish, told him, "Okay, smart guy, I'll see to it you don't get any pictures at all!" Fish turned to Miller and said, approximately, "Thanks, you son of a bitch."

At some point the back door of the garage was opened to let the flash-powder smoke out and let natural light in for the official police photographers and their tripod-mounted, eight-by-ten-inch view cameras and glass-plate negatives. Standing as far back as possible, at the rear of the truck where the dog had been tied, they were able to include all the bodies, from Pete Gusenberg collapsed onto a chair at the left to Albert Kachellek, otherwise known as James

Clark, at the far right. Barely recognizable in the foreground of this police photograph is the .38 Colt Detective Special that presumably belonged to Frank Gusenberg.

As the garage filled up with newsmen, cops, ranking police officials, and the coroner, the reporters and photographers tried to get enough information to call into their newspapers' rewrite men in time for an afternoon "extra." Getting anything at all was difficult. Official statements, beyond condemnation of the savagery, were out of the question, and some offhand quotes obviously were made up. Rumors that the murder victims were members of Bugs Moran's gang circulated rapidly, but efforts to identify them led to numerous mistakes which made it into print before time permitted even basic fact-checking. It was probably one of the few times in Chicago history when the detective bureau, the police department, the state's attorneys, the county coroner, and even the mayor's office did not compete with one another for newspaper attention. At least not until the bodies had been removed and the various officials had gotten their wits about them.

Sergeant Loftus had gone to the Alexian Brothers Hospital to check on Frank Gusenberg, who had so many wounds it was surprising that he was still conscious or could even speak—not that he said much. His remark that cops had shot him didn't make sense. Police in the Thirty-sixth District would not have been involved, nor would any cop in uniform. If the shooters were some rogue detectives, they would have been in plainclothes, which was about all that Loftus had learned before he left the crime scene. By the time he returned, some order had been restored.

Police Commissioner William Russell and Corner Herman Bundesen had arrived, and two detectives were dealing with the bodies while others dropped empty .45-caliber shell casings into paper sacks obtained from a nearby store. Loftus bagged and labeled the snub-nose .38 which had been left in place on the garage floor. He noted that the hammer had been cut down to eliminate the thumb lever, which might otherwise catch on the material in a pocket, and that the serial number had been ground off.

One by one the bodies were loaded into police wagons parked in the alley outside the back doors and were taken to Braithwaite's, a private mortuary at 2219 Lincoln Avenue which would serve as an unofficial annex to the county morgue downtown. Its chapel, filled with wheeled embalming slabs that stank of death and chemicals, did not exclude a few flies.

The first was Pete Gusenberg, who with his younger brother Frank were Moran's main gunmen. He was about forty, lived part of the time at 434 Roscoe, and had a police record dating back to 1902 for such crimes as burglary and robbery. These had earned him three years in the state prison at Joliet before 1923, when he was sentenced to three more years for his part in the Dearborn Station mail robbery of over three hundred thousand dollars with Big Tim Murphy. He and his brother had badly wounded Capone shooter Machine Gun Jack McGurn in a telephone booth at the McCormick Hotel smoke shop at 616 Rush Street on March 7, 1928, and the next month ripped his car with a Tommygun but missed the driver.

The two were also the presumed killers of Capone's Unione Siciliana Presidents Tony Lombardo and Patsy Lolordo after the Aiellos teamed up with Moran. This would soon allow Tony Aiello to become president in exile, for the war was not yet over. Now Pete was slumped awkwardly over a wooden chair which still supported his body, head and shoulders hanging over the back, and the seat of his pants ripped by bullets to reveal white underwear.

The second was Albert R. Weinshank, owner of the Alcazar Club, a nondescript speakeasy at 4207 Broadway, but more importantly, an official in the Central Cleaners and Dyers Association. He had toppled straight over backwards, arms at his side, face up, with blood running out of his eyes and nostrils.

Corpse number three was Adam Heyer, found on his back with a silk scarf bunched around his throat. He lived at 2024 Farragut Avenue and had a criminal record that included a year in jail for robbery in 1908 and then a year in the state penitentiary after a confidence-game conviction in 1916. He was part owner of Moran's Fairview Kennels dog racing track. Heyer had leased the garage the previous December through a downtown broker who still had the building for sale, and was carrying $1,399 in cash. According to detectives, he was the "brains" of the mob.

Next was John May, a young mechanic and father of seven who lived in a poor neighborhood at 1209 West Madison Street. He had eighteen dollars in his pocket plus two St. Christopher medals deformed by machine-gun slugs. His early life of crime consisted of safecracking, which he evidently abandoned in favor of the fifty dollars a week he earned working on North Sider cars and trucks. After falling on the garage floor he must have kept moving, for much of his head had been blown away by a shotgun blast.

A fifth body lay at the feet of the others, stretched out along the base of the whitewashed, and now bullet-pocked, brick wall. This was "James Clark," the alias of Albert Kachellek, who had graduated from a four-year course at Pontiac State Reformatory in 1905 in time for an armed robbery that in 1910 netted him another year at Joliet. Police considered him well-versed in all of the criminal arts, as well as a "hardened killer."

Last in the line of bodies, still wearing his hat, was Dr. Reinhart Schwimmer, a twenty-nine-year-old optician, whose presence in the garage at first puzzled the police. It turned out that he, like Moran, lived at the Parkway, and he had fitted the Gusenbergs and some of the others with eyeglasses. It looked as if Schwimmer simply had been in the wrong place at the wrong time, but then the mystery deepened. Police soon learned that he was a serious gangster groupie who not only enjoyed doing business with some tough mobsters but liked to pal around with them. In return, they treated him as something of a mascot or, in some ways, a mentor. He was educated, well-groomed, polished, and when dining with "the boys" at the Parkway or other place where "gentlemen" congregated, he demonstrated proper manners and even acted as their spokesman when the occasion required.

Schwimmer capitalized on this relationship by letting others believe he was in the rackets, simply by neglecting to mention that he wasn't. He also neglected to mention that he usually was broke, letting the Gusenbergs pick up his tailoring and food tabs and loan him spending money. He often depended on his aging mother to cover his past-due rent at the hotel. Schwimmer didn't exactly slave away at optometry, although he had an office on Lincoln Avenue near the Biograph Theatre and was in the process of moving farther up the street. He also had to keep a step ahead of two ex-wives, one of whom was hounding him for child support and the other probably for alimony. He was on his way to meet his mother for lunch that Thursday and had stopped off at the garage to drink coffee with his buddies. He and the others didn't make it to supper.

A greater mystery was the absence of Bugs Moran. If this mass murder was intended to wipe out the North Siders, and it looked that way, several were missing. Weinshank and Heyer were Moran's main men in racketeering and dog racing respectively, Heyer kept the books, and the Gusenbergs and Kachellek (alias Clark) were the gang's top gunmen. But nobody in the group at 2122 North Clark specialized in bootlegging and gambling; those would have been Frank Foster, Willie Marks, and Ted Newberry—other late arrivals. The newspaper extras mistakenly included Foster among the victims, but the body was actually that of Schwimmer.

Because the witnesses to the fake detective car's departure were likewise fooled into thinking the men being marched outside with their hands up were mobsters, and there was still much confusion, the police first guessed that Moran and possibly others had been kidnapped and would soon be found in a ditch. Some papers mentioned this in their first editions, before they learned that one of the "cops" had gotten behind the wheel of the car. By evening, reporters and police were trying to talk to anybody who had seen anything, and although memories did not agree on every detail, the event was coming into sharper focus. For that matter, the police and the press initially called the bloodfest "the North Clark Street Massacre."

Al Capone was still a Cicero mobster in the public's mind and not instantly suspected in the crime, as most people today assume. The only thing that seemed certain the first evening was that the uniformed men and the official-looking Cadillac all were phonies. At least that seemed certain to most people. The newsworthy exception was the head of federal Prohibition forces, Major Fred Silloway, who, before the blood had dried on the "cartage" company's concrete floor, had called a press conference that gave several of the more sensational papers in other cities an opportunity to go tabloid.

MURDER COPS HUNTED IN MASSACRE, clanged the *New York Daily Mirror* over a full-page photo of the bodies, while Milwaukee's slightly more sedate *Wisconsin News* had an artist sketch a cutaway garage scene next to a five-column, double-deck headline that read, CALLS CHICAGO POLICE KILLERS OF GANGMEN (the litter of corpses was discreetly published across six columns on page three). Other papers also jumped on the story, some headlining it, others saving it for a paragraph a little farther down the front-page column where various wild theories were reported for the record.

It was Major Silloway's belief that the squad car and the police were real, and that he would have the names of the murderous cops by nightfall. But his scenario turned into a two-way stretch, maybe a three-way. It boiled down to a truckload of Moran hooch being hijacked, possibly by cops. This, he said, would have irritated Moran to such an extent that he would stop paying the police for protection, and this would have irritated the police enough that they would not only keep his booze shipment but also murder the whole bunch, or as many as they could find in the garage that Thursday morning.

Needless to say, this did not go over well with the police, from the district cops to the detective bureau to the state's attorney's investigators.

Major Silloway's bombshell was worse than a dud; it blew egg in his face. While the Silloway scenario was locally deemed ridiculous, the reputation of the Chicago police was bad enough that their involvement in the murders didn't seem totally out of the question.

When reporters asked Commissioner Russell about Silloway's charges, he smiled and declined comment, except to say that the crime would be solved in "a day or two." When they kept asking, he coolly replied, "I'd just as soon convict coppers for the job as anyone else." But when asked if he would visit Major Silloway's office to discuss the matter, he blasted back at the reporter: "If Silloway has any evidence in this case, he ought to come to us with it!" At some point Detective Chief Eagan snapped, "There are a lot of things believed about this thing, but give me the facts!"

Later that day detective bureau Captain Schoemaker did meet with Major Silloway for nearly an hour, but neither would say what was discussed. Before the end of the month, a thoroughly discredited Silloway was transferred out of Chicago, and two weeks later he was fired.

Meanwhile, back on North Clark Street, three squads of officers had started going house to house and store to store, talking to everybody and learning a little. They spoke to Mrs. Max Landesman, who lived above Sam Schneider's tailor shop next door to the garage, and she repeated her story: While ironing she'd heard a noise from the garage that sounded like shooting, had looked out her front window in time to see the phony detective car speed away, had gone downstairs to investigate but could not get the door open, and had sent another boarder, Clair McAllister, down to give it a try. McAllister's story tallied closely with that of Jeanette Landesman, who had called the police.

Sam Schneider could have added some details that would be of interest later, but at the police station he said only that he'd seen two men standing in front of his shop looking toward the garage and three men getting into the car to leave.

Mrs. Josephine Morin happened to be looking out the front window of her third-floor apartment at 2125 North Clark, almost directly across the street, and saw everything, including men in uniform with guns and men in topcoats with raised hands getting into a Cadillac and driving south. Her account differed slightly but not significantly from those of Elmer Lewis, whose truck had clipped the Cadillac when it turned in front of him, and James Wilcox, the coal truck driver who had heard backfiring sounds and seen the men leave the garage, and was probably the second person to investigate after McAllister had forced open the door.

The canvassing officers hit the closest thing to pay dirt when they talked to Mrs. Minnie Arvidson at 2051 North Clark, the proprietress of a nearby rooming house. Patrolmen Connelley and Devane of the Thirty-sixth (Hudson) District took her statement on February 18:

> She told us that a man came to her Sunday, January 27, 1929, and said he wanted a room for his friend and himself (a room each). . . . She said, "Alright, I have 2 rooms at 2139 N. Clark St." He didn't ask to see the rooms then but gave her $1.00 and said, "We'll be here tomorrow and pay you the balance and take the rooms." Price was $8.00 each room. Monday afternoon, Jan 28, 1929, the other man came and gave her $15.00 which was the balance for two rooms for a week. This man took a front room on the first floor. They told her they were taxi cab drivers and asked her if she had a garage to rent so they could keep their cabs there, but she didn't have any to rent. . . .
>
> The following Monday, Feb. 4, 1929, Mrs. Arvidson went to their rooms to collect her rent and she found the man in

the rear room had vacated his room and was in the front room with his friend. They said they couldn't afford to keep two rooms, that they would both stay in the front room which she agreed to, for $9.00 a week and they paid the $9.00. The following Monday, Feb. 11th, 1929, she hadn't been over there and then they were going out about 6.00. They gave $9.00 to Mr. Hardway, a roomer, to give to Mrs. Arvidson, when she came over. They told her they were working nights, as Taxi Chauffeurs, but she doesn't know what kind of Taxis they drive. . . . She described those men as follows:

#1 30-35, 5-8, 150, slim build, fair complexion, brown hair, wore shell rim glasses, pearl gray fedora hat, dark overcoat.

#2 28-30, 5-10, 155 lbs., slim build, light complexion, blond hair, thin long face, tan soft hat, gray or brown overcoat. . . .

We interviewed Mrs. Alvin Pfeifer, 2139 N. Clark St., a roomer on the second floor at above. She said she saw the man described as #1, Thursday, Feb. 14, 1929, around noon. He spoke to her and said, "Isn't it terrible, this murder across the street." He had a newspaper in his hand and went out, that is the last she saw of him. Mr. Hardway, another roomer at 2139 N. Clark St., said he thought he heard them in their room Friday morning, Feb. 15, but didn't see them and was not sure. Mrs. Arvidson said that when the newspapers are quoting her as identifying pictures of her roomers, they're wrong.

(Signed) Devane and Connelley

Minnie Arvidson had the dubious pleasure of meeting Byron Bolton and James "Jimmy the Swede" Morand (or maybe Jimmy McCrussen), the principal lookouts who, as things turned out, mistook someone else for Bugs Moran and called the killers prematurely.

Patrolmen Devane and Connelley stumbled onto what would seem to be another lookout roost that didn't fit the time frame but was dutifully recorded. Mrs. Michael Doody at 2119 North Clark told them she had rented her third-floor front room to a man who gave his name as Morrison, occupation cab driver, and who moved in the latter part of December. He would come in about nine every morning, and two other men would arrived about thirty minutes later. They usually brought their own lunch, and would leave about 3:30.

She described her roomer as around "30 years old, 5-9 or 10, 160, dark complexion, wore puttees and a khaki shirt, looked like an Italian." One of his friends was "28-30, 5-9, 175, stout, light complexion, and hair, gold hose and knicker pants, long dark overcoat, and gray cap"; the other man was "35, 5-6 or 7, 140, medium build and complexion, shell rimmed glasses, black derby hat and dark clothes and overcoat." This first team of lookouts was eventually pulled out, and then late in January the second team came in.

Mrs. Doody and another resident "partly" identified one of several pictures as that of Henry [sic] Keywell, an ex-convict with a brother named Phil who were members of Detroit's Purple Gang. This is how Harry and Phil Keywell made it into most accounts of the massacre—and never made it out again—although both had acceptable alibis for the morning of February 14.

Several other witnesses turned up who would soon testify before the coroner's jury and receive some newspaper attention. However, just hours after the massacre the district police, the detective bureau, the state's attorney's office, and Coroner Herman N. Bundesen himself were all conducting their own investigations, more or less independently, and most of their records have vanished. Some were actually stolen, while others were eventually buried in unmarked files or otherwise lost forever.

Many details were missed because each agency had its own agenda and turf to protect. They often worked at cross purposes, and information gathered by competing investigators was sometimes jealously guarded, or at least not shared. Even Police Commissioner Russell was sometimes in the dark or so overloaded with theories or dead-end leads that no centralized operation could be mounted.

XIII

HOODS IN HIDING

I N THE FIRST FEW DAYS after the murders, theories multiplied like rabbits. They included hijackings, Purple Gang problems, refusal to pay protection, a falling out between the Aiellos and the North Siders, the cleaners and dyers feud, the aldermanic election, labor racketeering, a Canadian distillery war, the killings of Lombardo and Lolordo, a traitor in the ranks, and the matter of two mystery gunmen who had been following Pete Gusenberg.

Near the bottom of the list was local bootlegging, because it was so commonplace that it certainly didn't merit a massacre. Chicago's estimated ten thousand speakeasies (three thousand more than the number of saloons licensed before Prohibition) were now operating territorially, and Capone had been spending so much time in Florida that some police officials thought he was actually out of the business. At this time there seemed to be only a limited awareness that the Chicago Syndicate was reorganizing under the management of Frank Nitti, whose name rarely appeared in print, along with Jake Guzik and other mobsters.

In the absence of tangible leads, everybody initially tried to outdo one another in deploring the bloody deed. The day after the massacre, Commissioner Russell declared, "It's war to the finish. I've never known of a challenge like this—the killers posing as policemen—but now that the challenge has been made, it's accepted." Assistant State's Attorney David Stansbury, head of his agency's massacre team, said, "I've heard of brutal gang slayings in Chicago but never anything quite equal to this. The gangsters, by their very boldness, have written their own doom." And high-ranking federal agent Pat Roche, not wanting to be left out, stated, "Never in all the history of feuds or gangland has Chicago or the nation seen anything like today's wholesale slaughter."

Various investigators also promised a quick solution, "tonight" or "in two or three days." A week later, Stansbury gamely announced, "We have purposely given out the impression that we were following half a dozen theories of the time in order to lead the killers to believe we don't know what we're doing. We are following one trail, and we believe the end is in sight." If there was any trail at this point, it was the wrong one, as future events would show.

Annoyingly enough, in January Commissioner Russell had conducted massive raids that netted nearly five thousand "suspects"—mostly loiterers, "vagrants," bums, panhandlers, bartenders, speakeasy customers, and anybody else who somehow didn't "look right." But no bona fide hoodlums were arrested, as far as the newspapers could determine.

The "cleanup" might have continued but for an exodus caused by the massacre. For instance, on the evening of February 14, the bartender at the Idle Hour Café, 7704 Ogden Avenue in Lyons, was surprised to find his establishment full of "Capone men" from Cicero. Usually two or three delivered his beer and booze and left, but this night it seemed as if everyone from that suburb and others had fled their homes and usual hangouts to congregate at his joint, as customers, evidently figuring that the police would be descending on every nitery in the Greater Chicago area.

Meanwhile, State's Attorney John A. Swanson issued a command—dramatic if somewhat unclear— to "close up the town or go to jail." This upstaged Commissioner Russell at city hall only long enough for him to command his own police: "Booze running and booze selling must be wiped out, and the minute you men leave this room, the drive is on. Get that!"

Reporters filed their stories and then quickly hit the streets to see if the city, after nearly a decade of Constitutional Prohibition, was actually going dry. Half the city's "booze joints" were supposed to be closed by noon and the rest by evening, according to reports from city hall, but a *Chicago Journal* newsman reported that "within the shadow of the city hall, all in an hour's time," he had "purchased beer and whiskey in four places." At the first stop, in a hotel, he asked the bartender, who was not exactly shaking in his boots, "Jim, what do you think of this tightening up?" Jim answered, evidently referring to deliveries, "Oh, I've been expecting some orders all day but haven't gotten them yet. You never can tell how the thing will turn out."

By Saturday, however, the city's "saloonkeepers" were expressing anger at the gangsters for constantly warring with one another. This only brought the police down on taverns, because they knew where those establishments were. "The working people want their beer, and we've been going along, giving them the best we could, and a pretty good glass of it, all things considered. Why can't the big shots go along and be satisfied making thousands while we make dollars?" This was the consensus as paraphrased by one reporter, who soon found only about fifty "cheaters" ignoring the authorities. Beat cops were under pressure even from their district captains to "keep the lid on" and to keep that warning "ringing in the keepers' ears."

All this began immediately after the massacre, when relatives were still identifying bodies and Chicago cops were arresting anybody without obvious means of support. Their counterparts in other cities were also nabbing anyone who looked suspicious and was coming by train *from* Chicago. By now there were so many suspects—none linked to the massacre—that the police didn't know what to do with them in the absence of even circumstantial evidence. The local hoods who *might* have known something, anything, were carefully avoiding their usual haunts or shooting at anyone, and the pall of peacefulness that descended upon Chicago was almost spooky.

Wall Street's stock market crash was still eight months away, but real depression had come early to Chicago. The average citizen had never expected or experienced anything so frightening as a dry city. And the silence of Mayor Big Bill Thompson was almost deafening.

While the cops were running in circles and the whole country was following the chase, Braithwaite's funeral parlor had become a scene of personal melodrama. Despite the efforts of police to maintain order, reporters were able to corner sorrowing family members who had come to spare grief-stricken mothers or wives the pain of seeing their fallen black sheep. A few relatives were hoping for clues to hidden cash, and some were there purely out of curiosity.

And while detectives were questioning relatives, others were hot on the trail of the three cars and seven trucks parked in the garage. At least that was the number finally arrived at, for the count varied from one police report to another. And the trail led nowhere. The cars included a Chrysler, a Ford sedan and a Ford coupe. The trucks included two Reo Speedwagons, a White, a Mack, a Dodge, a Diamond-T, and a Ford. Most of the plates came back stolen, switched, unrecorded, or issued to bogus names and addresses—except for the Ford truck registered to Frank Snyder, the alias of Adam Heyer, at 2122 North Clark. And that wasn't helpful since "Snyder" had leased the garage at that address. It was also the only truck labeled S-M-C Cartage Company," and no one has ever decided what SMC stood for, unless it was something as mundane as Snyder Moving and Cartage.

Still among the missing were Bugs Moran and his lieutenants, Ted Newberry, Frank Foster, and Willie Marks, as well as every other notable hoodlum in town. Those who had any gang connections at all were far enough down the food chain to feel safe, not realizing how desperate the police were to arrest anybody for the murders.

Al Capone's name cropped up briefly in some papers because of his problems with Moran, but he had the best alibi of all. Not only was he two thousand miles in Florida remodeling the large estate he'd finally purchased on Palm Island in Miami's Biscayne Bay, but on the morning of the massacre he was keeping an appointment with the Dade County solicitor to reassure local authorities that he was behaving himself. Also present was an assistant district attorney from Brooklyn, who was seeking (but not getting, of course) information about the murder of Frankie Yale. Later historians would use that meeting against Capone, for the timing seemed too perfect, but they ignore the fact that such a conference could not have been set up on short notice, and that Capone had spent the previous few days traveling to and from Nassau.

The phone calls between Chicago and Florida that supposedly stopped three days before the massacre no longer seem as undisputed as other writers have made them out to be, and in any case would have been more suspicious if Capone had been home to answer them. The monthlong purpose of the lookout teams across the street was to watch for Moran and then quickly call the shooters, not Al Capone.

XIV

The Coroner and the Crime Lab

CORONERS IN ILLINOIS IN 1929 held a unique position. They were elected officials who served for four years, could succeed themselves, and once in office were answerable to no one. The Illinois Constitution required that each county have a coroner to investigate unnatural deaths and return a finding as to cause. These legislative protections created political mavericks who ran their own shops, courted the press, and often made a personal impact on crime and the criminal justice system.

Unlike most of his predecessors in Cook County, Herman Bundesen not only had the style to get elected coroner in 1928 (and that was usually the deciding factor) but also possessed a rare combination of medical training, intelligence, good judgment, and dedication to serving the community. Any one of these traits might have derailed his bid for the office had local politicians known. His earliest history is vague but included a stay in an orphanage, an impoverished childhood, a newsboy's aggressiveness, an ability to outrun the police (so far, so good), and a stint in the National Guard that settled him down enough to obtain an education which ultimately earned him a medical degree from Northwestern University in 1909.

After five years of private practice, he was named an epidemiologist in the Chicago Health Department, and in 1921 he was courageous enough (thanks to Prohibition, reform was in the air) to attack the Chicago Police Department for unhealthy conditions in its district stations. A year later he was appointed by Republican Mayor William Hale Thompson (then seen as a reformer himself) to serve as Chicago Health Commissioner. Bundesen retained that post under a real reform mayor, William Dever, and attracted sufficient attention for his David-and-Goliath fights with milk producers and other food industries to win the hearts and minds of his fellow Chicagoans.

His greatest achievements were in the field of child care—sending nurses on home visits, teaching mothers proper breast-feeding, and dispensing copies of his own child-rearing book, *Our Babies*. Thanks to Bundesen's emphasis on breast-feeding, safe low-cost milk, and similar concerns, Chicago's infant mortality rate dropped below that of any other large American city.

Despite many healthcare advances that were widely approved by the public and the press, he was sacked by the re-elected Thompson in 1927 for refusing to include Republican political literature in health pamphlet mailings. His many friends in both parties quickly found him a job as health director of the Chicago Sanitary District, a position that had not previously existed. The city's sanitary districts had long been controlled by patronage-system "bosses," of whom one newspaper editor wrote, "No bolder band of pirates ever sacked a public treasury."

In 1928 Bundesen switched parties to run for coroner against Thompson-backed Republican Oscar Wolff and won by a whopping 950,000 votes. Wolff had been described by newly elected Chicago Crime Commission President Frank Loesch as "amazingly incompetent" and the "most asinine official" Loesch had ever had to deal with. Loesch himself had been waging a one-man war against gangsters and corruption and had saved the nearly moribund commission from possible extinction when its most generous supporter, Julius Rosenwald, president of Sears, Roebuck and Company, threatened to quit and take his money with him if Loesch was not its president. Loesch and Bundesen were the first signs that Chicago was beginning to take its crime problem seriously.

Loesch already had thrown a scare into the community's businessmen by describing how a Michigan Avenue jeweler had to send his salesmen to customers in Evanston who were afraid to come into the city, and how an elderly Indiana woman refused to walk from the Palmer House Hotel to the nearby Marshall Field's department store for fear of being shot. Such examples worried the financial backers of the Century of Progress World's Fair, on which work had already started. The St. Valentine's Day Massacre of 1929 was hardly a step in the right direction.

With not a single worthwhile clue, Bundesen refused to go out on a limb by embracing any of the theories that soon would break under the weight of different, clumsy investigations. Instead, he impaneled a jury of prestigious members of the community, each a recognized professional totally above reproach. He understood that even a blue-ribbon coroner's jury did not rise to the level of action that Chicagoans were needing, so he ordered that the massacre be reenacted the next day, Friday, in the cold North Clark Street garage where the killings had taken place. He wanted it staged as closely as possible to the real thing, including the dog. Only the gunfire would be left out.

He and his staff had started making phone calls the afternoon the crime was discovered, and by late in the day he had corralled a panel of six wealthy, influential, and independent men willing to meet the next morning in a dingy squad room of the Hudson Avenue police station. A firearms expert who would join the group later said this "showed great foresight [because] here was a crime of beyond-average proportions," and Bundesen wanted to investigate it "with the assistance not of a jury of the usual composition but made up of men beyond the average." A private investigator, William Donohue, was personally selected to do work the police could or would not do and go where they could or would not go.

Foreman of the jury was Burt Massee, president of the Colgate-Palmolive-Peet Company, already installed in its new thirty-six-story skyscraper at the corner of Michigan and Walton. Its crowning touch would be the "Lindbergh Beacon," a revolving searchlight so powerful that on a clear night it supposedly could be seen from the western shores of Michigan.

The other five jurors were Walter E. Olson, president of the giant Olsen Rug Company; Dr. John V. McCormick, lawyer and dean of the Loyola University Law School; Fred Bernstein, lawyer, president of the Covenant Club, and superior court master in chancery; Major Felix J. Streyckman, prominent lawyer and attorney for the Belgian consul in Chicago; and Walter W. L. Meyer, master in chancery for the Cook County Circuit Court. No aldermen, policemen, or politicians, in other words.

In talking to Massee, Bundesen found that he had a juror who was fiercely dedicated to solving this crime of crimes. Massee told the coroner that he had discussed the murders with his personal attorney, Charles F. Rathburn, an influential Chicago lawyer, and had asked if a coroner's jury foreman had the authority to secure scientific aid to help in the investigation. Rathburn had said yes and added that he had served on a discussion panel a few months earlier with Major Calvin Goddard, a pioneer in forensic ballistics who had opened a private laboratory in New York City.

During his years in the army, Goddard (later promoted to the reserve rank of colonel) had developed a special interest in the rifling of gun barrels that left distinctive marks on their bullets when examined under a microscope. What attracted the first serious attention to Goddard's work was its application in the famous Sacco-Vanzetti case. Although too late to save both men (avowed anarchists) from execution, Goddard established that the guard killed in a Boston payroll robbery had died from a bullet from Niccola Sacco's gun, a Colt pocket automatic, and not from Bartolomeo Vanzetti's Harrington & Richardson revolver.

Coroner Bundesen, violent-death expert in his own right, told Massee to call Calvin Goddard immediately. Massee had to explain to Goddard that no public funds were available for this work but that he (Massee) would pay for it out of his own pocket. He did the same for private investigator Donohue. This was a case of such nationwide interest that Goddard personally might have taken it on gratis, but it involved moving himself, his equipment, and his staff from New York to Chicago for an indefinite period. With Massee footing the bill, Goddard jumped at the opportunity. The country's first officially recognized, full-service "crime lab" was soon in operation.

The morning after the massacre the jury panel congregated uncomfortably at the Hudson Avenue station, which was already packed with reporters, photographers, policemen, prosecutors, federal investigators, politicians, bail bondsmen, and anyone else who could talk his way past the cops at the door. Coroner Bundesen was fully in charge of the proceedings, and at 10:08 A.M. the coroner's clerk called the mob to order. Bundesen began by announcing that there would be no smoking and that "this inquest shall be conducted in an orderly fashion." He continued, "All conversation will be stopped. If anyone talks, the police will take him out and argue with them there." In a lighter tone he added, looking at the reporters, "We want to get along with you boys."

Then the principals were loaded into detective squad cars and taken to Braithwaite's on Lincoln Avenue to be officially sworn in. There, the Hudson Avenue bedlam was repeated as photographers jockeyed for an unobstructed view of the bodies, lined up side by side, on seven slabs jammed close together in a dimly lit chapel about the size of a modern living room. Stained-glass windows allowed colored light to illuminate the bodies with sheets drawn up to their faces, or what was left of them, with torn and bloody clothing piled at their feet.

The jurors lined up as far to the rear as they could, pressing their backs to the far wall, some averting their eyes from the corpses. The three physicians who conducted the post-mortem examinations stated in an officious monotone that each body had been raked by twenty-five to thirty bullets, including some fired into them after they were down. Those were best guesses, since two had been blasted with buckshot.

The jurors raised their right hands and swore they would endeavor to make every effort to determine how these men came to their deaths—a legal formality, since the immediate cause was obvious. Bundesen's last official order was to "release none of the bodies until they are formally claimed and positively identified."

Schwimmer, May, and Weinshank already had been claimed by relatives, but the ritual had to be observed before proceeding to the garage for the re-enactment.

Here the police were nearly overwhelmed by crowds on both sides of Clark Street, with more onlookers in the alley, when Bundesen arrived with his own horn-honking entourage. This included the jury, Police Commissioner Russell, Deputy Commissioner Thomas Wolfe, Acting Deputy Commissioner John Egan, Assistant State's Attorneys Harry Ditchburne and Walker Butler, Detective Captain William Schoemaker, and even federal investigators, who so far had no federal crime to investigate but decided they would be remiss if one turned up and they weren't on top of it.

Some represented the federal Prohibition Unit and felt obliged, or at least privileged, to attend in case they discerned a Volstead violation. A few were agents of the Justice Department who were using the confusion over license plates to possibly invoke the Dyer Act, which prohibited interstate transportation of a stolen vehicle. This was purely a convenience law to bypass the complicated paperwork needed to return a hot car recovered in one state to its rightful owner in another, but it would later provide a handy excuse for federal agents to pursue bank robbers. The feds were a pain to the locals, but they had badges and impressive-looking United States Government credentials, so it was better not to argue.

After more elbowing and shoving to clear the murder scene still sticky with blood, Bundesen took charge of the garage like it was a movie set. Three officers were chosen to play the shooters, using unloaded shotguns instead of Thompsons, which the police now had in their arsenal but weren't eager to display until they themselves were in the clear. (Newspapers had not yet let go of Major Silloway's initial claim that the killers were rogue cops on a personal mission.) Other plainclothes police and even a reporter were drafted to play the victims, facing the wall with their hands in the air.

A space was made for the jurors, whose sharply creased trousers and carefully polished shoes seemed out of place on greasy, blood-stained concrete in a bootlegger den jammed with tightly parked cars and trucks, some loaded with unassembled vats and other brewing equipment.

The scene complete, Dr. E. L. Benjamin, a coroner's physician, began reading from the report he had compiled with medical examiners Dr. S. D. Gunn and Dr. A. G. Schmidt. He described where every machine-gun slug had pierced a particular victim, and as he did so Bundesen jabbed his forefinger lightly into the back of the individual, who then crumpled to the floor and assumed the position of the body he represented.

The detective standing in for Pete Gusenberg slumped onto the same chair as had Gusenberg and accidentally bumped his head, causing the audience to grimace. Bundesen took over the reading and touched a reporter recruited to play Weinshank. The man turned, reached for an imaginary gun, and as he then slumped to the floor the coroner pointed to where the other slugs had hit the victim in the chest and abdomen.

Confusion arose over Bundesen's belief that the recovered revolver was Weinshank's, and he indicated where it was found about in the middle of the floor. Also, he believed the dog was Weinshank's and named Fritz, instead of May's dog named Highball, as writers later decided. In any case, Fritz, or Highball, or whatever, still tied up, suddenly broke into a mournful howling that caused the crowd to move away, until somebody's uneasy laugh broke the tension. The revolver, police later concluded, was Frank Gusenberg's.

During the reenactment, the jurors and spectators displayed varying reactions. Massee listened intently. Streyckman, seated on a pile of wooden staves for making vats, looked on solemnly. Meyer chatted with men around him. Commissioner Russell, impressive in a white muffler and heavy dark overcoat, walked in and out of the room. The dog had quieted down but still whined and yelped and tugged at its rope trying to back away.

This bit of showmanship satisfied the press, which satisfied the public and kept Bundesen at the forefront of the investigation without having to seize on some theory that would not hold up, order an arrest that would not stick, announce that a solution to the crime was imminent, or otherwise compromise his role as a serious professional who would withhold judgment until all the facts were in— or at least partly in, which would require more meetings at irregular intervals over the next ten months.

To keep things moving, Coroner Bundesen reopened the inquest at 1:15 P.M. at the Hudson Avenue police station with the introduction of Maurice T. Weinshank, an attorney at 110 West Washington and the uncle of Albert Weinshank. Maurice denied any knowledge of who might have killed his nephew, an official with the Central Cleaners and Dyers Association and before that the circulation manager for a Chicago newspaper. Central Cleaners was at the center of the warfare between Moran and Capone, in case no one was reading the papers, and a "circulation manager" was the polite name for a captain in the war that had finally cooled between William Randolph Hearst's *Herald and Examiner* and Colonel Robert McCormick's *Chicago Tribune*, both of which had employed sluggers and hoodlums to keep the opposition's papers out of street-corner newsstands.

The newspaper truce evidently had left Albert so restless that he transferred his talents to the cleaners and dyers, and once Morris Becker teamed up with Capone, that only confused matters further by the addition of racketeering as a murder motive. Attorney Weinshank knew nothing about such things, of course, and said only that gangster Weinshank was supposed to meet with him late that morning to make travel plans for the February 27 prizefight in Miami between Jack Sharkey and Young Stribling (won by the former in ten rounds). The rest of his answers were "I don't know," and in angry frustration Assistant State's Attorney Ditchburne sent the witness back to practice his law.

The next witness was Henry Gusenberg, who acknowledged that Peter and Frank were his brothers but had no idea of what they did for a living, or what they were doing in the garage. He described himself as a simple, honest, hard-working motion-picture projectionist, although he could have added that his projectionists union recently had been taken over by Capone. That didn't come up, and Henry Gusenberg also was dismissed.

Myrtle Gusenberg, wearing an expensive fur coat, said she had married Pete under the name of Gorman the previous June in the belief that he was a prosperous real estate broker; otherwise, she alternated between sobs and indignation while providing no useful information. The only tidbit she revealed was that Pete had called home to have her cancel his Thursday morning dental appointment because he had to attend a meeting.

Frank Gusenberg's married life was twice as interesting: He had left behind two expensively outfitted "bullet widows" who glowered at each other. Ruth Gusenberg said she had married Frank five years previously, while Lucille claimed three years of marriage to the same man. Both refused to discuss their late mutual husband's affairs. Reporters were consumed by curiosity but kept their peace. Bundesen had already seen the *Tribune*'s banner headline, DOCTOR KILLED IN MASSACRE, and could imagine an even spicier one proclaiming, MASSACRE DOCTOR & BIGAMIST! He let the matter go.

Coroner Bundesen personally questioned victim Adam Heyer's seventeen-year-old son, Howard. His fear of retribution was so great that he refused to allow photographs, but Adam admitted that his father was general manager of the Fairview Kennel Club. This was Moran's dog track operating northwest of the Chicago city limits under the protection of a court injunction, and which dodged state gambling laws by the clever subterfuge of denying that it encouraged gambling. In other words, it had no indoor windows with signs that said PLACE YOUR BETS HERE.

Juror Meyer, wearing a smart bow tie and heavy black horn-rimmed glasses, piped up, "Didn't you know who owned that track?" Before the witness could answer, Ditchburne jumped to his feet and said, "I would rather that you didn't go any further on that line of questioning." Reporters held their breath while Meyer, a prominent lawyer not about to be silenced, snorted, "Is this state's attorney kidding me? That's Bob Crowe's track." Ditchburne told juror Meyer that an investigation was being made along that line and "any revelation now would be premature." Which was the end of that and of any investigation which might have added dog tracks or the War of Sicilian Succession as yet other bones of contention among Capone, Moran, Aiello, and New York's Frankie Yale, who already had been killed by Capone's American Boys.

No telling whose name or names were on the ownership papers, but Robert E. Crowe had been the Cook County state's attorney and a powerful Republican political boss trounced in the Pineapple Primary. His integrity could be judged by his appointment of an unsavory character named Ben Newmark as chief investigator with a staff of forty Chicago police officers who roamed the county making "show" raids. Never known to turn down a bribe, Newmark and his men were so notorious that Crowe himself characterized them as "Ali Baba and his forty thieves." Their laughable expense reports even included receipts for illegal booze.

Next on the stand was Mrs. Marie Neubauer, housewife and sister of victim James Clark. Tearfully, she said that she had lost her husband in late January to an accident, and now her brother was dead. She explained that Clark's name was actually Albert Kachellek and that he used Clark to "cover things up . . . so that nobody would know anything." She added that Kachellek was "always in trouble." Her emotional state was so obviously fragile that the questioning quickly and mercifully ended. In the weeks and months that followed, and in later years, she complained that writers copying previous writers kept wrongly identifying Kachellek as Bugs Moran's brother-in-law.

Pathos was permissible when it came to Mrs. Josephine Schwimmer, sixty, crushed with despair and swaying as she took the stand. AGED MOTHER BRINGS TEARS TO MANY EYES, read the line that introduced her testimony as reported in the newspapers. When news of the killings broke and her boy was listed among the dead, she had asked a younger friend to identify the body, and news photos of her taken at the inquest—tiny, tearful, and clearly grieving in a simple dark dress and cloche hat that almost hid her face—bothered even hardened reporters.

> She was the widowed mother of the slain Dr. Reinhart Schwimmer—her only child and her single joy—and her quavering voice took on a pathetic firmness while she insisted that his presence was—must have been—purely accidental.

That colorful quotation was published in the *Chicago Herald and Examiner*, which gave her a personal sidebar that was equally heart-rending but raised a few other questions.

'ALWAYS A GOOD BOY!'
DOCTOR'S MOTHER SOBS
* * *

> No, no, no, my son was not a gangster, cried Mrs. Josephine B. Schwimmer, gray-haired mother of Dr Reinhardt [*sic*] H. Schwimmer. . . .
>
> "He was always a good boy, my son, until he got to going around with that North Side gang about a year and a half ago. I pleaded with him and warned him to break away from them, but he seemed to like to boast about knowing reputed 'toughs' and of having an 'in.'"

Tears rolled down the mother's cheeks as she told the detectives how she had waited for her son on the night of the murder. Although he maintained a legal residence at the Parkway Hotel [as did Bugs Moran], he often spent the night at her home at 2837 Burling st.

GIVES CONFLICTING STORIES

Reported by some to be the owner of a hair and scalp treatment establishment at 159 N. State st., and by others to be a fortune teller with a studio at the same address, she gave several conflicting accounts of her son's relationship to the Moran gang.

In one story she said that Dr. Schwimmer, an optometrist, had gotten to know Peter Gusenberg because he sold him a pair of glasses. He became friendly with Gusenberg, she said, but was never a member of the gang.

"He must have just happened into the garage yesterday to see his friend," she said.

She told Lieut. William Cusack of the detective bureau, however, that her son "couldn't break away from the gang. He surely would have left them if he had been able to."

Still another newspaper report told how, in her role as fortune teller and "soothsayer," she had predicted the violent death of her son:

WARNED OF DOOM

"I told him months ago that his doom was coming," she is reported as saying. "I warned him, but he had no faith in me."

Lieut. Cusack said that Dr. Schwimmer had a .45 revolver and a bill of sale for a Lincoln car at $4400 from "P. J. Gorman," the name often used by the gangster Gusenberg. The doctor was a rather attractive fellow, said the lieutenant, and whenever the gang needed a smart, well-dressed talker to put over something in a "grand" manner, they called on him. He "fronted" for a lot of them.

He revealed that the doctor had been "picked up" with the North Side hoodlums several times recently.

Some of this may have been copspeak used when someone had been running with a bad crowd and obviously enjoying it, or otherwise was not quite what he seemed. Eyebrows were raised when a gun was found in Schwimmer's hotel apartment, which he could not afford. The fact that his stricken mother was a little odd herself—and on first-name terms with "Mr. Pete"—also caused the police to wonder.

That Reinhart had two former wives by the age of twenty-nine did not create a favorable impression either, and the $162 he was carrying when killed disturbed Mother Schwimmer, who had kept him in pocket money much of the time and picked up his rent at the Parkway when he moved offices from one building to another on North Lincoln Avenue.

At least one paper suggested that Schwimmer's North Sider connection went back to O'Banion's day. However, the side-view newspaper photo of a man purported to be Schwimmer at O'Banion's funeral bore little resemblance to the body on the floor of the garage.

Next to be sworn was Ella Schulte, the friend of Mrs. Schwimmer who had first approached the police to confirm that one of the bodies was Reinhart's. Out of fear of some kind of retribution she refused to give her own husband's name to the press but under pressure divulged it to the court reporter.

The last two witnesses were James May and Mrs. Lucy Powell, the brother and sister of the murdered John May. James would say only that he knew his brother drove a truck and lately had been working as a mechanic. His sister claimed to know even less but said that May's widow was "at home—hysterical." In the course of this bland testimony, some reporters whispered cruel jokes about the absence of protection afforded by John May's two mangled St. Christopher's medals, which had failed to stop bullets.

McCormick's *Chicago Tribune*, extremely Republican and therefore no fan of Bundesen, now a Democrat, reported that by the end of the long day's hearings, "Nothing of value to the investigation was obtained," while Hearst's *Los Angeles Examiner* described the day's events (especially the reenactment) as "thrilling and exciting."

The day had ended on a testy note as Coroner Bundesen dueled semantically with State's Attorney Ditchburne. The coroner formally asked if anyone present had any reason why the inquest should not be closed. "You mean adjourned," said Ditchburne. "No, closed," said Bundesen. Evidently the coroner was referring to the inquest proper, concerned with the bodies, while Ditchburne was referring to the overall massacre investigation. Rephrasing his request, Ditchburne formally asked for a two-week continuance, which Bundesen—it was his jury, after all—allowed that he would grant.

XV

THE WOOD STREET FIRE

T HE FIRST SESSION OF THE coroner's jury hearings was a bust as far as anyone learning anything new, but it had to be done for the record. The tension between Coroner Bundesen and Assistant State's Attorney Ditchburne had been obvious from the start, and Police Commissioner Russell was called upon to prevent a potential turf war. He did that with enough diplomacy to satisfy both combatants, proposing an investigative strategy that gave both parties roles best suited to their different styles and expertise.

Which left Russell with other agencies to accommodate. At the outset he had joined State's Attorney John Swanson in handing down an order that a wide-open Chicago would become a bone-dry Chicago, and that he would have the heads of any district captains who thought otherwise. In the past such edicts had been periodically issued and routinely ignored, for police captains had long enjoyed something close to sovereignty in their districts. To suddenly be held accountable for the police work of their men put the district commanders on the spot, but the grumbling was done in the privacy of their offices. It was Chicago tradition to have no knowledge of bars or speakeasies within their jurisdictions, and so these also escaped the notice of their otherwise vigilant beat cops.

The detective bureau had even greater concerns. The order that each man account for his activities at the time of the massacre would have resulted in something approaching a rebellion, so the dirty work was happily shoved off on the staff of the state's attorney's office. The state's attorney's investigators liked playing cop when a major crime was committed, but strictly speaking they were not part of the police command structure; however, the two hundred or so detectives who might be accused of insubordination thought it best to humor them.

The detectives' real concern, which they did not make public but allowed one or two favored reporters to overhear, was that a major crime wave might take place if an estimated thirty thousand bootleggers and gun-toting hoodlums suddenly found themselves out of work. As a rule, the detectives knew where the hoods hung out, who they worked for, who their friends were, what they were up to in a general sort of way, and who they probably had knocked off, even when they couldn't prove it. If someone's name was in the news as a suspected killer or racketeer, who would invariably have an alibi, it was often sufficient just to announce that he was sought, and the suspect, flanked by lawyers, would turn himself in. Many detectives and criminals were on first-name terms whether they liked each other or not, and after engaging in banter that passed for interrogation, they usually walked back out, maybe cracking some jokes that left their adversaries chuckling.

Bugs Moran, for instance, was still missing but sent a message to Chief of Detectives Egan with the convincing assurance that he did not know and could not guess the identity of the shooters. He refused to blame either the Detroit gang (the Purples) or the "Cicero gang" (Capone). He reportedly said, "We don't know what brought it on. We're facing an enemy in the dark." Actually, an enterprising reporter had tracked Moran to St. Francis Hospital in Evanston, where he checked in under an assumed name on the same day as the massacre, claiming he had the flu, and four days later checked out again and disappeared. The reporter learned nothing of value but quoted Moran as saying, "Only Capone kills like that!" (When Moran's words reached Capone in Florida, he responded, "They don't call that guy bugs for nothing.")

Also missing was Jack McGurn, Chicago's perennial murder suspect, whose absence increased suspicions about Capone and who is still regarded by many as the massacre's paymaster. (Although McGurn obviously knew the killings were planned, he evidently didn't know when and had holed up in the Stevens Hotel two weeks previously. Georgette Winkler believes Capone left the planning to Frank Nitti, his cousin whom she was beginning to distrust, and the payoffs to Frankie Rio, who was caught in the middle.)

Anxious for news of any kind, reporters could get nothing from their usual tipsters in either the law-enforcement or criminal communities, and could turn up only a report on the booze situation in Detroit. During nice weather, Canadian bootleggers had used speedboats to whisk their wares to the American side, switching to light trucks when the river was frozen over. But now they were complaining that the relatively mild winter had made it treacherous to drive loads across the thin ice on the Detroit River. Cash-and-carry rules were instituted: Let American booze trucks break through the ice.

And while the Canadians officially frowned on smuggling, the country's liquor industry was booming like never before and the government could hardly keep a straight face in meetings with U.S. authorities to discuss the problem. As of January 1929, it was still entirely legal for a vessel departing from Canada to declare that it was bound for an American port with a cargo of liquor.

At this stage, the best that some newsmen could come up with was the report that a telephone repairman had been at the garage several times, including the morning of the massacre, to make certain the phones weren't tapped. He had left about thirty minutes before the shooters arrived.

Another witness, of sorts, was a young woman who lived in the vicinity of the Moran garage and patronized the nearby Parkway Riding Academy when she went horseback riding in nearby Lincoln Park. A few days before the massacre a male companion had pointed out some men he said were "West Side gangsters," without explaining how he knew this. To someone in Lincoln Park, this narrowed it down to those around North Avenue, who probably dressed like gangsters in spiffy clothes, expensive hats, and spats—something that made them stand out from ordinary-looking Chicagoans.

If West Side gangsters, they would be have been connected with the Circus Gang, headquartered at the Circus Café on North Avenue, but more likely they were some of Moran's North Siders. Either way, all she could tell police was that she had seen some of the same men in the alley she took to Lincoln Park, which passed behind the SMC Cartage Company garage. This wasn't very helpful, but police withheld her name and asked photographers not to take her picture.

A witness of some prominence was H. Wallace Caldwell, President of the Chicago Board of Education—or, rather, his chauffeur, who called the attention of Mr. Caldwell to what looked like a detective squad car which had sped through a red light on the Near North Side in an apparent rush to get somewhere. The chauffeur described the driver as missing a front tooth, which would become a source of great interest as the investigation continued.

Potentially the best witness of all was the teenager George Arthur Brichet, who had been walking in the alley behind the garage and evidently saw more than anyone else. He noticed what looked like a detective squad car parked partly out of sight in a lot across the alley and said that when the back doors of the garage were opened to admit a truck, two uniformed men and one in a topcoat, guns drawn, slipped in behind it. Believing a raid was in progress, Brichet hoofed it around the short angular block to the front of the garage, apparently missing the shooting but arriving in time to see two "cops" with guns marching two other men in overcoats, hands raised, out to another detective squad car, which then sped south on North Clark Street. He claimed to hear one of the men in the alley address another as "Mac," which the police guessed would be Jack McGurn, who had not yet been picked up. This also accounted for the differing number of men, in and out of uniform, seen leaving the garage by other witnesses.

The firing squad and lookouts must have numbered seven or eight, the police now guessed. The scenario was still unclear, but it was backed up by the claim of Mrs. Landesman's elderly mother, who often passed the time looking out her bay window onto North Clark, that she had seen *two* squad cars, one of which had left before the shooting. What now made sense, though it was not reported, was that the killers didn't just go in and out the *front* door, as virtually every account describes.

For one thing, the front door almost certainly was locked, and a uniformed policeman, especially a stranger, was not likely to be invited in. Even if allowed to enter, he, one or two others in uniform, and finally the men with machine guns and a shotgun, would have had to make their way single file between closely parked trucks and cars from the office back to the killing wall—a distance of some thirty to forty feet. It would have been much simpler for the men in uniform to enter from the alley, disarm the seven victims, and then open the front door for the shooters, whose squad car on North Clark Street would discourage any nosy pedestrians from wondering about the sounds of gunfire—or backfiring, as some witnesses thought they heard.

The widely accepted story that the victims were gathered to unload a truck of Old Log Cabin whiskey, supposedly hijacked from Capone, seems to have been Major Silloway's original acorn growing into an oak. It reappeared in the *Tribune* several days later, about the same time another reporter speculated that the Moran gang had congregated at the garage to drive trucks to Detroit to pick up a booze shipment. A telephone call from Detroit to Bugs Moran had indeed been made the day before, but the Detroiters, like the Canadian distilleries, also had adopted a cash-and-carry policy.

In any case, booze hijacked from Capone made a better story, and the tale evolved from there into an even more elaborate ruse: one truckload sold to Moran at a bargain price, with the promise of a second load that would arrive on February 14—a Valentine's Day present for Bugs is the way it's usually portrayed in movies and documentaries. In the 1967 film *The St. Valentine's Day Massacre*, scripted in the style of a documentary, that scenario is beefed up slightly by having the hijacker complain that he was cheated on his first delivery, so Moran would have to be there in person.

So far, so good, except that the men Moran assembled were not working-class bootleggers dressed to unload fifty or a hundred cases of liquor, even Old Log Cabin, which should have taken up too much floor space for yet another truck to squeeze in and still be able to back out. Nor were they dressed to make what in those times was a full day's uncomfortable drive to Detroit and back. The men, in full gangster formal attire plus jewelry, were Moran's board of directors—one was his rackets specialist, another his dog-track manager—plus his three top gunmen, one of whom had cancelled his dental appointment to attend the meeting, and another who was wearing a carnation. The three or four who didn't reach the garage in time were Willie Marks, Moran's number-two man; Ted Newberry, his gambling chief; possibly Frank Foster, believed to have recently shot a Capone union official; and Moran himself.

The ruse or reason that was used to assemble these members of the Moran gang (not counting Dr. Schwimmer and May, the mechanic) may never be known. However, it's safe to assume that the meeting was called on short notice, probably for the purpose of a killing or some other immediate and drastic action that would make waves and needed agreement among the gang's leadership. In the absence of conference-call telephone systems (which anyway might have been tapped), it could be brief and held in an unheated garage, so as not to arouse the curiosity of the Parkway Hotel management or doorman, who would almost certainly remember the collective arrival of Moran's top warlords on an occasion that was not Bugs's birthday.

Likewise, Claude Maddox and his Circus Gang were more than a local nuisance. Not only were they invading unions that Moran had his eye on, they also were bombing stills and speakeasies that the North Siders and the Aiellos were supposed to be protecting. A factory-size distillery was operating within their expanding boundaries, and it was said to be Capone's. So there's the possibility that Moran had been tipped off by friends in high places that the Capone Outfit or Maddox or both were planning to make some move the North Siders could not or would not tolerate. The tip might even have been false, deliberately leaked to someone they knew would run with it to Moran. How quickly Moran decided to move would have been the time frame for the lookouts to start watching the garage.

The one thing that probably can be discarded is the hijacked-whiskey story. If a delivery had been scheduled, one or two lookouts in a parked car could have signaled Moran's arrival, and he

"Scarface" Al Capone (left) is the best-known of America's Depression-era gangsters. His rise to power and the emergence of nationally organized crime syndicates are due in large part to U.S. Prohibition, which spawns massive political corruption and drives law-abiding citizens to underworld purveyors of illicit alcohol. The murder of vice lord "Big Jim" Colosimo (bottom right) in 1920 is the first big gangland slaying of the period.

THE GRAFTERS

"LIFE IMPRISONMENT FOR A PINT!"

THE AGE OF BARBARISM.

CHICAGO DAILY TRIBUNE

COLOSIMO SLAIN; SEEK EX-WIFE, JUST RETURNED

Racketeers protected by Chicago's political machine increasingly shake down the city's business community during the 1920s and '30s as rival gangs vie for control of the lucrative bootlegging business. The 1924 "handshake murder" of North Side Gang leader Dean O'Banion (below) by South Side factions sparks a violent series of clashes, including the September 1926 drive-by hit on Al Capone's headquarters in Cicero's Hawthorne Hotel by a caravan of machine-gunners led by Hymie Weiss (bottom right).

Chicago Herald and Examiner

Chicago Daily Tribune FINAL

Daily 815,635
Sunday 1,248,707

VOLUME LXXXV—NO. 36.   WEDNESDAY, FEBRUARY 10, 1926—40 PAGES.   PRICE TWO CENTS

MACHINE GUN GANG SHOOTS 2

Italy Seizes Tyrol Arms Cache; 50 Held   RAKE SALOON IN BEER WAR: Find Bezner Guilty; Given 20 Year Term   SMALL'S FINAL PLEA REJECTED;

NEWS SUMMARY   TEMPTED

Chicago Daily Tribune

Daily 614,869
Sunday 968,556

VOLUME LXXXIII—NO. 27.   TUESDAY, NOVEMBER 11, 1924—30 PAGES   PRICE TWO CENTS

KILL O'BANION, GANG LEADER

CONGRESS MAY   NEWS SUMMARY   ARMISTICE DAY FINDS THE WORLD, INCLUDING THE BALKANS AND MEXICO, PRETTY MUCH AT PEACE   BEGIN HILL SUIT   Shut 4 Up in Bank Vault in   3-GUN FLORIST

KILL LOMBARDO, MAFIA CHIEF

Three weeks after the Hawthorne drive-by, Weiss and bodyguard "Paddy" Murray are cut down in front of Holy Name Cathedral by Capone shooters in a machine-gun nest across the street (top). An unused nest (in circle) is found later. While Mayor "Big Bill" Thompson (above left, with aviation hero Charles Lindbergh) keeps Chicago wide open, Frankie Yale, O'Banion's murderer, becomes New York's first Tommygun victim (above right), launching the War of Sicilian Succession. In a matter of weeks the war will also claim the lives of Capone-supported Unione President Tony Lombardo and his successor, "Patsy" Lolordo (left).

A neighbor investigating popping sounds that came from a garage at 2122 North Clark Street on the morning of February 14, 1929, stumbles upon a grisly scene: six dead men and one nearly so, all riddled by bullets (above and right). On the floor is a revolver (circle and inset), which is documented by Officer Tom Loftus and later determined to belong to Frank Gusenberg.

Victims at the SMC garage include: (above from left) North Siders Frank and Peter Gusenberg, Albert Kachellek (alias James Clark), and Adam Heyer; Albert Weinshank (far left) and driver John May; and their optician pal Reinhart Schwimmer (not pictured), whose mother, Josephine (below), downplayed his ties to the gang and sobbed to reporters, "He was always a good boy." The killers executed the North Siders prematurely as their intended target, George "Bugs" Moran (left), had not yet arrived at the scene.

As word of the killings spreads, crowds of curious onlookers gather in front of the SMC garage and in the alley behind the building as the dead are removed from the scene. The only survivor of the execution-style murders is an Alsatian shepherd (above left) belonging to driver and mechanic John May.

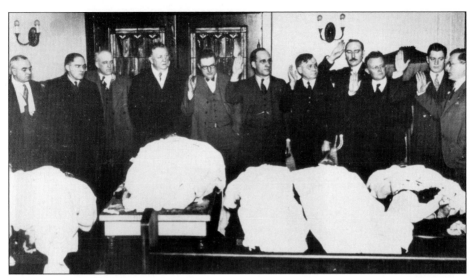

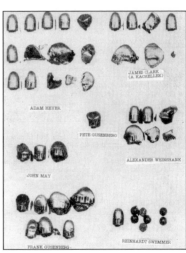

Members of a blue-ribbon coroner's jury of prominent Chicagoans are sworn in as they survey the bodies at Braithwaite's mortuary. The victims had been riddled by some 20–30 machine-gun slugs, and two had been blasted by a shotgun. Newspapers collectively denounce the wholesale slaughter as each scrambles for a fresh angle on the killings.

Crowds again surround the SMC garage (below) on the day after the killings as Coroner Herman Bundesen carefully restages the massacre (above) for jury members, using police and a reporter as stand-ins for the shooters and victims.

NORTH CLARK STREET DOOR THROUGH WHICH KILLERS ENTERED

OFFICE

The "American Boys" known to have composed the St. Valentine's Day execution squad: (top, left to right) Gus Winkler and Robert Carey; (center) Ray Nugent and Fred Goetz; (bottom) Byron Bolton and Fred Burke. Two or three others probably participated as lookouts, but Burke and Goetz wore the police uniforms and slipped in through the back door of the garage, then left by the front door after "arresting" two presumed bootleggers in civilian clothes.

WHO WILL PROHIBIT THIS?

Shall Chicago Stand for This?

In the days following February 14, nearly every daily newspaper in the country features the massacre, many with editorial cartoons singling out Chicago and its bootlegging wars.

NO WORDS can add to the force of this cartoon. Chicago stands ashamed before the civilized world. Lawbreaking in this city has reached its climax in a mass murder that makes law-abiding people everywhere gasp with horror. Chicagoans who feel themselves dishonored in the dishonor of their city will rally to its defense and, if necessary, appoint a committee to take the municipal government out of the hands of the public servants who have betrayed their fellow citizens.

—Providence Bulletin

The Score-Keeper

An editorial cartoon depicts Chicago's rampant gangland violence as a Soldier Field sport (top). A few days after the slayings, the executioners' phony squad cars are discovered, one dismantled and burned in a Wood Street garage (above left), which leads police to the Circus Café, the other blasted in Maywood, (above right) but largely ignored by the police and press. Most observers initially attribute the post-massacre murders of three Capone mobsters to the Moran gang (left).

The arsenal found in the house of Fred Burke (above) after his killing of a Michigan policeman eventually leads to his capture. The tiny "S" stamped onto a short run of bullets (right) helps tie Burke to the massacre. Major Calvin Goddard (seated at left below) uses forensic ballistics to link Burke's Tommyguns to both the massacre and the earlier murder Frankie Yale in New York.

Plate 17. .45 automatic pistol bullet of U. S. Cartridge Company make with cannelure, fired through Thompson gun.

Plate 18. .45 automatic pistol bullet of U. S. Cartridge Company make without cannelure, fired through Thompson gun.

By 1930 Capone is transformed into a national "crime czar" headquartered at Chicago's Lexington Hotel (below right). Scarface Al is mistakenly accused of "reviving" warfare with surviving remnants of the North Side Gang and blamed for the murder of Tribune reporter Jake Lingle, at a time when his principal foe for control of the Unione Siciliana is Joe Aiello (below left).

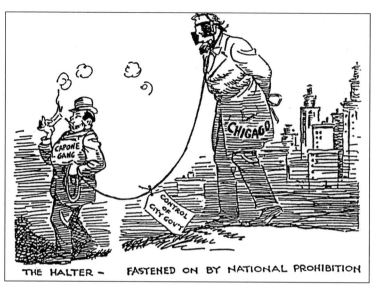

THE HALTER - FASTENED ON BY NATIONAL PROHIBITION

Before and after his imprisonment, Capone remains the predominant symbol of Chicago crime, despite the defeat of Big Bill Thompson by Anton Cermack. The new mayor's efforts to "clean up" Chicago lead to the shooting of Capone's successor, Frank Nitti, whose name had not even appeared on the first two "Public Enemy" lists.

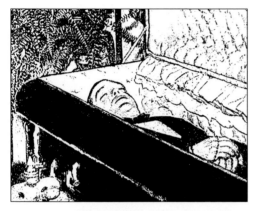

The 1935 arrest of Byron Bolton on a kidnapping charge leads to a "confession" of his part in the massacre and throws FBI Director J. Edgar Hoover into fits of denial. The bureau already has the memoirs of Gus Winkler's widow, which support a more detailed account of the murders soon wrung from Bolton, but does not share them with local police for a year as they implicate two prominent politicians and Chicago's chief of detectives. With Prohibition on the ropes, Gus Winkler's loyalty to Capone has earned him control of Chicago's North Side and the enmity of Frank Nitti, whose gunmen kill the last of the "American Boys."

Officer White
Isolation

INMATE REQUEST FORM

Have Dr. Lewis examine Capone in his cell. He is not to be taken to the hospital or night sick call.

NAME Al Capon

                                Captain Martin
NUMBER 84610

DATE 12-20-35

REQUESTED BY INMATE

I need to see the doctor

While Hoover frets that murder (not a federal offense) will derail the nation's first "War on Crime" against bank robbers and kidnappers, syphilis catches up with Al Capone in Alcatraz. Frank Nitti's bullets end Jack McGurn's efforts to renew his ties with the Syndicate. A despondent Nitti fatally shoots himself in 1943 (below) near his home in Riverside.

was clearly the main target of the hit. The Gusenbergs certainly would have been a bonus as far as McGurn was concerned, or if friends of Tony Lombardo and Patsy Lolordo had a say in the matter, since it was "common knowledge" that the Sicilian community had broken *omerta* enough to finger the Gusenbergs in their slayings.

Moreover, Newberry and Foster made peace with the Syndicate over the next year, and Newberry reputedly was on its payroll (working with Gus Winkler, no less) when casino operations revived.

Young George Brichet, who had seen the "cops" go in and the "cops" come out, was hurried to safety in a Loop hotel and probably questioned extensively, as were the girl on horseback and several others. Their testimony would have been recorded in another session of the coroner's inquest, but that particular transcript has long since vanished from each of the several places that would have received copies. Today the file on the massacre which resides at the Chicago Crime Commission includes an internal memorandum from 1929 noting the transcript's absence, and stating that it disappeared soon after it arrived from the coroner's office.

After the first few days of canvassing by the cops, the claiming of bodies, the coroner's initial inquest, orders to "round up the usual suspects," proclamations of wars on criminals, and baseless assurances of quick solutions, Chicago's major hoodlums were still in hiding. The authorities were still baffled, Mayor Thompson had gone fishing (or someplace), and the speakeasies were padlocked, with only the most trusted regular customers allowed to slip in through the back door.

Then, exactly a week after the massacre, Commissioner Russell decided the lull in police activity was making his department look ineffectual and issued a new edict:

> Cause district commanders to have a search made of all garages, both public and private, barns, sheds, in fact any type of buildings in the alleys for the purpose of ascertaining and reporting any places suspected of having miniature breweries, whisky stills, alcohol stills, whisky or beer trucks, liquors or beer stored. . . .

It is ordered that district commanders use every available man in order that this search may be thoroughly and quickly executed.

Division commanders shall give this matter their personal attention.

It's hard to say whether this order worried the hoods or the public most. But before it could be executed, an impressive fireball lit up the inside of a garage on the alley behind 1723 Wood Street, barely two blocks from the Circus Café, and out ran a man well singed by what appeared to be a gasoline explosion, because it made more of a *whoosh* than a *bang*. While local residents called the fire department, the scorched man ran south down the alley to North Avenue, then four short blocks east to the North Avenue Hospital, which was more like a large clinic, at number 1625, just west of Ashland. Tony Capezio must have looked like a lobster that had just escaped from the pot, but before he was seen by a doctor, he realized that he could survive his burns more easily than the cops, and he hurried back outside.

Firemen quickly doused the garage fire and discovered the remains of an automobile. The police nabbed John Wiesnefski, who rented the house on Wood Street but didn't use the garage. Wiesnefski sent the police to his landlord, Leo Joppett, who lived on Wabansia and owned both the house at 1723 Wood and the garage behind it. He explained that a man calling himself Frank Rogers had rented the garage on February 12, paid a month's rent in advance, and had given his address as 1859 West North Avenue. That, in retrospect, was pretty stupid.

While several detectives examined the burned-out interior of the garage and discovered much interesting evidence, others headed for the address given by "Frank Rogers" and found that it was a kind of annex to the Circus Café at number 1857, jointly owned by Claude Maddox and Anthony "Tough Tony" Capezio. Bingo. The massacre investigation was back on track, and the newspapers had a field day.

The police quickly determined that they had found what was left of a 1927 Cadillac touring car, just like detective squads used, plus a Luger pistol, grips for another gun, a siren, and even the hat and overcoat of the man who had been laboriously cutting the car apart with a hacksaw and acetylene torch. Commissioner Russell's order to search every garage, shed, and outbuilding panicked the car dismantler, who evidently didn't know that most automobiles of the day used a mechanical pump to draw gasoline from the main tank up to a canister mounted on the firewall behind the engine, and from there the gas was gravity-fed to the carburetion system. These canisters were often the size of a coffee can, and cutting into one with a torch usually resulted in a spectacular but short-lived fireball that thoroughly scorched but rarely killed the cutter.

Something else excited the police at the North Avenue address given by "Frank Rogers." It not only was next door to the Circus Café and across the street from the apartment of the late Patsy Lolordo, it apparently was being used as an indoor shooting range. The café itself had recently closed and was being stripped of fixtures, but at the address listed by "Rogers" police found guns and overcoats indicating that several of its occupants had fled out the back door as soon as the garage blew, or as soon as the burn victim sounded the alarm.

The man they would like to have found was Claude Maddox, otherwise known as John E. "Screwy" Moore, whom detectives had picked up in a raid there as recently as January 26, hiding in a back room with a fully loaded hundred-round drum magazine for a Thompson, plus many boxes of ammunition. They knew Maddox from election- and union-related shooting scrapes dating back to 1924 and assumed that he had kept a hand in the labor rackets up to the time Capone and Moran went head-to-head in the cleaners and dyers war of 1928.

Maddox had some kind of living quarters at the Circus Café but had given his home address as 1642 Warren Avenue on the Near West Side. He was the leader of the Circus Gang , which was causing a lot of grief for Moran and the Aiellos and, with café co-owner Tony Capezio, was considered a Capone beachhead wedged between the Aiellos in Little Sicily and Moran's North Side mob. Its members included veterans of the old 42 Gang, such as Jack McGurn, Tony Accardo (then driving for McGurn), and Rocco de Grazia, plus former punks from the Patch, an area of fluctuating boundaries on the city's Near West Side comprising nearly a dozen distinctive European cultural communities.

The Circus was also a hangout for the boys from St. Louis. Although it went unreported at the time, detectives already had found in one of the lookouts' rooms a letter to one Byron Bolton from his parents, who farmed near the downstate towns of Thayer and Virden. They also found (according to Mrs. Winkler) an empty bottle of doctor-prescribed medicine for Bolton's tuberculosis, a common disease at the time. What the cops didn't yet know was that Bolton had spent time in St. Louis, driving for Fred Burke, which technically made him another of the American Boys.

Chicago detectives were closer than they realized to cracking the case. How they kept some of their moves out of the newspapers until later is one of the mysteries of inquisitional journalism. Every newspaper had one or more crime reporters who usually were privy to insider gossip as well as confidential information, and the police and the press played one another with "off the record" tips—usually the kind that also reached the competition and then became a matter of "you read it here first."

The detectives had made quite a newsworthy visit to St. Louis, based on evidence seized from a Maddox office at 1134 North Ashland, and they came back with what should have been a blockbuster. Authorities there were familiar with the use of police uniforms by criminals, and the criminal best known for that stunt was Frederick R. Burke, believed to be the alias of a Thomas A. Camp, born in Kansas City, who was wanted all over the Midwest for murder and bank robbery. One of his early arrests had provided police with quite an odd weapon—a German "broomhandle" Mauser, introduced in 1898 as the first successful semi-automatic pistol holstered in its own removable stock. The weapon later was factory redesigned into one version known as the Schnell-Feuer, which also could be fired on full automatic, like a machine pistol.

Moreover, Burke had a partner in crime who called himself James Ray, the alias of Gus Winkler, who would later start going by the names Rand and Reed and eventually Michaels. Burke was as much a killer as a robber, and besides taking part in the Milaflores Massacre in Detroit on behalf of the Purple Gang, he and Winkler had more recently knocked over the American Securities Company in Toledo, home of Ray "Crane-Neck" Nugent (whom Georgette

Winkler knew as "Gander") when he wasn't kidnapping Detroiters or Chicagoans.

The cops already knew where to look for the Toledo robbers. Fred Goetz, alias Shotgun George Zeigler, also had participated in the American Securities job, which nearly ended the crime careers of the American Boys before they made it big in Chicago. The money was in a portable safe, but Nugent had forgotten to bring any explosives. So, the Five Stooges (in this case) decided to load the safe into the back of a car, take it to Nugent's garage, and use his tools to open it there. Nearly everything that could go wrong did, including a police chase, but the robbers somehow lost their pursuers. At the garage they managed to get the safe open just as a cop walked in. Grabbing their loot and their guns, they made yet another getaway, but not before Goetz had shot and killed the policeman.

In their rush to escape, Goetz left behind his coat, in the pocket of which was the address in Cicero where he was living with his Irene and Byron Bolton. According to Georgette Winkler, this freelance robbery sent the Chicago police on a hunt for Goetz and Bolton, forcing everyone to move again. This infuriated Capone, who didn't need the mud of armed robbery and a cop-killing tracked into the rackets empire he was trying to run like a regular business, Torrio style.

XVI

THE ST. LOUIS CONNECTION

IT NOW SEEMS STRANGE THAT Chicago's detectives came back from St. Louis convinced that Fred Burke and "James Ray" were at the SMC garage the fateful morning of February 14, and that one of the lookouts was their Toledo fugitive Byron Bolton, and that Fred Goetz was involved. Despite this, they still dropped the ball.

The police immediately named Burke and James Ray as two of the killers—and fleshed out their theory with a visit to the Bolton family farm in Central Illinois. Nobody was home except some children, who said only that Bolton had "gone to Texas." They even discovered a trunk which evidently had served as a shipping crate for two Thompson submachine guns, sent there from Cicero on March 18.

After the fire in the Wood Street garage led them to the Circus Café and Claude Maddox (who also wasn't home), Al Capone became the new main suspect in the massacre. This was fueled by the fact that the cops had not yet found Jack McGurn—who was initially construed to be the "Mac" that young George Brichet had heard one gunman call another at the back door of the garage. Nobody knew of McGurn going by the name of Mac, but it made sense, unless the shooter was using the generic "Mac" that was a popular substitute at the time for a person's name. Then Maddox displaced Capone again when police decided that the Circus Gang, allied with Big Al, was the "new" mob in town.

By this time, the Chicago police were convinced that some or all of the killers were former Egan's Rats members led by Fred Burke, whom the newspapers had nicknamed "Killer" Burke, and the mysterious James Ray. They also surmised that the shooters' local chief was Claude Maddox, another former Rat and the major beer purveyor in the Cragin District who was looking to expand his horizons.

It wasn't yet clear whether the slaughter on North Clark was in retaliation for the murders of Tony Lombardo and Patsy Lolordo over control of the Sicilian Union, which would also involve the Aiellos; or the shooting at Capone's friend McGurn; or part of the cleaners and dyers war, which involved Maddox-controlled unions; or the Capone outfit's incursions into Moran's North Side; or a combination of these. The dog tracks figured in somewhere, but police probably didn't know that the late Frankie Yale had commissioned the Aiellos to muscle in on Capone's Hawthorne Kennel Club (also called the Laramie) near Cicero, which had been hurting Moran's Fairview Kennels near the village of Orchard Place, now the site of O'Hare International Airport. He had also threatened to burn the track.

Without citing his source, Detective Chief John Stege declared that the killers were "out-of-town assassins" who had been paid by the head—the more Moran men they murdered, the more money they made. The figure reported by Stege was ten thousand dollars apiece, but if a bounty actually was paid, it's likely that the figure was lower, since the killers failed to knock off Bugs Moran. It's also possible that the killers were docked for slaying the noncombatants, optician Reinhart Schwimmer and mechanic John May.

The police continued arresting anyone who might help their investigation, which again was going nowhere, except in one area that would become significant long after the books on the massacre were closed. They had been doggedly tracking ownership of the dismantled Cadillac found in the Wood Street garage by means of numbers stamped on the frame. These told them the car had been purchased new by County Commissioner Frank J. Wilson and thereafter had belonged to Kavanaugh Motor Sales on Irving Park, Irving H. Reger on North St. Louis Street, the Northwest Cadillac Sales Company on Irving Park, and finally the Cadillac Motor Sales Company—conveniently located across the street from the Metropole Hotel, Capone's first stop upon his return from Cicero and a block south of his Lexington headquarters as of 1928. There it was purchased for $350 on December 15 by one James Morton, who said he was from Los Angeles. According to the salesman, Morton showed no interest in any other car.

Stege, the deputy police commissioner and chief of detectives, expressed doubts that the buyer's name was Morton or that he was from Los Angeles, but no stone would be left unturned. California was cranky about its cars, and before an automobile could be offloaded from a train, for instance, a resident of the state had to produce a certificate from the police in the city where he had bought the vehicle proving that he was the lawful owner. Further, any Californian driving home in an out-of-state car or truck had to have it licensed within three days.

Stege wired the Los Angeles Police Department to find out if they had a record of a resident named James Morton, and the reply was no. At least nobody by that name had arrived in Los Angeles connected with a Cadillac purchased in Chicago. The LAPD did have a warrant for one Magnus Olson, with a criminal record in five states, and they wondered if he would do. Stege thanked his California colleagues and resumed the search, using the factory numbers on the tires.

He had not yet gotten back those results when shortly after midnight on Wednesday, February 27, another car blew up.

This vehicle was a black 1926 Peerless touring car, identical to two still in use by Chicago detectives. It was parked off the road at First Street and Harvard Avenue in the western suburb of Maywood, which was in Syndicate territory, and blowing it up would not seem to be the best way to destroy evidence of a crime. The explosion awakened the entire neighborhood, which was immediately swarming with Maywood cops, who took one look at the police equipment scattered about the scene and called their Chicago colleagues.

Because the bomb (either black powder or dynamite) mainly wrecked the car's hood and radiator, Deputy Commissioner Stege decided it was a plant to throw off investigators. It's also possible the explosion was premature, since near the car were such incriminating items as a police-type gong, two spent shotgun shells of the brand used at the massacre, a red notebook belonging to massacre victim Al Weinshank, and license plates with the Chicago detective squad prefix 787, which had been stolen in the town of Lombard some two months earlier.

Either way, the blast didn't make sense, but the absence of any blood, body parts, or other signs of injury reinforced Stege's belief that the car had been planted to confuse the cops, although it only confirmed the use of two vehicles, as some witnesses were insisting. The automobile's serial number showed the last purchaser to be a "Patrick Gleason," whose address turned out to be a vacant lot. To support his "plant" idea, Stege announced that several of the gangs had such cars, disguised to look like detective squads, and more would probably be found burned or abandoned.

The phony-police-car debate was eventually taken up by *Chicago Daily News* columnist Robert J. Casey, who made considerable sport of the subject, opining that second-hand "Death Cars" were so plentiful that it made no sense to buy new ones. His columns always began with a few lines of doggerel, and this time he wrote:

> *The squad cars, death cars, gangsters' hacks*
> *Across the town make smoking tracks.*
> *While motorcycle coppers ride*
> *Along the edges of the tide.*
> *Patrolmen flivver through the night*
> *And alky truckmen rise and fight.*
> *And that's Chicago as we've seen*
> *Presented on the stage and screen.*

But ah! 'Twas just the other day
We read of one lad gone away
Reflecting credit on the town:
A milkman's horse had run him down.

Anyone trying to understand the massacre investigation from local newspaper accounts would have had to conclude that nobody knew what they were doing. Including the newspapers. The several police agencies trying to solve the crime were reversing themselves every few days, contradicting one another, and hotly denying there was any dissension within their ranks or between their leadership. The tracking of the Wood Street car to Claude Maddox had made Al Capone the massacre mastermind for a few editions until unnamed "authorities" decided that "they did not believe the Cicero mob chieftain was directly involved in the murder of the seven Moran mob members." Suspicion suddenly fell on Maddox himself, and the names of corrupt City Collector Morris Eller, gangster Danny Vallo, and Lolordo's brother Joseph were mentioned as helping Maddox assemble a new, bigger, and better gang—one allied with Capone but operating independently.

According to the *Tribune*, in a story expanding on a theory of the state's attorneys, Maddox not only was miffed that Moran followers had killed John Clay, his top man in a cleaners and dyers union, but he also "coveted some of the Moran domain on the North Side" for his bootlegging operations. McGurn, here gratuitously identified as a Sicilian who had changed his name from Gebardi or Gibaldi (or sometimes DeMore or DeMora, his stepfather's name), was now working with Maddox and said to be lusting for both personal and patriotic revenge against the Gusenbergs, who had been trying to kill him. The story continued:

> "A council of war was held at the Circus cafe, 1857 West North avenue, which had a machine gun annex next door at 1859 [the address given by Tony Capezio when he rented the Wood Street garage], used by Maddox and which was across the street from Pasqualino Lolordo's Italian American club, and the obliteration of

the whole Moran gang was decreed, the investigators disclosed.

Maddox, McGurn, and Lolordo [Patsy's brother Joseph] couldn't get near the Moran booze depot at 2122 North Clark street without an alarm being given, and the idea of dressing two killers as policemen apparently was conceived.

"Lombardo recalled the two big men that took part in the Yale murder, and Maddox knew them from former membership in the St. Louis Egan's Rats," [Assistant State's Attorney David] Stansbury said. McGurn had the money to pay them, and Burke and Ray were called into the war council. The rest is gang history in Chicago. . . .

That fairly garbled account of the massacre at least covered part of the territory and brought in Burke and Winkler (both as "Ray" and under his real name). Considering the murder of his brother, Joe Lolordo supposedly had been given the "honor" of manning one of the machine guns at the massacre, but that was just more of the nonsense then circulating.

Stege, hot on the trail of Burke and Ray, but far off course, remained convinced that the Maywood car, which was out of his jurisdiction, had less investigative significance than did the Wood Street car, which was in his jurisdiction. The fact that the first car had been bought off a lot near the Metropole and Lexington Hotels, and that Capone occupied both, did not seem to interest either the police or the press, who might have thought that significant—especially when they learned the purchaser had used a phony name, and that the mystery man dismantling it led them to the Circus Café.

Eventually Stege conceded that the Maywood car, which had been impounded by Chicago police, was *not* a plant because of Weinshank's notebook and the stolen plates with the 787 detective squad prefix. Moreover, the name and address of the man who bought the Peerless were as phony as those given by the purchaser of the Cadillac.

There was also the puzzling matter of an abducted dentist, Dr. Loyal Tacker, whose office was near the SMC garage. Tacker had pulled a tooth under highly unusual circumstances on the morning of the massacre and had reported this to Chicago police. On the evening after the Wood Street explosion, he had been knocked unconscious by some men who drove him, bound and gagged on the back floor of a touring car, to Detroit, where they inexplicably dumped the dazed dentist in a gutter to be rescued by local cops.[9] His wife, almost nine months pregnant, was greatly relieved.

XVII

"SEIZE M'GURN FOR MASSACRE"

T HE BIG NEWS ON FEBRUARY 27 was the capture of Jack McGurn. Actually, he had been in not-so-deep hiding for at least two weeks with his "Blond Alibi" in the Stevens Hotel—just three floors away from the state's attorney's special group of massacre investigators who were also staying there. McGurn had been reading the papers and knew he was at the top of Stege's wanted list, but he said that he and Louise—"Mr. and Mrs. D'Oro," honeymooners— had been going out in the evenings to the theater and other "nice" places where police were not likely to look.

The arrest hardly came as a surprise, and he had made no move toward his guns when Detective Chief Stege, Lieutenant William Cusack and Sergeant John Mangan burst into the room, probably on a tip from hotel management or staff. McGurn was hustled over to the detective bureau for a lineup (then called a "show-up") and was immediately identified by at least two witnesses, as he probably expected.

As the first notorious gangster to be arrested, McGurn didn't expect royal treatment, since he'd been hiding under investigators' noses. But he wasn't too ruffled, either, bantering with his grim-faced captors as though the arrest were just another cross he had to bear. Asked about the abduction of Tacker, he replied, "I never saw him and never kidnapped him. He probably got lit up and ran away for a night with some Jane and had to fix up a yarn for his wife."

Asked for his theory on the massacre, McGurn said, "Aw, a squad of cops probably. They probably had been doing business with Moran and found things getting hot and had to bump 'em all off." As for the SMC Cartage Co.: "I don't know anything about the garage. I'd never have been able to get inside it alive. The Gusenbergs would have shot me down the minute they saw me."

Later, Lieutenant Cusack asked, "Who's the girl?"

"She's my wife," McGurn answered.

"She must have bleached her hair wonderfully well," Cusack remarked, "as your wife has black hair and black eyes."

"Aw, suit yourself," McGurn replied with annoyance.

McGurn wasn't happy about his sleeping arrangements and asked the turnkey to fix him up with something more comfortable.

"No, sir," was the answer. "Stege told me to put you in this cell and keep you, and here is where you sleep."

Miffed, McGurn rolled up his coat and vest for a pillow and used his overcoat for a cover. When he awakened, however, McGurn was back in good form and began joking with the prosecutor.

"How are you this morning?" he asked.

"Very well," Ditchburne answered.

"But you didn't look so well last night," McGurn continued. "You fluttered around like you had the jeebies."

Then McGurn ignored gangland tradition and willingly posed for photographers. "Make me look swell," he said. "Going to take my girlfriend's picture, too? Who is she? Oh, just a little lady I been helping out. The cabarets aren't doing much business now, you know."

With the arrest of McGurn, which the *Tribune* reported under the banner headline SEIZE M'GURN FOR MASSACRE, State's Attorney Swanson fairly crowed. "This crime has now been solved," he told reporters. "There is no question about it. The prisoner has been viewed by witnesses who declare positively that he is one of the killers. I also know the motive and have known it for days."

This rankled Stege, who was still trying to track down more of the hoodlums on his wanted list. He had collared McGurn himself, but Stansbury had beaten him to the headlines. And he still hadn't found Frederick R. Burke, formerly Thomas Camp, and James Ray, the alias of Gus Winkler, whose name investigators knew but thought might be the alias of St. Louis hood Milford Jones.

That trail had dead-ended in a fashionable Detroit gambling club owned by none other than Al Wertheimer, the brother of Henry Wertheimer, who had been kidnapped more than a year earlier presumably by Burke and held in Chicago by Winkler and his friends. Early press reports from Detroit had the whole group in custody, but the local cops had nailed only Wertheimer and two other Detroiters at the exclusive Amiwah casino in the city's fashionable Indian Village district, and they had to be released because of mistaken identity.

However, that arrest brought up the names of Chicago's Big Tim Murphy and Nicky Arnstein, who with Wertheimer had opened a gambling operation in Chicago, only to have police close it down. Everybody, it seemed, knew everybody else. And since Burke had used that Chicago club as a hangout, it now sounded as if the earlier kidnapping either was a friendly one, or the hoodlums involved were quick to forgive.

The thing Chicago reporters sensed most was the increasing dissension between Stege and the state's attorney's people. Stege had recently reversed his position on the Maywood car, declaring it important because of Weinshank's notebook and because a distinctive fountain pen that had been lost by Dr. Tacker had been found behind the vehicle's rear seat cushion. However, his men were complaining that their efforts were being obstructed or duplicated by the state's attorney's troops, and when Stege set a morning meeting to iron out differences, Stansbury stood him up. Asked by reporters if he and Stege could not agree on how to conduct the massacre investigation, Stansbury barked, "It's an outrageous lie. The inquiry is proceeding."

Two days after McGurn's capture on February 27, he was still cooling his heels in the detective bureau lockup waiting to be booked when Rocco Fanelli, one of Stege's seventeen "most wanted" was "seized" by detectives at Taylor and Halsted Streets. It's also possible that he got tired of hiding and turned himself in to the first friendly squad he could find. Both he and McGurn were charged with the massacre murders.

The police also picked up two members of the 42 Gang, including Sam "Gin Gin" Giancana, not in connection with the massacre but for general questioning about crime in the so-called "Valley," south of the Loop. Giancana's nickname of the day did not catch on, but "Momo" did when he eventually achieved mob leadership. A contemporary of Tony Accardo, a 42 Gang member known by police to be McGurn's young driver, Giancana would become Chicago's organized-crime chief some twenty years later and was linked to the massacre through wiretaps.

Acquitted cop-killers Albert Anselmi and John Scalise were rounded up, mostly out of habit, and charged with the massacre, and a minor courtroom uproar occurred when they were arraigned on March 8. Mob attorney Thomas Nash decided to ask the arresting officer, Sergeant Fred Valenta, if (as the formal complaint stated) he had "just and reasonable grounds" for believing Scalise had any connection with the Moran gang murders, and the officer answered, "No."

Assistant State's Attorney Russell Root "sent an SOS" to Stansbury and Ditchburne, who rushed to the courtroom in time to request a delay. However, both suspects later "walked," as did Rocco Fanelli, who was finally released when his lawyer persuaded the judge that, with his Coke-bottle spectacles, Fanelli's eyesight was too poor to hit any kind of target, even with a machine gun.

On the lighter side, McGurn's Blond Alibi entertained the police by chain-smoking cigarettes with an indifference to ash trays and displaying a flippant-flapper attitude, which was enhanced by her outfit and makeup. The *Daily News* described Louise Rolfe as a twenty-two-year-old former St. Louis cabaret entertainer "dolled up" in a black silk crepe dress trimmed with lace, string of pearls, expensive squirrel coat with gray fox collar, and an "exquisite emerald-cut diamond ring" on her right hand, plus "mascaraed eyes and eyebrows thinned down to so extreme a line that one of the police officers asked a girl reporter how it was done."

It turned out that one reason local mobsters were so hard to find was their certainty of being arrested as massacre participants. What witnesses police could find were identifying nearly anyone the cops seemed to "like" for the crime.

A real problem was one George Bevan, who was somewhere in the vicinity and had come up with an eyewitness account which practically duplicated that of the teenage boy. The man looked a lot like a bum, and eventually police decided that he had his own mini-racket going: Identify everyone, if that's what it took to keep the cops happy and him housed in a warm police station, where he was fed, watered, bedded, and coffee'd around the clock. After a few days, police wised up and put Bevan back out in the cold, never to be heard from again.

Not yet heard from, however, was Al Capone. After his visit with the Dade County and New York authorities the morning of the massacre, he assumed he'd soon be hearing from the various agencies that had gotten thoroughly tangled in their Chicago investigation. The summons came out of left field in the form of a U.S. Marshal's subpoena to appear March 12 before a federal grand jury that was ostensibly investigating bootlegging but also was looking into the matter of Capone's back taxes. Since this would put him within reach of state and local authorities—and grand jury officials promised as much—Capone convened his lawyers and doctors and pled pulmonary illness. Federal Judge James H. Wilkerson postponed the appearance until March 20, and when that date was missed, he held Capone in contempt.

Other bad news had been coming the Big Fellow's way. An assistant district attorney from Brooklyn had been at the February 14 meeting with Capone at the Dade County courthouse, and a week later the same prosecutor, Louis Goldstein, was back again to discuss the murders of Frankie Yale and Arnold Rothstein, especially since the names of Burke and Ray (Winkler) had surfaced in the course of their own investigation into Yale's demise. Capone nearly charmed the pants off Goldstein, judging from one account in a New York paper:

> "It was exactly 12:25," said Mr. Goldstein, "when a bright, light blue town car, beautifully shined up and polished, with a uniformed chauffeur driving it, and three men riding inside, drove up to the courthouse. Our appointment was at 12:30. At exactly that hour Capone walked briskly into

the room as if he were going to the meeting of a board of bank directors. He shook hands with Taylor and the others. I was introduced and he shook hands with me.

"'Well,' he said, smiling, 'what can I do for you?'"

The Brooklyn attorney went south on official business. He came back brown and bronzed, affable and cheerful, but utterly unwilling to talk, at least about his questioning of Capone. He admitted that Capone answered all the questions he put readily and, at times, gleefully. . . .

"I simply can't talk about the results of my trip," he insisted, and that was that.

However, Mr. Goldstein learned a lot of things about Capone and about Al's mode of living. He found him a big, well set up man, strong, with stubby hands. His eyes are coal black and they are like some kind of black steel, powerful and at times magnetic. His face is swarthy [and clean-shaven, except for its scars which give] him that name of "Scarface," which he doesn't like.

He has a strong, well-molded chin. He is six feet tall, says Mr. Goldstein, and he must weigh nearly 200—a second edition of Jack Dempsey, who, by the way, is his friend who dines frequently at the guarded house on Palm Island. Capone is powerful, moves quickly and silently, and appears to take in at a glance every detail of everything that happens. And he would not sit with his back to the door.

He wore a checkered coat, white flannel trousers, sport shoes and a light-gray fedora hat that was spotless. His stubby fingers were well manicured. His hands were white and soft, although they seemed muscular as well. . . .

He has given generously to every charity. He has supported every municipal undertaking. He has been polite. The Florida which sniffed at him when he arrived has learned to like him. Perhaps all the liking isn't tempered with love. Perhaps there isn't an entire trust. Mr. Goldstein says that the amazing thing about Capone is that he is so decently affable.

But his worst enemies in Chicago never could and never did say that he wasn't a fine person to know as long as one didn't cross him. . . . That's the story behind "Scarface Al" Capone now. . . .

Capone also charmed the pants off reporter Wilbur E. Rogers, who wrote the article about Goldstein's visit and impressions. Rogers ventured the opinion that Capone was through with the rackets, had "turned over a new leaf," and had "become a sporting man. No more gang life for Capone, no more races with death, no more scheming and plotting either to kill or be killed. . . ."

> "It appears that Capone, although he has reformed, by his own statement, can't entirely make the reformation stick. There are still dangers, for in the background of his life there are gang wars and the vicious undercurrent of gang life. He's living on a nest of dynamite, and his past is always there to explode in the present, regardless of how he feels about it himself.". . .

This assessment of Capone, published ten days after the St. Valentine's Day Massacre, could not have been more flattering if it had been written by Big Al's public relations staff.

By the time Rogers's column saw print, detectives had returned from St. Louis with the names of Burke and "Ray" as suspects, and the pair again started running for cover. Gus Winkler headed to Louis Campagna's house in Cicero, while his wife, Georgette, went to Sunday Mass. When she returned briefly to her home, Mrs. Campagna was there waiting anxiously. She told Georgette to hurry inside, find a large package Gus had left in a closet, and get it to him as quickly as possible. But no sooner had Georgette started looking than a call came from someone at "the Syndicate" telling the women to get out quickly, leaving Louie's wife and Georgette nervously holding the bag.

Gus already had fled with "Lefty Louie" (as Campagna was also known), and Georgette and Mrs. Campagna and her two children headed to Louie's mother's house with a carton that weighed about fifty pounds. They were allowed to leave the kids there but not the mystery package. They tried another friend of the Campagnas and again were turned away. In desperation, Georgette called Frankie Rio (she spelled it Reo) who said he would come for it himself. He arrived a short time later with some young gangsters-in-training plus hotel directions, and sped off with the carton, but not before curiosity had gotten the best of the two frightened women. They had opened the package as if it were a bomb, and in a way it was. Inside were a police uniform and two bulletproof vests.

In their rushing about, neither woman had dressed for the storm that was drenching the city. By the time they had reached the Paradise Arms Hotel at 4114 West Washington by cabs (one of which had broken down, forcing them to hail another), they were soaked, freezing, and miserable. Making matters worse, if only a little, Mrs. Campagna checked them in as sisters, raising the eyebrows of the desk clerk, who saw before him two nightgowned floozies with coats but no luggage, one large and dark-complexioned and the other small, light-skinned, and blond. When Mrs. Campagna opened her purse to pay for the room, Georgette saw a gun and nearly panicked. Mrs. Campagna looked surprised and said, "Oh, it's nothing. I always carry one when I'm with Louie."

The next day Georgette said good-bye to her pistol-packing partner and ventured out to buy clothes, but after that she remained holed up at the Paradise for a week anxiously waiting to hear from Gus. He called the following Monday and told her to meet him at Louis "Doc" Stacci's O. P. Inn in Melrose Park. Georgette would soon learn this was a hideout and hangout for gangsters and outlaws, and its walls could easily have been decorated with signed photos of every celebrity criminal in Chicago and the Midwest.

Over the next five years the inn would become notorious, brokering the information that led to the so-called Kansas City Massacre in 1933 and harboring such criminal luminaries as John Dillinger, Pretty Boy Floyd, Machine Gun Kelly, Verne Miller, and the Barker-Karpis Gang.

But this was still April 1929, and the Winklers could meet safely at Stacci's. Farther away was better, however, and Gus took Georgette to a resort cabin owned by the father of Capone bodyguard Phil D'Andrea and located, as chance would have it, deep in the woods outside St. Joseph, Michigan. It was a designated hideout for Italian mobsters, as many as ten at a time, but now it was populated mainly by Campagna, Bob Carey, Fred (or George) Goetz, and several others.

The crowd stayed there for two or three weeks, getting on one another's nerves and receiving some scares that turned out to be false alarms. But the Winklers had had enough, and the couple moved to an apartment in Gary, Indiana, while Bob Carey relocated to nearby Hammond.

A day after settling in Gary, which must have been in late May or early June, Gus returned from some mission to say that he'd encountered Fred Burke at a bar in Calumet City. Apparently, he hadn't seen Burke since around the time of the North Clark Street massacre, when the two had made it a point to go separate ways. Burke had taken a scenic route, ending up in Kansas City, where he evidently hooked up with Harvey Bailey, one of the most successful bank robbers of the 1920s. He knew Bailey from earlier criminal endeavors and stayed with him or relatives at the Bailey farm near Green City, Missouri.

Gus told Georgette that they were invited to join Burke and his then-current lady, Viola, at a camp he had outside Grand Rapids, Minnesota, a small town about ninety miles west and slightly north of Duluth. They drove up together, and Winkler and Burke thoroughly enjoyed their reunion and were beginning to relax. Their only regret was having to bring along Bob Carey, whose heavy drinking had earned Capone's disapproval. Burke and Winkler started playing golf every day, but Burke's sobriety rarely lasted till evening. Gus put up with his carousing companions better than Georgette did, but for the first time in weeks she felt safe.

What was not yet making much news was the discovery by Major Goddard that some of the .45-caliber bullets plucked from the body of New York's Frankie Yale matched slugs fired into the St. Valentine's Day Massacre victims. When this bombshell was first dropped, it failed to explode. This was mainly because the press was not familiar with the science of forensic ballistics and what Goddard's discovery meant: that the men who killed Yale were indeed from Chicago, land of the Tommygun, and were working for Al Capone.

In fact, New York authorities seemed to have a better fix on Capone than the police agencies in Chicago, which were practically warring with one another over the various massacre theories and were seemingly unaware that there was a criminal conspiracy sufficiently organized to again qualify as a Syndicate. With Capone in Miami or traveling in disguise, the day-to-day operation of Big Al's mob had been taken over by Frank Nitti, working out of an obscure office in the Loop.

It was the New York police who laid out a convincing case (even before the incriminating slugs were found) that Yale was killed for double-crossing Capone and seeking to extend his operations to Chicago. They also laid the massacre directly on Capone's doorstep. It was as though New York, less distracted by civic anarchy and gang warfare, had proclaimed Capone the national king of crime months before he started receiving front-page coverage in Chicago.

The fact that Capone received more massacre-related coverage in newspapers in New York and other parts of the country might have had something to do with the goodwill he fostered among the Chicago reporters. No one doubted that newsmen depended on confidential informants in gangs and in government to keep them "in the know," especially when the information was "off the record." But when *Chicago Tribune* crime reporter Jake Lingle was murdered in the Michigan Avenue pedestrian underpass at Randolph Street on June 9, 1930, the killing shocked the entire city. Local police and politicians joined in giving Lingle a martyr's funeral that rivaled that of a fallen governor (or notorious mob boss), and the *Tribune* vowed terrible revenge. The newspaper's outrage was shared by its competitors, which also regarded reporters as noncombatants entitled to the same level of protection as Red Cross workers.

Then underworld leaks began to surface that the *Tribune's* sixty-five-dollar-a-week journalist had secretly amassed a small fortune in mob money for reporting things not quite like they were, and that when he was shot in the back of the head at close range, Lingle had fallen not only on his face but on a diamond-studded belt buckle that Al Capone gave as gifts to his special friends.

While the *Tribune* made what excuses it could, syndicated columnist Harry T. Brundidge traveled from St. Louis to Miami for an impromptu meeting with Capone. When the Big Fellow told Brundidge at the outset that he would deny anything the columnist wrote, Brundidge quoted him as saying that, and then proceeded with the interview. Capone, while conceding the visit from Brundidge, predictably said the two had only toured his estate and talked about fishing, but the column Brundidge wrote afterward ran in dozens of newspapers, along with testimony the columnist had already given to a Chicago special grand jury which had blown the whistle on the city's corruption and the lid off local police reporting.

Capone, Brundidge wrote, said that the mob had become so securely entrenched in city and county government that reformers were wasting their time, and that the corruption extended to members of the journalistic community. As a result of Brundidge's revelations, a handful of politicians actually were sacrificed by their bosses, by ballot, or sometimes by bullet, with no shock to the Chicago political system. But the newspaper housecleaning came as genuine surprise to many people, although the surprise lay less in the fact of the corruption than in the fourth estate's admission of it.

Several Chicago papers—some six major dailies were serving the city at the time—discovered they had reporters, editors, or circulation managers who were in bed with Capone, in most cases, or with Moran. Brundidge named names, costing some their jobs, and must have made himself many enemies in the profession. Only a syndicated columnist from out of town could get away with what locally would have been considered a betrayal of trust among friendly rivals who often exchanged favors. Brundidge made no friends in Chicago, but his news syndicate benefited from what looked like a courageous display of journalistic integrity—a reporter doing his duty "without fear or favor." At least nobody shot him in the head.

In a city with so many gangs operating in so many wards, rampant political corruption, a powerless crime commission and badly fragmented law enforcement community, and a mental-absentee mayor who was either out of town or fuming at the British monarchy, it would not have been hard for investigators and newsmen alike to miss the forest for the trees.

Meanwhile, back in Chicago, Coroner Bundesen tried to remain outside the fray, closeted with Calvin Goddard, who had moved his New York laboratory to rooms provided by the Northwestern University Law School on East Erie Street, practically on the lake. Goddard had given him a crash course in the lands and grooves of gunbarrel rifling, processes for chemically restoring ground-off serial numbers on firearms, and other forensic technology more refined than eyeballing bullets and sniffing gun muzzles.

The first two Thompsons tested by Goddard turned out to be false alarms. One Tommygun was discovered by a janitor under a loose floorboard in the closet of slain Frank Gusenberg's apartment at the Parkway and kept by the hotel manager until police got wind of it. That gun wasn't likely to be one of the murder weapons anyway, and Goddard's tests quickly proved that to be the case.

Much more excitement attended the discovery of a Thompson in the possession of South Side beer runner Steve Oswald, and most newspapers jumped to the mistaken conclusion that it had been used in the massacre. That lasted about one edition, until Goddard ruled it out, too. In the coming weeks he also ruled out dozens of Thompsons grudgingly surrendered for testing by the Chicago and suburban police departments, which did much to spike the theory that the massacre had been committed by rogue cops.

The sparring between Bundesen and the state's attorney's office revived following the massacre, with Bundesen now hinting that he had new leads and new witnesses, and the state's attorney complaining that the work of his investigators and police was being impeded by the coroner's inquest hearings. When the second session was opened on February 23, Assistant State's Attorney Ditchburne had somehow disappeared from the scene and been replaced by Walker Butler. It had already been reported that Bundesen had received and shrugged off two death threats, and all parties were predicting imminent results, but the coroner bowed to the prosecutor's insistence on more time and ordered a postponement until March 2. That session also was postponed, with no published explanation. The evolving public impression was that even the hottest leads were cooling off, and that many witnesses were proving less useful than had been hoped.

One incident around that time reminded readers that Bundesen was still on the job. He learned that the Lincoln sedan owned by massacre victim Albert Weinshank, which authorities deliberately had left parked for a time across the street from the murder scene, had since been towed by police and recovered by Weinshank's uncle, Maurice, on a writ of replevin. On March 13 Bundesen wrote to State's Attorney Swanson urging him to permanently impound the other cars and trucks seized at the garage pending a more careful examination.

It was another month before the coroner's inquest was reconvened. On April 13 Bundesen, rejecting the smaller meeting rooms at the County Building or the County Morgue, assembled his panel in the largest one at the new headquarters of the Chicago Police Department, 1121 South State Street. In attendance (like it or not) were Police Commissioner Russell and all fifty-five deputy chiefs and district police captains, one judge, one assistant attorney general, three assistant state's attorneys, and an assortment of city and county officials, demonstrating the power of the Bundesen's office during that period of Chicago's history.

As might be expected, the press turned out in droves—police-beat reporters, star reporters, and photographers. Teams of messengers stood ready to motorcycle the wooden four-by-five-inch film holders to their respective papers. All three assistant state's attorneys assigned to the massacre were present, including Harry Ditchburne, who had vanished for a time, and his associates David Stansbury and Walker Butler.

Bundesen set the tone by reading "Who's Who in Chicago Gangland," a recently released Chicago Crime Commission report describing the violence attributed to local mobsters. He emphasized the section which reported that two hundred gang-style murders in recent years had resulted in only one conviction—a statistic that caused police officials and county prosecutors to squirm in their seats. He then discussed the importance of adopting the forensic ballistics technology which Calvin Goddard had been trying to sell to the country's law enforcers without great success. His captive audience had no choice but to watch a convincing demonstration, complete with large photographs and projected slides, showing how each gun left unique impressions not only on any bullet fired from it but also on the bullet's casing, as well.

Most investigators had at least some familiarity with the rifling marks left on a projectile by the grooves cut into a gun's barrel. Goddard earlier had collaborated on a device that could measure the left- or right-hand twist of a gun barrel's rifling and also the degree of spiraling. This "helixometer," as it was called, could reveal both a gun's make and model, and further examination of a bullet under Goddard's twin microscopes with their split-field optics could match it to the gun that fired it.

Moreover, Goddard explained, every firing pin left a distinctive imprint on the cartridge primer. Therefore, by using the same method of examination described above, it was possible for investigators to match a shell casing to a specific weapon.

The important thing, Bundesen emphasized, was to collect and carefully preserve every bullet or casing from a crime scene for later microscopic examination. In other words, don't carry them around loose in a pants pocket with keys and coins that could impart other markings.

Thus, the St. Valentine's Day Massacre marked the start of a new forensic-sciences era in criminology. In part because the Chicago Police Department was so deeply distrusted in matters of crime control, Goddard's first full-service Scientific Crime Detection Laboratory was attached to the Northwestern University Law School and operated mainly by trained civilians for the next several years.[10]

After discomfiting the cops with lessons on ballistics, serial number restoration, and such, Bundesen called his first witness. Possibly for the sake of irony, this was the police chief of Cicero, Martin Wojciechowski. His department had no submachine guns, the chief insisted, only shotguns—five of them. Bundesen requested these for testing, as empty twelve-gauge shells had been recovered at the massacre scene.

The second witness was Rocco Passarrella, the Melrose Park police chief for the past eleven months. Passarrella admitted that his department had one Thompson and five shotguns, which Bundesen's experts could test. He said the Thompson had been purchased in Chicago from the Detective Publishing Company, which also sold police equipment, and whose owner, the same Al Dunlap who was involved in the McSwiggin murder investigation, would figure prominently in the gun hunt that Bundesen had started.

Finally, Bundesen called Major Goddard himself. Goddard recounted his employment by jury foreman Burt Massee in late February, and the work he already had done on the slugs and shell casings from the North Clark Street garage. What he then described would ultimately make Goddard internationally famous, at least in law enforcement circles, as the pioneer whose findings in a high-profile murder case would once and for all establish forensic ballistics as the most important crime-fighting tool since fingerprints.

Like a professor lecturing a class, Goddard said he had been given seventy spent .45-caliber shell casings and thirty-eight bullets, fourteen "in fairly complete form," most taken from the bodies of the victims and a few found on the floor of the garage. Using lantern slides and greatly enlarged photographs, he showed how the marks on these exhibits indicated that the killers had used two Thompson guns, one with a fifty-round drum and the other with a twenty-round box magazine, and a shotgun. He added that the .45-caliber ammunition used had been manufactured by the U.S. Cartridge Company in 1928.

It wasn't mentioned at the time, but this ammunition was the same as that seized when police raided Maddox's Circus Café and may have been from a short run whose bullets were factory-marked with a small "S" indented in the side of the cupro-nickel jacket, just visible above the brass shell casing. This seemingly minor difference would prove significant a few months later in connection with Fred Burke.

The coroner's jury was sufficiently energized by this display of crime-fighting enthusiasm that it wanted to tackle the problem of gangland violence generally. As the session concluded, a jury spokesman announced: "Coroner Bundesen and Major Goddard have made such a contribution to the cause of science, and the testimony taken today has opened such a wide field, the jury desires a continuance in order that all the cases in hand may be further developed."

Bundesen agreed to hold more sessions when new developments warranted, and Goddard immediately prevailed on the city's police department to provide him with its collection of slugs and shell casings recovered from crime scenes. Back at his office, using an annotated list supplied by the cops, he scribbled some handwritten calculations on a legal pad and discovered that about 11 percent of Chicago's gangland killings since 1926 had been committed with Thompson submachine guns.

XVIII

MACHINE GUNS FOR SALE

C ORONER HERMAN BUNDESEN RECONVENED THE inquest jury on April 19, 1929, in Room 1123 of the County Building. He announced that the session would begin with a report by Major Goddard directed at police departments in all large cities and at Chicago's in particular. Goddard recommended the adoption of fully equipped firearm-identification bureaus staffed by persons who were not only well-trained and competent to examine guns and bullets but also capable of giving expert witness testimony at trials. Chicago's special contribution to gangland murder, he added, was the machine gun, which had made its debut in the local beer wars and whose use in 11 percent of the mobster slayings in the city far exceeded its kill rate in any other municipality.

Goddard and Bundesen then discussed other unsolved Chicago murders from the recent killings of Tony Lombardo and Patsy Lolordo that might have been related to the massacre back to the 1926 machine-gunning of Hymie Weiss, the successor to Dean O'Ban-ion. It was becoming evident that Bundesen's panel was turning into a phenomenon previously unknown in the city: a runaway coroner's jury of determined crime-fighters.

The first witness called was Edward Weidner, manager of the gun department of Chicago's premier sporting goods business, Von Lengerke and Antoine, commonly called VL&A, with a retail store at 33 South State. Weidner said that in 1927 a man calling himself Vincent Daniels walked in off the street claiming to be the inventor of the "Daniels submachine gun." He explained that his gun was not yet in production, so he needed others to send to a buyer in Mexico and for his own experimental work. He bought ten Thompsons for cash and offered to work as a sales representative for VL&A. Weidner said he hired him and sold him nine additional Thompsons.

Daniels's special approach to gun-selling was to take orders from select customers, then purchase the guns under his own name for cash, and later sell them personally. Many of the individuals and companies Daniels said were buyers later turned out to be fictitious, but VL&A liked cash sales, apparently liked Daniels, and in the absence of any legal regulation of Tommyguns at the time, was perfectly happy with the arrangement. To put VL&A's conscience at ease, Daniels had displayed a letter appointing him a Prohibition agent for the district of Los Angeles, said he was a Polish war veteran, and claimed to be a Mexican government spy using his connections to sell guns south of the border, where a rebellion was in progress. Which side was obtaining the guns was of no great concern to VL&A.

Further testimony revealed that Daniels, whose real name proved to be Danielski (Danialski, in some accounts) and who claimed to be living at Chicago's Hollywood Beach Hotel, also went by the alias of David Goldberg. It was under that name that he did business with the Thompson gun's New York company, the Auto-Ordnance Corporation, which kept its stock in a building on the grounds of the Colt's Patent Firearms Manufacturing Company in Hartford, Connecticut. In January 1928 he ordered seven guns from Auto-Ordnance and had them shipped to his Mex-America Company "warehouse" at 1548 West Taylor Street in Chicago. This facility amounted to a sign hanging in the window of an Italian cobbler's shop in Little Italy, which just happened to be next door to a gambling joint operated by Johnny, Willie, and Red Bolton—leaders of one of Chicago's gangs at the time.

Bundesen next called Captain William L. Schoemaker, one of the most respected members of the Chicago Police Department. "Old Shoes," as he was known, had been assigned by Commissioner Russell to work full time on the massacre, and he was asked about the two Thompsons found in the home of Charles Cleaver. The testimony wasn't clear on this point, but "Limpy" Cleaver and some other hoods were suspected of using Tommyguns, acquired from VL&A or Mex-America, in pulling a $135,000 mail-train robbery in the Chicago suburb of Evergreen Park on February 25, 1928.

An attorney named Wiesbrod interrupted the proceedings to quarrel with the coroner about the hearsay approach to matters apart from the massacre, which he said jeopardized the rights of his client, Vincent Daniels. Assistant State's Attorney Stansbury supported Bundesen in denying the objection, but the line of questioning was sidetracked nevertheless.

The inquiry turned to other gang crimes and investigations, including the machine gun found in Frank Gusenberg's closet, which had come from Daniels by way of VL&A, prompting Schoemaker to remark: "Anybody that buys a machine gun is buying it for the purpose of murdering somebody." Without concerning himself with legalities, he said simply that a law should be passed making the sale of machine guns to gangsters punishable by life in prison.

In what would be another long day of hearings, Coroner Bundesen managed to elicit some laughter by announcing that he had been "severely criticized by witnesses, by the jurors, and particularly by the press for the rather inhuman treatment of running this inquest for ten or twelve hours without any breathing spell." And with that, he called a recess.

At 2:30 Bundesen re-opened the hearings and summoned one of his most important witnesses, Peter Von Frantzius, whose sporting goods shop was at 608 West Diversey Parkway, in the Rienzi Hotel. Although Von Frantzius's store was in the middle of Moran territory, he was an equal-opportunity gun dealer who did not discriminate among gangs or overly scrutinize his customers if a sale could be made without clearly breaking Chicago's handgun law. His most frequent visitors had included the late Hymie Weiss as well as other members of the North Side mob.

Von Frantzius had started a mail-order business at his mother's home in 1922, and by 1925 he had opened the shop on Diversey as well as a catalog operation, both called simply Peter Von Frantzius. The catalog included a police equipment section displaying the usual Sam Browne belts and other hardware, plus the Thompson gun and bulletproof vests from an Elliott Wisbrod (no relation to lawyer Wiesbrod), making him a competitor to firearms dealer and magazine editor Al Dunlap.

Von Frantzius readily stated that he bought submachine guns from Auto-Ordnance by way of Colt's, which had manufactured that company's entire stock of fifteen thousand guns in 1921 and 1922. It did not come out in the inquest testimony, but police disinterest in fully automatic "street-sweepers" had led the Auto-Ordnance Corporation to slightly modify the original gun to fire only semi-automatic, calling it the Model of 1927. Those weapons found even fewer buyers, but the following year the fully automatic gun, with a heavier breech-block that slowed the rate of fire from about 800 rounds per minute to 650, was adopted by the U.S. Navy as an auxiliary weapon and labeled accordingly by means of an overstamp.

Displaying a measure of discomfort, Von Frantzius admitted selling two Thompsons for two hundred dollars each to a man who had merely shown him a badge and said he was William McCarthy of the Indiana State Police. At least one of those guns had turned up in the apartment of beer-runner Steve Oswald on South Racine Avenue. Bundesen previously had shown a special interest in the weapons because of the "Major Silloway theory" that real police had committed the massacre, but by now he could report to the jury members that Indiana had no state cops named William McCarthy.

Under further questioning Von Frantzius admitting to selling "probably fifty" Tommyguns since going into the business, inadvertently establishing how slow the Chicago police had been to pick up on this item of gangland ordnance.

Von Frantzius also told how the same Daniels who later represented VL&A had approached him as early as 1924 to purchase machine guns for Mexico. At that time the dealer had ordered a Swiss-made Bergmann 7.65mm submachine gun (called a "machine pistol" in Europe) which Daniels had taken to the Mexican consul general in San

Antonio, Texas, in the hope that it would be demonstrated for the Mexican secretary of war and ultimately land him a contract.

No contract was forthcoming, although the enterprising Daniels had somewhere, either in Chicago or San Antonio, hired a gunsmith to mill off the Bergmann logo and restamp the gun with his own name, making it the "Daniels submachine gun." This was the only inventiveness to which Daniels could lay claim, and while a few Bergmanns did get into local circulation, the Chicago gangster community found them difficult to conceal and awkward to fire from a speeding car. Thus, the submachine gun of choice remained the Thompson.

The next inquest witness was an ex-prizefighter named Joe Annerino, alias Pepe Genero, both with the usual spelling variations, who operated a fruit store in an Italian neighborhood on Chicago's South Side. He had been periodically arrested for killing three of his friends or neighbors, Mike Vinci, John Minnati, and Charles Peppe, and now he had been arrested as a suspect in the massacre. While he admitted knowing Capone mobster Charlie Carr, of the massacre he testified, "I don't know nothing [and] I ain't got nothing to say because I don't know nothing." For once he probably was telling the truth.

Von Frantzius was recalled to the stand several times to try to explain how he determined that his machine-gun buyers had a legitimate use for such weapons. At one point Captain Schoemaker laconically commented, "Presuming that there was a legitimate use for a fifty-shot machine gun."

When Schoemaker was recalled to testify about Alex Korecek's earlier sale of machine gun No. 4656 to Charlie Carr, he referred to Carr as a notorious henchman of Al Capone. No particular note was made of this comment, but it was the first time Capone's name had come up during the hearings, and to emphasize his point about Carr, the captain characterized him as a pimp and whorehouse proprietor. The house in this case was well-known as the Stockade, mainly because of its construction, and was located on Harlem Avenue just south of Ogden Avenue. It was owned by Capone's brother Ralph and continued to operate as a brothel into the 1950s.

Schoemaker recalled that when Korecek was taken to see Carr in the police chief's office after selling the gun used to kill Assistant State's Attorney William McSwiggin in 1926, Korecek turned away and cried, "Oh, my God. . . . I will die, I will die." Korecek eventually regained his composure enough to gasp that he would never testify against Carr in court.

Calvin Goddard returned to the witness stand to describe how he had used an acid solution to raise the serial number which had been ground off the Thompson used to kill Dean O'Banion's successor, Hymie Weiss, in 1926. The gun had jammed after firing thirty-five rounds, and in their flight from the upstairs apartment next door to Schofield's Flower Shop, the killers had thrown it onto the roof of a dog house in an alley a block away.

Bundesen interrupted Goddard's testimony to mention that the gun in question had been sold by Wisbrod to the Hawthorne Kennel Club, controlled by the Capone gang and managed by Edward O'Hare.[11] This sent newsmen running in search of telephones to call in the new development to rewrite desks, and because of the late hour Bundesen concluded that day's session. With his usual flair for the dramatic, the coroner added that the hearings would be resumed on a Sunday or at midnight or "whenever events developed that require immediate action."

Eleven days later, on April 30, the inquest jury reconvened at the County Building and the hearings began to pay off—at least in exposing an even darker side of the Chicago machine-gun business. Up to this point, local dealers had displayed a measure of fear (to the extreme in Korecek's case) or negligence masquerading as naiveté bordering on stupidity.

The first witness was Louis Scaramuzzo, whose shop was at 803 South Halsted Street. Police had suspected Scaramuzzo was a major supplier of guns to the criminal community, and he responded to Bundesen's questions with wisecracks. He didn't keep records or books, he said, because nobody asked him to, and anyhow it didn't matter because he didn't know the names of the people who bought guns. After a few minutes of verbal dueling,

Bundesen told Lieutenant Erlanson to "lock him up" until he got his memory back.

Half an hour later Scaramuzzo's memory showed little improvement, but he did recall that the previous summer he had taken a man—he didn't know his name—to Von Frantzius to buy a machine gun. Otherwise, the fellow was from "out of town" and wore a pin-striped suit and gray fedora. Von Frantzius later testified that Scaramuzzo said the man was one of his good customers and "O.K. in every way; just take care of him." A few days later "the man" had his machine gun and Von Frantzius had his cash.

The next witness was James J. Reynolds, secretary of Von Lengerke and Antoine. He testified he had had sold two machine guns to the Laramie Kennel Club. These brought to three the number of Thompsons sold to the dog track's president, Eddy O'Hare, who operated it for the Torrio–Guzik–Capone mob. Reynolds added that VL&A had sold seven Thompsons to the Gopher State Mines in Minneapolis, a corporation that didn't exist. To other questions about machine gun sales and VL&A records, Reynolds maintained a straight face but claimed the records had been thrown out or could not be found, or possibly the transaction had never been recorded.

Now it was Stansbury's turn to explode: "To send this man out to bring in something is to give him notice not to have it there when he goes to get it." The only way to get any such information, he said, was to send an officer with a subpoena, and he ordered that all of VL&A's books be brought in.

During his turn on the stand, O'Hare admitted purchasing four machine guns, ostensibly for the protection of money wagered at his tracks in Illinois, Wisconsin, and Missouri. He said he had bought the club four or five months previously from Johnny and his brother Jake Guzik, who had risen in the Capone Outfit's ranks from panderer to accountant and paymaster.

The last witness of note was J. W. Shipman, president of the Haber Screw Machine Products Company, 864 West North Avenue, on the southern edge of Little Sicily. He said that in January 1928, when a machine gun was sold to a "Mr. F. H. Miller" of the company, it was called Haber Die and Stamping, and its president was politician and later alderman Titus Haffa. Shipman was then a company vice president and said he didn't know any Mr. Miller.

To preserve a measure of secrecy, Bundesen held the April 30 inquest session in Room 500 of the County Building, his private office. The reason for the secrecy was special witness Frank V. Thompson of Kirkland, Illinois, who had an office at 738 South St. Louis and would prove to be a major player in supplying Thompsons to the Chicago underworld, especially to the Capone mob. In the course of intensive questioning by Bundesen, individual jurors, and Assistant State's Attorneys Butler and Stansbury, an increasingly sinister picture emerged, involving unidentified purchasers, dummy crates shipped out of the city, bizarre meetings in secret places, the systematic removal of serial numbers, and other efforts clearly intended to conceal the identity of machine-gun buyers.

From the summer of 1928 to February 1929 at least ten submachine guns went to Frank Thompson and several more to other mystery men. Some were shipped directly to Thompson at either his home in Kirkland or at a hotel in Elgin, Illinois, some coming from the Auto-Ordnance warehouse at Colt's and others delivered in person by Von Frantzius.

Some were returned to the store to have their numbers ground off by an obliging Austrian gunsmith named Valentine Juch, who worked in the back room. Both Von Frantzius and Thompson claimed this was done at the suggestion of the other. Juch admitted removing the numbers from about ten machine guns and fifteen handguns, a service provided (according to other sources) for two dollars per weapon. Most of this information was revealed at a session convened May 1 to hear only Von Frantzius. During one illuminating round of questioning, Ditchburne asked Von Frantzius point blank:

"What was your impression as to the reason that these people whose names you tried to suppress wanted those machine guns? You took all the precaution, didn't you, to keep the names from being discovered and the addresses, and you shipped out decoy packages, you took the numbers off. You knew these guns were not going to legitimate hands?"

In a surprising burst of candor, Von Frantzius answered, "I will tell you frankly that I was interested in the sale of them."

Coroner Bundesen decided that more than enough information had been revealed for one day and adjourned the session.

After the February 14 massacre, one of Thompson's regular customers, who called himself Joseph Howard, was unfazed by the
uproar the murders had caused and wanted four more machine
guns. But after a secret meeting with Von Frantzius at the Logan
Square terminal of the Chicago "el," Thompson abruptly discontin-
ued his Tommygun brokering and lammed it to Canada until things
cooled down.

XIX

The Fall of Al Capone

D URING THE THREE MONTHS FOLLOWING the massacre, public attention focused on the efforts of police to solve the crime, with scant interest given to periodic bulletins on the inquest hearings that were so far yielding little useful information. Even when Calvin Goddard determined that the same machine gun used to kill Frankie Yale in New York had also been used in the slaughter on North Clark Street, the press—at least in Chicago—virtually ignored Al Capone. The newspapers did, however, keep their readers up to date on the war of words among police commissioners in several cities describing their respective battles against crime.

The Yale murder had helped trigger a war against crime in New York, where Commissioner Whalen, a month before the massacre, said his roundups already had mobsters fleeing to Chicago. Commissioner Russell quickly responded that his police still had plenty of bullets and would send the hoodlums "back in boxes." Not to be outdone, Detroit's police commissioner posted a bounty—a ten-dollar gold piece—on the head of any dead criminal. And playing catch-up, the commissioner in Memphis issued "shoot to kill" orders to end that city's crime wave. A week after the massacre, when Whalen declared that his deployment of police "strong-arm" squads would prevent New York from becoming another Chicago, Russell was busy and let that remark slide.

Al Capone's delay in appearing before a federal grand jury had earned him a citation for contempt, which made front-page news quite apart from the massacre. This in itself was no big deal, even though he knew the government was sharpening its income tax knives. Whether illegal income could be proven—and if proven would be taxable—was still in dispute, in spite of the Supreme Court's *Sullivan* decision that it was, with a few "ifs" thrown in that still left room for legal maneuvering.[12] Capone did not yet realize this was the beginning of the end, especially in light of the underworld earthquake the massacre had triggered.

Gang wars were now brewing in previously peaceful New York, and in May 1929 the Big Fellow made a command appearance at the country's first nationwide organized crime conference, in Atlantic City. An earlier conference in Cleveland had involved only Sicilians, whose conspicuous arrival and arrogance earned them something less than "respect" from local police who raided the meeting on a tip.

The Atlantic City conference drew top mob leaders or their emissaries from the East Coast and Midwest, who collectively made it clear to Capone that he needed to drop out of sight for a while—at least until the massacre blew over, if it ever did. From Atlantic City he went by train to Philadelphia on May 16 and (of all things) a movie, after which he walked into the arms of some detectives he already knew and cheerfully submitted to arrest for gun possession. Capone ordinarily left gun-carrying to his bodyguards, in this case Frankie Rio, but it was either that or be killed, is the nearly unanimous belief of crime historians. The shocker was the speed with which he was jailed on a guilty plea—sixteen hours from arrest to cell—and the length of his sentence: the one-year maximum. Chicagoans gasped at what seemed to be the swift, sure justice meted out in Pennsylvania. At last Capone rated banner headlines and found himself featured by name in front-page editorial cartoons.

If Capone thought he had restored order in Chicago by sacrificing three of his principal mobsters to appease the opposition, he was wrong. On May 8, police in Hammond, Indiana, had found the bodies of Albert Anselmi, John Scalise, and Joe Guinta dumped at a remote spot outside their town—probably as a courtesy to Chicago cops—and the first reports suggested that the killings were retribution by Bugs Moran and the remnants of his gang.

The underworld grapevine held otherwise, and a variety of gruesome accounts began to circulate. That the men had been killed by or on orders of Capone was soon accepted by mob-watchers, who came up with a scenario that has played well ever since. The colorful and complicated story has Capone learning of a betrayal contemplated by the three, staging a roadhouse banquet at which they were honored guests, and, for the floorshow, personally beating them into bloody pulps.

Morgue photographs of the bodies do not support this version; the victims appear to have been slugged and well shot up, but that was the community standard for "ride" killings. Also, the banquet story often involves different roadhouses, fifty or more gang members, clubs ranging from sawed-off baseball bats to bowling pins, and a Capone with time to make elaborate arrangements before going berserk. The story sounds like a few elements of fact that have been embellished into a great and grisly legend that no writer could pass up.

In any case, the massacre left Moran in deep hiding and Capone in deep trouble with a new generation of major hoodlums—men like Frank Costello, Charles Luciano, Meyer Lansky, Max Hoff, Charles Solomon, Abe Bernstein, "Nucky" Johnson, and Frank Nitti, with elder statesman Johnny Torrio presiding. These mobsters did not need a mass murder to generate national hysteria when their objective was nationally organized crime.

The jailing of Capone was a ticket to stardom that he didn't need or want. Locked up, he became a true celebrity gangster, fair game for editorial cartoonists and journalists with soaring imaginations to demean or lionize or torment, depending on the particular point the editor wished to make: that crime did not pay, that crime did pay, that crime could be a ladder of "upward social mobility." The last was certainly true, as Fred Pasley indicated in daring to write the seminal book *Al Capone: The Biography of a Self-Made Man*, published in 1930.

The fact was, many Italian and Sicilian immigrants did pull themselves up by the bootstraps of home-cooked alcohol; many low-paid cops put their children through college on payoff money; and more than one state and national leader owed his family's fortune to Prohibition.

Also true was that before 1929, an unpublicized Capone wielded power exceeding that of almost anyone in public office. But after the St. Valentine's Day Massacre and ten months in a Pennsylvania prison, his real power rapidly slipped away. He became a staple character for newspaper editorial cartoonists and previously timid columnists; the subject of dozens of books and magazine articles, ranging from intellectual journals (*Forum*, *The Literary Digest*, *Harper's*) to slick mass-circulation magazines (*Collier's*, *The Saturday Evening Post*); and the only "gangster" ever to make the cover of *Time*.

XX

SMOKING GUNS

D URING THE SUMMER AND FALL of 1929, the actual massacre shooters had amused themselves by golfing, drinking, and fishing at Fred Burke's resort in the woods outside Grand Rapids, Minnesota. They might have stayed there longer if Syndicate funds had not stopped coming through. During Capone's enforced vacation in a Pennsylvania prison, those in Minnesota reluctantly decided they had to return to Chicago and shake the money tree.

Frank Nitti was running the shop, supposedly sending funds to Burke and Gus Winkler by way of Phil D'Andrea, who had disappeared when the funds stopped and when finally tracked down claimed he had lost the whole wad on the horses. He begged Winkler not to tell Capone, who would have blown his top at both him and at Nitti, who, with Jake Guzik and Ralph Capone, was soon to become a tax-law test case himself. Winkler said nothing to Capone, and with Outfit affairs in disarray probably used this to his advantage. It gave him some leverage over Nitti, who was still accountable to Capone, and saw it as a means of regaining power in the organization, whether Nitti liked it or not.

Gus and Georgette Winkler were then holed up at an apartment hotel in Gary, and Bob Carey was in nearby Hammond. Ray "Crane-Neck" Nugent had earlier joined Ralph Capone in Miami, where Nugent was opening a tavern. Burke and Viola had found their perfect lakeshore cottage near Stevensville, Michigan, not far from George and Irene Goetz (as Georgette Winkler called them, although Fred Goetz and Irene Dorsey never married), and were living under the *nom de crime* of Mr. and Mrs. Frederick Dane when this assortment of master criminals managed their greatest screw-up yet.

Bob Carey introduced Gus to Harvey Bailey and some of his outlaw gang at Burke's watering hole in Calumet City. They were sitting on a fortune in bonds just looted from the Farmers' and Merchants' Bank in Jefferson, Wisconsin, on November 7. Winkler wanted no part of this, but Carey talked him into dropping the bonds off at Burke's place.

Burke was at home drunk and getting drunker. So were Carey and his new girl, Babe. But the bonds were left there anyway, and the next day Gus received a emergency call from the Syndicate in Chicago. There was big trouble in Michigan that would reopen the massacre investigation.

It seems that the previous evening of December 14, a soused Burke had driven into St. Joseph, where he rammed another car. It was only a fender-bender, but when the other motorist wanted five dollars to repair the damage, Burke ignored him and drove off. (It was not that different from the driving displayed eight months earlier by the same "Killer" Burke, if some witnesses were correct, when a phony detective car made a bad left turn onto North Clark Street and was hit by Elmer Lewis's delivery truck.)

Twenty-four-year-old patrolman Charles Skelly saw the commotion from in front of the police station, and as the driver of one car began leaving the scene with the other in angry pursuit, Skelly jumped on the running board of the second vehicle. That car managed to curb the offender's vehicle and as Skelly approached it, the driver picked up a gun, probably a .45 automatic, and shot him three times through the window before speeding off in a northerly direction. Skelly died three hours later at St. Joseph's Sanitarium hospital.

Such a crime was catastrophic in the quiet lakeside community, and Michigan police set up roadblocks as rapidly as possible. Searchers found the wanted car a short distance from town, a wheel broken in yet another collision, this time with a power pole. The driver was gone, having commandeered another car at gunpoint, but papers in the wrecked vehicle yielded the name of Frederick Dane and an address near Stevensville (commonly referred to in news stories as St. Joseph, the larger town to the north). Police quickly descended on the house and there found Viola Dane, who said her husband wasn't in and hadn't been home that evening, and asked what all the fuss was about.

Viola was taken into custody and a search of the cottage, including an upstairs closet she said was always locked, turned up a windfall of machine guns and other firearms, ammunition, bulletproof vests, and almost $300,000 in bonds, about a third of them stolen in the Wisconsin bank robbery a month before. Shirts embroidered with "FRB" suggested that the man they were hunting might be the now-notorious Frederick R. Burke featured on so many wanted posters, and a call to the Chicago police left no further doubt.

Word of the discovery soon reached Herman Bundesen, who wired the Berrien County district attorney at the courthouse in St. Joseph asking him to hold all the guns and protect the machine guns and shotguns, especially. The Berrien County DA not only did that, he personally drove them to the Chicago coroner's office. The machine guns were immediately given to Goddard, who compared bullets fired from them with bullets taken from the bodies of massacre victims Schwimmer and Kachellek, alias Clark, and discovered them to be perfect matches. Moreover, the bullets from one of the guns matched some of the bullets taken from the body of Frankie Yale.

This was the most important development in the entire massacre investigation, and the Yale connection would have made it a double-whammy, if someone had followed up on the information. However, New York police apparently didn't mourn Yale's loss enough to pursue the matter with any great diligence.

Bundesen released his information officially at what would be the last session of the coroner's inquest, held on December 23, 1929. Because of the illness of juror Bernstein and the absence of juror

Olson, who was out of town, their places had been taken by Major A. A. Sprague, a former commissioner of public works, now board chairman of Sprague, Warner & Company; and Cyrus R. McCormick, Jr., official of the International Harvester Corporation, Rhodes Scholar at Oxford, and grandson of the inventor of the McCormick reaper.

Goddard, as quiet and unassuming as a country clergyman, knew the drill well. He described receiving the two machine guns found at Burke's place, serial numbers 2347 and 7580, and explained how he was able to raise the ground-off serial number 7580 to visibility by applying an acid solution. Without ceremony or hesitation Goddard stated that the two weapons were the same Thompson submachine guns that had been used in the massacre, and also described the firing-pin and extractor marks on the shell casings that supported his findings.

He added the minor but interesting detail that the .45-caliber ammunition made by the U.S. Cartridge Company included the short run of bullets manufactured in 1928 and marked with a telltale "S" which had been recovered both as slugs fired into the massacre victims and as unused cartridges seized by police at the house of Killer Burke. The same brand of .45 cartridge had also been found at the Circus Café.

To thoroughly impress members of the jury and the press, Goddard used slides, drawings, charts, and a blackboard to prove his findings. At one point juror McCormick left his seat to peer through Goddard's comparison microscopes at the test bullets and the slugs recovered at the crime scene. A good time was had by all.

The massacre put the science of forensic ballistics firmly on the map, providing evidence through laboratory work that had not been accomplished by months of intensive effort by hundreds of Chicago detectives and state's attorney's investigators.

After Goddard finished his presentation, Bundesen turned to Deputy Police Commissioner Stege, who wrapped up the case in the conventional manner. He described how a Chicago police fingerprint expert had gone through the house near Stevensville, lifting prints from a salt shaker and other items which matched those of Frederick R. Burke, wanted by the police in several states for bank robbery, kidnapping, and murder.

Stege was followed by the final appearance of gun dealer Von Frantzius. Consulting records submitted previously, Bundesen reported that submachine gun No. 7580 had been sold to Victor Thompson, otherwise known as Frank V. Thompson, in care of the Fox Hotel, 100 Douglas Street, Elgin, Illinois. Bundesen said Von Frantzius already had admitted selling such guns to parties in Illinois, Indiana, and Michigan. When Von Frantzius had nothing to say on this point, Bundesen continued. He said that Thompson, who already had been arrested on the basis of Goddard's findings, had testified during an earlier session to selling No. 7580 to one James "Bozo" Shupe, a perennial police suspect in criminal mischief, who had been killed on Chicago's West Side.

The trail of gun No. 2347 should not have been hard to follow after it left the Auto-Ordnance Corporation, for it was purchased by Deputy Sheriff Les Farmer of Marion, Illinois, on November 12, 1924, when the Shelton and Birger bootlegging gangs in the southern part of the state had been feuding with the Egan's Rats. In a case of bad timing, Farmer reportedly had hooked up with the Rats before they were destroyed as a viable gang, after which the gun somehow found its way to Burke. And Burke eventually found his way to Detroit, where other St. Louis criminals were trying to coexist with the Purple Gang and rival bootleggers known as "the Little Jewish Navy."

How much of this was known to the inquest jurors isn't clear, for the story of how Deputy Farmer came into possession of No. 2347 was recounted by the U.S. Treasury Department's star crime-buster, Pat Roche, in an Associated Press story datelined Chicago, December 18, 1929. But the jury had plenty to work with and retired to deliberate, which required little discussion beyond how to word its verdict:

> [The seven victims] came to death on the 14th of February in premises known as 2122 N. Clark Street as a result of gunshot wounds received from bullets fired from a machine gun in the hands of a person or persons at present unknown to this jury at above location on February 14th at about 10:30 A.M. From testimony presented to us, we, the jury, recommend that the said Burke, now a fugitive from justice, be apprehended and held to the Grand Jury on a charge of murder as a participant in the said murder

and that the police continue their search for other said unknown person or persons and when apprehended that he or they may be held to the Grand Jury on the charge of murder until released by due process of the law.

This layman effort to cover all legal contingencies did not yield a verdict that would have pleased an English professor, but it provided the stamp of official certainty that the guns found at Burke's had been used in the St. Valentine's Day murders. *The Chicago Daily News* headlined a simpler version: BURKE EXECUTIONER IN MORAN GANG MASSACRE. That was a little overstated for trial purposes, for no one had witnessed Burke using the guns. But given his criminal notoriety, even the best defense attorney would have had a hard time raising enough "reasonable doubt" to conquer the mountain of circumstantial evidence.

Burke's main alibi witness would have been his "paramour," Viola, who claimed that he had left the house the morning of February 14 and returned much too soon to have driven to Chicago and back, and whose veracity probably would have underwhelmed a jury. A fellow criminal would have provided no better alibi. Long-time bandit Harvey Bailey later complained in his 1973 autobiography that the two of them were minding their own business, drinking beer in a Calumet City tavern on that memorable Thursday morning when the heat generated by the massacre made Burke a prime suspect—and ruined their lucrative bank-robbing business.

A possible alibi witness might have been Georgette Winkler, whose husband, Gus, was one of the murder crew and on the lam. Her memoirs mention Gus encountering Burke in a Calumet tavern,[13] giving at least some credence to Bailey's story. In her brief reference to the mistakes discussed at her house after the massacre, she does not include Burke as one of the gunmen (although she would include him later in an FBI document). Ray and Winkler had yet to be identified as the same person, despite a Michigan police official correctly naming him and others as regular visitors to Burke's place, just as New York police believed he, or "James Ray," and Burke had killed Frankie Yale.

Burke was quickly "swallowed up by the haunts of gangland," according the International News Service, leaving his wife, or "consort" (in the absence of a marriage certificate), Viola, about thirty-seven, in the clutches of the cops, who charged her with receiving stolen property. Police called her a bandit queen who, as Mattie Howard, neé Brennamann, had served a term in the Missouri State Penitentiary for murder. Actually, Burke had headed back to Missouri, with a few stops elsewhere, and would spend more than a year there as "the most dangerous man alive" and "the most desperate criminal alive" in spite of rewards totaling one hundred thousand dollars for his capture, "dead or alive."

In a nationally syndicated news story datelined Chicago, INS writer Francis F. Healy listed the crimes for which Burke was suspected and otherwise described him with the journalistic eloquence of the day as the "former terror of the Egan's Rats gang in St. Louis":

> Stranger than fiction and more horrible than the murder intrigues of medieval times has been the life of Burke, according to police investigations. Graduated from the Egan's Rats, an education noteworthy in criminal annals, Burke went further and organized his own group of fiends, murderers and bank robbers. Murder, it would appear from his records, was an incidental step in his undertakings. . . .
>
> Burke has long been connected by rumors with rum smuggling at Detroit, running of liquor into Chicago, hijacking of liquor and alcohol, bribery and alleged political corruption and the crimes previously mentioned.
>
> NIPPED IN BUD
>
> Witnesses here have identified Burke as one of two men (the other said to be James Ray or Gus Winkler) who posed as policemen to line up the Moran gang and mow them down like animals. Only the cunning of a super-criminal would conceive that angle—the police uniforms, Commissioner Stege points out. The Moran gang, contemptuous of police, will willingly lineup to be searched for weapons, but would have fought like rats had they known the "policemen" were rival gangsters.
>
> Of the murder of Frankie Yale in Brooklyn, many theories present themselves to detectives. Possibly the best theory is that Yale harbored a desire to "muscle in" on Chicago gangsters and that his murder "nipped him in the bud."

As a bank robber Burke has been identified by a score of witnesses. Peru, Ind., officials have identified his picture as the leader of the smooth-running gang which invaded the bank and with superlative daring made off with $50,000 from the First National Bank. The same evidence connects him with robberies at Louisville and Lexington, Ky., and at Jefferson, Wis.

This concluded the front-page story in the *Columbus Evening Dispatch* which took up the paper's entire lead column except for fourteen lines, leaving the type compositors just enough space for a little box reminding readers, 7 SHOPPING DAYS TO CHRISTMAS!

When the arsenal and loot were found at Burke's house near Stevensville, most members of the execution squad scattered, if they hadn't already. Burke headed back to northern Missouri. The Winklers went to Campagna's house until they could find a place in Berwyn, but they soon left for the relative safety of Texas before returning in March—about the same time Capone was leaving the Pennsylvania prison and Frank Nitti was being indicted on tax charges similar to those that Capone would face later.

Capone also would have to face a city crime commission revived under the crusading leadership of Frank Loesch. The Chicago Crime Commission was the first organization of its kind in the country, formed in 1919 by the Chicago Association of Commerce "to promote the efficiency and activity of all officers and departments of the State, County and City administrations charged with the duty of the suppression, prevention and punishment of crime." It was a watchdog with no teeth. And in the absence of any police powers, its financial support had been weakening along with its eyesight, which was trained more on the surviving Prohibition gangsters of the Twenties than on their successors who were busy expanding into the rackets.

By 1928, corruption in Chicago had climbed so far above the national average that Loesch had been compelled to enlist the aid of Capone to avoid a repeat of April's Pineapple Primary during the national elections that fall. An Ohio newspaper editorial reprinted in Chicago brightly suggested that the Second City simply fire its entire police force and hire a new one.

The immediate resumption of gang warfare after the November election of hapless Big Bill Thompson—who proclaimed Chicago wide-open and then went out to lunch—required desperate measures. There was even talk of declaring Chicago an occupied city under a seventy-year-old Civil War statute so federal troops could place it under martial law. That frightened gangsters, businessmen, and citizens alike.

After Capone finished his stretch in the Pennsylvania pen and returned to Chicago in March 1930 to resume control of his empire, he found there was a new sheriff was in town. He wasn't exactly Wyatt Earp backed up by a posse of Doc Hollidays looking to rid Tombstone of the Clantons and the McLaurys, but Alexander G. Jamie seemed like a good idea at the time.

A month before Capone's release, Colonel Robert Isham Randolph had formed a "citizens committee" that would soon be known as the Secret Six,[14] essentially an independent "secret service" that would complement the crime commission. Carefully protecting their anonymity (except for Colonel Randolph), six wealthy businessmen employed Jamie, a former U.S. Justice Department operative, to recruit a small army of likewise unidentified Prohibition agents, undercover men, special prosecutors, guards, private detectives, wartime Secret Service men, certain hand-picked Chicago cops, and possibly some former Texas Rangers and Canadian Mounties.

This private crime-fighting organization was extralegal bordering on the illegal and even the criminal (when it came to unauthorized wiretaps and ad hoc gun battles), but it was widely embraced by the press, businessmen, and citizens willing to overlook its close resemblance to vigilantes. It wreaked havoc on illegal breweries and made things hard on low-level bootleggers, but it had little effect on racketeering, and eventually careless recruiting methods allowed the infiltration of unorganized criminals who liked its cloak of righteousness. After some conspicuous excesses began to worry even lukewarm civil libertarians, members of the crime commission felt obliged to disband the group before they themselves had to call for federal troops or the Illinois National Guard.

Before that was seriously contemplated, however, the Chicago Crime Commission conceived what unexpectedly became its greatest publicity stunt: a "Public Enemies" list.[15] The term *public enemies* had been coined, or at least used in speeches, by the commission's finance director, George A. Paddock, during the 1920s, and it appealed to both the group's veteran operating director, Henry Barrett Chamberlain, and its latest president, Frank Loesch. It had the potential of focusing public attention, complete with newspaper commentary, on the city's top gangsters, and on April 24, 1930, the commission released an unprecedented roster of Chicago's twenty-eight top "Public Enemies" in an order more numerical than meaningful, not exactly current, and sometimes misspelled.

Thus, Al Capone became the country's first "Public Enemy No. 1," followed by:

2. Tony (Mops) Volpe
3. Ralph Capone
4. Frank Rio, alias "Frank Kline," alias "Frank Cline"
5. Jack Demore, alias "Jack (Machine Gun) McGurn"
6. James Belcastro
7. Rocco Fanelli
8. Lawrence (Dago Lawrence) Mangano
9. Jack Zuta
10. Jack Gusik
11. Frank Diamond
12. George (Bugs) Moran
13. Joe (Polack Joe) Saltis
14. Joe Aiello
15. Edward (Spike) O'Donnell
16. Frank McErlane
17. Vincent McErlane
18. Danny Stanton
19. Myles O'Donnell
20. Frank Lake
21. Terry Druggan
22. William (Klondike) O'Donnell
23. George (Red) Barker
24. William (Three Finger Jack) White
25. Joseph (Pepy) Genero
26. Leo Mongoven
27. James (Fur) Sammons
28. William Niemoth

Well intended and a big hit with the press as well as the public, the list was more relevant to the middle 1920s than to 1930, and it was initially considered a joke by most of the gangsters listed as well as by the cops obliged to arrest them. Many of the hoods had been in and out of court or police stations regularly on charges that would never stick, and some left bantering with officers as to how "we Public Enemies got to stick together." The cops themselves would laugh and wave good-bye.

Conspicuously absent from the list was the name of Frank Nitti, who was quietly running what Capone had called the Outfit (and Mrs. Winkler called the Syndicate) during Capone's ten months in the Pennsylvania prison. Nor was Nitti named in the next Public Enemies list circulated by the crime commission in 1931, although former North Side gangster Ted Newberry's name was there. He had defected to the Capone organization remarkably soon after the massacre, if not before. Moran had worried about a traitor in his ranks, and without putting a date on it, Georgette recalled the Syndicate giving Newberry quite a warm welcome upon his arrival.

Ted Newberry had been put in charge of the North Side territory previously controlled by Moran, who had fled to Windsor, Ontario, and other places north, for an extended vacation before venturing back to pick up what pieces he could in Lake County, Illinois, with the sufferance of the Roger Touhy Gang.

However, mob watchers of the day, inspired by "exclusive" reports in the *Chicago Herald and Examiner*, came up with the startling revelation that Capone and Moran had buried their hatchets and forged a great city-wide crime cartel to avoid continued bloodshed and pool their payoff money. This was picked up for a full-page article in *The Literary Digest* and was echoed in other papers and in the proliferating detective magazines, which had abandoned murder-mystery fiction in the 1920s in favor of exposé reporting.

Even Hal Andrews, one of the better-informed crime writers of the day and unlisted author of a best-selling *X Marks the Spot* picture book in magazine format, put together a plausible scenario for a 1932 *Real Detective* article. In it he correctly revealed Frank Nitti as Capone's successor ("you read it here first") and gave top billing to Ted Newberry on the North Side. But he mistakenly subordinated Newberry to Moran instead of to Winkler, who had remained a favorite of Capone's while Nitti did his jail time for taxes (along with Ralph Capone and Jake Guzik) and quietly consolidated North Side operations on the Syndicate's behalf.

Also absent, in other ways, was Fred Burke. After the killing of Officer Skelly and the discovery that his machine guns had been used in the massacre, Burke was back in Missouri hiding out with relatives of Harvey Bailey on a farm near Green City.[16] And it was quite a gutsy Burke who, while his "moll" Viola took the heat in Michigan, began wooing the daughter of another local farmer, Barney Porter, in nearby Milan.

Bonnie Porter was a pretty twenty-year-old student nurse in Kansas City, and after a whirlwind courtship she and Burke were married in Centerville City, Iowa, on June 17, 1930. Instead of becoming a Bailey farmhand in overalls, Burke had transformed himself into Richard F. White, a well-groomed and expensively dressed oil and real estate tycoon from Kansas City with fancy car and blushing bride. He even took up residence at the farm of his new father-in-law. But as bad luck would have it, Green City's only customer for *True Detective Mysteries* was a town character and thoroughly dedicated crime buff who eventually would become Burke's undoing.

Burke's expensive Hudson straight-eight coupe must have been the closest thing to a tourist attraction in Sullivan County, just south of the Iowa state line, where Model T Fords were outnumbered by mules and horses, and the Model A was a luxury car. So it was that the newcomer Burke, alias White, and his fine machine aroused first the curiosity and then the suspicions of a young odd-jobber, Joe Hunsaker Jr. Scarce as gangsters might be in a land of graded-dirt roads that frequently turned to mud, Green City's aspiring sleuth had noticed that Burke always stayed behind the wheel of his car while his passenger bought gas or groceries and any Chicago newspapers.

Hunsaker started following the car (somehow) and decided that the driver resembled the Burke he'd seen pictured in an issue of *True Detective*. He reported this to the sheriff, the police chief, a railway agent, and a few others who had small-town clout. In fact, the effort he put into tracking Burke's comings and goings aroused so much curiosity among other Green City residents that it's surprising Burke himself didn't become suspicious, especially when Hunsaker switched from work clothes to a business suit, making himself even more conspicuous.

Then Burke disappeared for several weeks, and Hunsaker worried that his quarry might have flown the coop, until he overheard Barney Porter tell someone that his son-in-law "Dick" would soon be returning from Chicago. He was practically a nervous wreck by the time Burke did come back, driving a brand-new Studebaker President coupe which Hunsaker later learned had been purchased at Joe Bergl's Auto Sales, next door to Ralph Capone's notorious Cotton Club in Cicero.

By now enough local lawmen had been pestered into agreeing that Hunsaker might be right and, backed up by out-of-town lawmen, they raided the Porter farmhouse at six A.M. on March 26, 1931. Bonnie's father tried to slam the door on the officers, but Burke, still in bed, didn't even go for his nearby revolver "while he was covered by three or four pistols and a submachine gun."

Burke was taken to the most secure jail in the area, ironically in St. Joseph, Missouri, a town with the same name as the one in Michigan where he had killed Officer Skelly. Police from several cities called to establish his identity and seek his extradition, and in spite of his presumed guilt in the "gangland crime of the century," the massacre was not Burke's greatest concern. When called to the jail telephone to talk to Chicago's new chief of detectives, John Norton, Burke brushed him off with a remark that he could beat any rap the city would try to hang on him. Chicago's paperwork may have been greater than Michigan's, or there may have been some deliberate meddling by politicians worried that an unfixed trial before a reform-minded judge would put them too close to the St. Valentine's Day action.

In any event, after an exchange of calls among governors and prosecutors, Illinois (and several other states) deferred to Michigan because of its air-tight case in the Skelly murder, and Michigan wouldn't let go anyway. Chicago authorities were permitted to question Burke but were only told how much he liked their city. When questioned by New York authorities, Burke parried even questions about his religion, saying he was a Hindu. Asked what he'd done with his turban, he said he had put it over a photographer's camera.

Burke was charged with Skelly's murder by Berrien County Prosecutor W. W. Cunningham, pled guilty before Circuit Judge Charles E. White in a Benton Harbor courtroom, and was sentenced to life in the Michigan state pen. Nearly a dozen other states were kept at a distance, and on July 10, 1940, Burke died in prison of a heart attack, without so much as a public comment about his jam-packed life of crime.

XXI

CAPONE MEETS UNCLE SAM

FRED BURKE PLEADED GUILTY TO Officer Skelly's murder in April 1931, the same month that Anton Cermak defeated Big Bill Thompson for mayor, and Chicago, preoccupied with the Depression, closed the books on the St. Valentine's Day Massacre. Coroner Bundesen's inquest remained the only official reminder of the event, but no further sessions were called before it, too, became history the following November 17 when Bundesen declared that "all who were under suspicion are dead save one and he has received a life penitentiary sentence." That seemed true at the time, and after Bundesen turned down appeals to enter that year's mayoral race, he returned to private life.

A Chicago coroner would never again wield so much power—nor would Bundesen's life remain private for long. Mayor Cermak soon appointed him the city's commissioner of health, putting him back in the realm of the living where he resumed his work for safer foods, better child care, and more sanitary hospitals. Bundesen held this position through the terms of three mayors and died with great honor and a national reputation.

The heat was officially off Winkler and the other American Boys, whose names had not even made the papers in connection with the massacre. The public was preoccupied with the economic disaster which had befallen the country in October 1929, and by 1932 desperate voters would elect Democrat Franklin Delano Roosevelt president on a New Deal platform that included, among many dramatic measures, the repeal of Prohibition. The president's view of the Depression as a national calamity requiring national solutions would greatly increase the powers of the federal government, not only in financial reform but also in crime control, much to the dismay of state's-rights congressmen.

When the abduction-murder of national hero Charles Lindbergh's baby in March 1932 raised such a outcry that Congress quickly made kidnapping a federal offense, then-President Herbert Hoover and his attorney general, William Mitchell, had resisted the move on the grounds that "You are never going to correct the crime situation in this country by having Washington jump in."

Roosevelt's approach was just the opposite, and while he planned the drastic measure of instituting a bank holiday to halt a national financial disaster, his new attorney general, Homer Cummings, declared America's first War on Crime.

Not that the Justice Department had many weapons to fight it with. Few crimes were federal offenses unless they could be construed as interfering with "commerce between the states," and those were a stretch: "white slavery" (an interstate prostitution law), interstate auto theft, and for reasons no one bothers to remember, the interstate shipment of prize-fight films. Even the new Lindbergh Law originally required the Justice Department to wait several days until it was presumed the kidnap victim had been taken across a state line and was now a "product" being transported in interstate commerce. (The law's waiting period has since been scrapped.)

But even without ammunition, Cummings possessed the country's biggest gun in the person of J. Edgar Hoover, director of the Justice Department's Division of Investigation, and Cummings intended to remedy the ammo shortage with his "Twelve Point Program" of federalized crime control. While a raft of new anti-crime laws fought their way through a Congress fearful that it might be creating a national secret police, Hoover used (some would say misused) the

Dyer Act to go after bank robbers whose only federal violation was interstate car theft. This was not unlike the Treasury Department prosecuting murderous gangsters for unpaid taxes.

The new Lindbergh Law was the only federal statute that could be used as it was intended—against kidnappers, whose years of safely snatching fellow criminals had emboldened them to begin abducting wealthy private citizens.

The general public had little objection to bending other federal laws, if that's what it took to bring the crime epidemic under control, especially since local authorities had been thoroughly corrupted by Prohibition and seemed powerless against gangsters and racketeers. Before President Hoover left office, he took a personal interest in the country's other best-known citizen, Chicago's own Al Capone, and made his destruction the primary mission of the Internal Revenue Service. And as events would soon prove, the power to tax could indeed be the power to destroy.

That remained the goal of the IRS when Roosevelt became president and replaced Mitchell with Cummings and his far more ambitious War on Crime. The public would soon be distracted from its Depression worries by an exciting national game of cops-and-robbers, even if many were not yet sure which side to root for. It would be J. Edgar Hoover's job to win public support for real law and order, but in that endeavor he would face a challenge from the news media, which, given the harsh economic times, often portrayed criminals in a sympathetic light.

In 1932, *The Literary Digest* introduced "Pretty Boy" Floyd to the country as "Oklahoma's 'Bandit King.'" The following year a captured Dillinger gang member would rationalize that "we only stole from the bankers what the bankers stole from the people."

Even Capone was on his best behavior, opening soup kitchens for the unemployed, and later, after losing his battle with the IRS, offering his underworld services to track down the person(s) who had abducted the Lindbergh baby, an act he guaranteed was not the work of any organized criminal gang.

The task facing newly elected Mayor Cermak was no less ambitious and difficult, considering that his "reform" platform was quite low to the ground. He had been elected in 1931 partly to rescue Chicago from Big Bill Thompson but also on his pledge to clean up the city in time for the Century of Progress World's Fair. It was mostly good luck and good timing that three major gangland crimes had already taken place during the waning days of the Thompson administration.

The Fox Lake Massacre of June 1, 1930, left three dead and two wounded at Manning's resort hotel in McHenry County northwest of Chicago and was initially headlined as a resumption of the Capone–Moran gang wars. However, the roster of victims argued against this theory, and the murders eventually would be attributed to wild-man Verne Miller avenging a friend's "ride" murder, which had put him in a bad mood.

The June 9 murder of *Tribune* reporter Jake Lingle in downtown Chicago had only demonstrated the depth of the city's corruption, and if the guilt of gunman Leo Brothers seemed further proof of that (he was represented by future Dillinger attorney Louis Piquett and received only fourteen years), it was still the first gangland murder conviction anyone could remember and therefore cause for celebration. That one of the jurors later complained publicly that he had been coerced into finding Brothers guilty didn't sur-prise jaded Chicagoans, who frequently knew beforehand what ver-dict was acceptable.

Five years earlier, Albert Anselmi and John Scalise had been acquitted of killing two policemen in a running gun battle because the officers had no warrant or probable cause to give chase. Their defense attorney practically doomed the Chicago jury system by explaining, "If a police officer detains you, even for a moment, against your will, and you kill him, you are not guilty of murder but only of manslaughter. If a police officer uses force of arms, you may kill him in self-defense and emerge from the law unscathed."

And that doesn't even count the bodies that had piled up in the Sicilian community for not contributing to the hundred-thousand-dol-lar defense fund in a case where the only complaint was from a juror who pleaded to be excused on the grounds that "I would have to carry a gun the rest of my life if I serve and found the two guilty. . . ."

Such trials were fairly rare, owing to a life-preserving inability to see shootings actually take place or recognize shooters. On August 1, 1930, Syndicate gunmen who still couldn't get a bead on Bugs Moran tracked North Side mobster Jack Zuta to the Lake View Hotel near Delafield, Wisconsin, and, after motioning other dance-floor patrons out of the way, riddled him with machine-gun bullets. Nobody was looking, except at the victim, or able to recognize any pictures of the suspected gunmen.

The so-called War of Sicilian Succession had been won in spectacular fashion on October 23, 1930, outside an apartment building at 205 North Kolmar, when Outfit gangsters were credited with setting up two opposing machine-gun nests that sent Joe Aiello running from one straight into the other. The careful planning had all the earmarks of a Capone operation, although the killers may actually have been New York Sicilians (or Capone gunmen sponsored by them) winding up that city's so-called Castellemmarese War before Aiello, already dodging Outfit guns, could make good his escape from Chicago to their city.

It was also Mayor Cermak's good fortune that much of the headline gunplay had since moved to New York. On April 15, 1931, the Castellemmarese War left Charles "Lucky" Luciano in virtual control of that city's underworld, following the murder of Joe "the Boss" Masseria in a Coney Island restaurant. Five months later, on September 10, Luciano had Salvatore Maranzano, his nominal superior and Masseria's former rival, shot to death in his Park Avenue office by hitmen masquerading as IRS agents.

On May 7, 1931, Francis "Two-Gun" Crowley (more outlaw than mobster) entertained a huge crowd of New Yorkers with a two-hour gun battle against 150 police trying to dislodge him, his girlfriend, and his buddy "Fats" Duringer from their apartment on an upper floor at 303 West Ninetieth Street.[17] The police won after Two-Gun was hit four times, but Crowley, already a cop-killer, lived long enough to be electrocuted at Sing Sing nine months later.

The excitement over the Crowley siege had only started to diminish when ongoing warfare between Dutch Schultz and Vincent Coll made more banner headlines on July 28. A carload of gunmen driving along on heavily residential East 107th Street shot up the Helmar Social Club at Number 208, missing their intended target but wounding five children, one of whom died. This earned Coll the nickname "Mad Dog," and on December 17, the day after his trial began for the "Baby Massacre," someone finally discovered bullets that could kill the often-shot "Legs" Diamond, master rumrunner and owner of New York's Hotsy Totsy Club, while still in his bed in an upstate rooming house.

Diamond had been wounded enough times in the Twenties to brag that he was bulletproof, just as Coll would soon declare himself conviction-proof when his guilty verdict was reversed. But on February 9, 1932, a call he was making from a drugstore at 314 West 23rd Street was disconnected by a blast of machine-gun fire, generally credited to Dutch Schultz, that took a fatal toll on both him and the telephone booth.

So it was that Cermak's mayoral victory on a campaign promise to make Chicago and the World's Fair safe for tourists seemed to be working in the absence of any more newsworthy killings or mass murders after he took office in April 1931.

Ostensibly a reform candidate, Cermak had his own strategy for ending Chicago's gang wars. It might not have been as inspired or sublime as the "O'Conner System" in St. Paul, Minnesota, which had kept that city nearly crime-free for years through the simple expedient of declaring it a safe haven for gangsters and outlaws so long as they left their guns at home (figuratively speaking), paid off a designated fixer, and obeyed the law as selectively enforced by Police Chief O'Conner and his successors.

Cermak's goal was the more specific one of breaking the Capone organization's stranglehold on the city's government (of largely Republican persuasion) by offering northwest suburban gangster Roger Touhy the use of the city's police force to destroy the Chicago Syndicate by hook or by crook, providing, of course, that Touhy would then return to suburbs outside Cook County. Touhy took a pass. He was Mr. Nice Guy, as gangsters go, had successfully turned down overtures from Capone, and anyway had his hands full keeping his wild brother Tommy under control. So Cermak next decided to exploit the increasing factionalism within the Syndicate itself, and this is where Winkler comes back into the picture.

Since the massacre, when Ted Newberry defected to the Syndicate, and the capture of Fred Burke in 1931, Capone had served his Pennsylvania prison time, emerged as the foremost symbol of Prohibition-era crime, and returned to Chicago in the mistaken belief that he could resume control of his empire. During five years of beer wars that had made the city the gangster capital of the world, he discovered that his great ship of crime that had survived the broadsides of a dozen gangs was leaking badly in the storm of the Depression, and that while he remained the nominal captain, Frank Nitti had taken the helm.

Nitti—whose name wasn't on the original Public Enemies list or even the next, was managing Syndicate affairs while Capone took the heat. Because he handled the money, he was an easier target for the tax cops than Capone, and when Nitti was finally arrested in the fall of 1931, he handed the tax cops a hollow victory by simply pleading guilty and doing an easy four months chauffeuring the warden of Leavenworth until his release in March 1932.

Mayor Cermak, through his own underworld ties, knew that Nitti would acquire de facto control of the Syndicate while the government used every trick in the book to gather evidence against Capone for the country's greatest gangland show trial. Capone would have pulled the same stunt as Nitti, offering to pay what he owed and take a slap on the wrist, but at the last minute he learned the fix wasn't in and pleaded not guilty. So the country was entertained by a courtroom carnival after all, and Capone was sentenced to eleven years. What happened in gangland's real world, now controlled by Nitti, remains a puzzle with several pieces missing.

GUS WINKLER MEETS HIS MAKER

ACCORDING TO GEORGETTE WINKLER'S ACCOUNT, Ted Newberry had gotten himself into serious debt with the Syndicate over liquor advanced but not paid for. While that alone might not have put him "on the spot," because of his popularity with the Gold Coast aristocrats, Gus Winkler believed he could bail him out by opening classy nightclub-casinos practically in the shadow of Chicago's historic Water Tower.

Besides the ritzy Chez Paree at 610 Fairbanks Court, there would be the 225 Club at 225 East Superior, also in the heart of the city's Gold Coast, and the expensively renovated Opera Club at 18 West Walton, two blocks from North Michigan Avenue's fancy Drake Hotel. But before these elegant nightspots were in full operation, Winkler was badly hurt in a car accident that landed him in the St. Joseph, Michigan, hospital.

Word of the wreck did not reach Georgette Winkler for several days, thanks to intentional foot-dragging by Nitti's men, and then she heard that he had lost an eye, was delirious, possibly dying, and could not have visitors. She finally managed to penetrate the cordon thrown up by Nitti, and with the help of Winkler's friend Joe Bergl, the gangland car seller, found Gus blinded in one eye, as she'd been told, but otherwise recovering.

To make Winkler's legal situation worse, local police had arrested him as one of the Bailey gang who on September 17, 1930, had robbed the Lincoln National Bank and Trust Company in Lincoln, Nebraska. That heist of some $2,870,000 in cash and bonds was the biggest bank job in the country up to that time.

Winkler's arrest was a simple frame-up engineered with the help of Alexander Jamie's Secret Six to recover the cash and negotiable securities. Jamie knew that Winkler knew the Baileys, and witnesses had conveniently identified Winkler as a member of the gang. As soon as he was able to travel, he was whisked to Nebraska to stand trial, and the only way he could clear himself was to raise the hundred-thousand-dollar bail bond and browbeat Bailey into giving up the loot. Which is how Winkler made the newspapers.

Georgette had been finding it harder and harder to reach Capone, who by this point was practically under house arrest by his own—or, rather, Nitti's—men, but Big Al managed to come to the rescue with the hundred-grand bail bond, Winkler kept his end of the bargain, and the charges were magically dropped. Although Chicago papers turned the event into a midnight melodrama cooked up by the Secret Six—with Winkler leaving a suitcase under a downtown corner street light at a given hour where it was picked up by an undercover operative—in truth, he simply carried it into the Loop office of Alexander Jamie and plopped it on a table. (Jamie told Winkler later they knew he wasn't involved in the robbery but figured he was the only man who knew the right people and, with Capone's help, could pull it off—essentially getting Capone to buy back the loot to keep his favorite gangster on the job.)

From the runaround she'd been getting from Nitti and his "Italian element," Georgette had developed a strong distrust of the new Syndicate regime. They had tried to keep her from seeing her husband in the hospital, and even Capone had to pull rank on his Nitti-appointed guardians just to talk to Georgette in person, or to make bail for Winkler once he had been transferred to Nebraska to stand trial. Gus Winkler now shared his wife's distrust and dislike of the Nitti faction, and two of his American Boys were missing in action.

Bob Carey (alias Sanford, Conroy, and Newberry, no relation to Ted) wasn't missing; he was dead. After he and his girlfriend ignored Capone's advice and started blackmailing businessmen with compromising photographs of them and his girl, Conroy soon found himself at odds with the mob and moved to New York, bottle and beauty in hand, and may have expanded into counterfeiting. Details are unclear, but New York cops concluded that on July 31, 1932, he went wrong in the head, shot his girlfriend in their apartment, and then shot himself.

Ray "Crane-Neck" Nugent simply vanished. He had followed Ralph Capone to Miami, opened a tavern, and then foolishly started buying his booze from opposition sources. Word reaching Georgette Winkler was that he had perished, probably in the Everglades, where he may have nourished an alligator, leaving a wife struggling to support her family in Toledo. She eventually filed the paperwork to have him officially declared dead.[18]

The Chicago mob was also feeling the effects of the Depression, but Nitti still didn't think Newberry was making the most of his opportunities and wanted more Syndicate involvement in his club operations. At first it looked as if Newberry was going to be demoted to flunky, but before his conviction Capone still wielded enough influence that the man brought in to help revitalize the North Side was Gus Winkler, with whom Newberry had developed a close friendship. Both soon were living in a luxury apartment building at 3300 North Lake Shore Drive near Belmont, the Newberrys on the thirteenth floor and the Winklers on the fifteenth. Edgar Lebensberger, who was clean on the outside but had his own underworld connections, and who "owned" the other gambling club on Superior, lived in an equally luxurious apartment at 1258 North Lake Shore Drive.

During the summer of 1932 Newberry was still in hock to the Syndicate, and it was all Winkler could do to keep the wolves away from his door. Nitti's men were leaving cabaret operations to Newberry and Lebensberger but were managing the casinos and putting pressure on Newberry to fork over much of the illicit liquor take.

Newberry also believed that, with Capone entangled in tax troubles and Nitti undermining his other North Side operations, he would soon be unemployed—unless he could take out Nitti first. Mayor Cermak, promising reform while taking his own cut from the gambling parlors, may have been thinking of his future more in terms of politics, but he had reached the same conclusion about Nitti, and at about the same time. Whether Newberry and Cermak were acting in concert is still unclear.

In any event, on December 19, 1932, a Chicago police detail headed by Detective Sergeants Harry Lang and Harry Miller—two of the mayor's underworld bagmen, but by other accounts paid five thousand dollars or more by Newberry—raided the Syndicate's downtown headquarters in Room 554 of an office building at 221 North LaSalle Street, where Lang pumped three bullets into Frank Nitti. He then went into another room and gave himself a minor flesh wound, so that when the press arrived he could claim that Nitti, although unarmed, had shot him first.

But Nitti didn't die, and two days later Cermak, Lang, and Miller highballed it to Florida. The man who did die was Ted Newberry, whose bullet-riddled body was found on January 7, 1933, outside Chesterton in northern Indiana. It seems that Newberry, at a party for Gus Winkler, had tipped his hand during a drunken conversation with Capone's personal physician, Dr. David Omens, and Omens took the story to Nitti. At least that's what Winkler suspected.

Lang and Miller were initially given commendations for their "gun battle" with Nitti until it came out in court, thanks to a uniformed cop who testified truthfully (and probably to his lasting regret) that Nitti simply had been gunned down. Nitti was cleared, but Lang and Miller had to turn in their badges and pay hundred-dollar fines for simple assault.

On February 15 Mayor Cermak was shot while talking to President-elect Roosevelt following an outdoor speech in Miami, and a dubious but persistent argument still holds that Cermak, not Roosevelt, was the intended target. The shooter was a small, mentally challenged, and hypochondriacal Sicilian named Giuseppe Zangara (voices in his aching stomach ordered him to kill all kings and presidents), who climbed on a bench to see over the crowd and loosed five wild rounds from a small revolver. Against long odds, one bullet hit Cermak, who would have survived with no more than a battle scar except for peritonitis that set in at the hospital and killed him three weeks later, on March 6. Two weeks after that, Zangara, who pleaded guilty to the crime, was executed.

Nitti survived his far worse wounds, and Winkler prospered—at least for a time.

With Burke serving a life sentence, Capone behind bars, Nitti in the hospital, and the country in the throes of the Depression, Gus Winkler worked hard to distance himself from the outlaw community whence he had come. Newberry's death deprived Winkler of his Chez Paree manager and aroused suspicions on the part of the Syndicate crowd, whose strength remained concentrated south of the Loop and in Cicero. His surrender of the stolen Nebraska bonds to the Secret Six had put him at odds with some of his old bank-robbing buddies, as well as the Syndicate, and his ambitious development of casinos on the North Side with the approval of Capone was widening his differences with the Italian element— especially when he made it a point to take himself off the Syndicate payroll. He was still a "member of the board," which had begun meeting at Nitti's house on Maple Street in Berwyn once he was on the mend.

Winkler's dealings with former Prohibition Bureau official Alexander Jamie was a two-way proposition, however. It gave him access to a man Georgette Winkler knew as Al Lehman (probably an alias), who kept Winkler posted on the bureau's activities for a monthly stipend of three hundred dollars, and who presumably tipped him off to impending raids on his cabarets and casino operations. Lehman also was tight with a girl employed at the U.S. District Court in Chicago and who provided (knowingly or otherwise) information on federal activities concerning Winkler and his associates.

An even better spy was a former state highway patrolman named Buck Kempster, who had been loaned, or assigned, by Governor Henry Horner to work with the Chicago office of the Bureau of Investigation. The Special Agent in Charge there was Melvin Purvis, who would later gain national fame (to Hoover's dismay) in the John Dillinger case.

Kempster, according to Georgette Winkler, was more crook than cop, and she said that one of Chicago's principal "fixers" was a man whose name sounded like Bartholomus, who had an uncanny ability to make bank robbery victims lose their memories and often made criminal charges disappear altogether. It cost Winkler several thousands of dollars to dispose of two bank jobs for which he'd been framed while trying to cultivate his new image of North Side respectability.

It was this same "Bartholomus" (possibly Edmond Bartholmey, a one-time Bensenville, Illinois, postmaster involved in a Barker-Karpis Gang kidnapping) who supposedly had such influential Washington connections that, for one hundred thousand dollars, he could have gotten Capone's conviction reversed or his sentence greatly reduced, an option the Syndicate refused to consider.

In the aftermath of the massacre, Capone's main function was that of a lightning rod that kept Chicago brightly illuminated as the nation's crime capital. This was bad for business, Cermak, tourism, the upcoming World's Fair, and Nitti, especially once Cermak was out of the way and a reconstituted Syndicate found it could carry on nicely with his successor, Edward J. Kelly, by keeping a low profile.

A major shakeup in the law enforcement community sidelined Detective Chief William Schoemaker in favor of John Sullivan, former chief of police in Cicero. For good measure, the monumentally corrupt Daniel A. "Tubbo" Gilbert was appointed special investigator by the new state's attorney, Tom Courtney.

To the increasing concern of the Syndicate, Winkler also met with the feds after Verne Miller sought his help following the Kansas City Massacre. Winkler was a friend of the captured bank robber Frank Nash, who along with five lawmen was slain there, and knew Miller as well. The prevailing belief at the time was that Miller had lost his head and shot everyone in sight. Later investigations would suggest otherwise, but this version of the attack was played in the nation's press as a case of Depression-era criminals so bold and bloodthirsty that they no longer had compunctions even against cop-killing. To U.S. Attorney General Homer Cummings, this demonstrated that the "underworld army" had declared "war on America," and America had to fight back.

Agents of the FBI (as it would later be called) were quickly authorized to carry guns without the formality of being deputized by local police. The newsreels showed J. Edgar Hoover in full rant before Congress, and the nation's new "G-men" armed with Thompson guns and tracer ammunition were soon pictured in nighttime target practice that made their shooting range look like the Fourth of July. With the nation's first Number One criminal finally behind bars, the nation's new Number One cop declared the Justice Department to be the nation's Number One crime-fighting agency—if Congress would just pass Cummings' new federal laws.

After the Kansas City killings, Miller's girlfriend Vivian Mathis had gone to Georgette Winkler for help and was told that Gus had said no—she and Miller were the last people he wanted anywhere around. On September 22, another display of outlaw audacity took place that put Chicago back in the headlines, and it was mistakenly blamed on Miller and Machine Gun Kelly,[19] with Pretty Boy Floyd thrown in for good measure. A carload of machine-gunners robbed Federal Reserve Bank messengers on Jackson Boulevard in the middle of the city, wrecked their car a few blocks away, and there killed police officer Miles Cunningham, but still managed to escape with loot consisting mainly of cancelled checks.

This turned out to be the work of the Barker-Karpis Gang, but Winkler was hauled in, among others, mainly because of the wrecked getaway car. It was internally armored and equipped with gun ports, bulletproof glass, a police radio, siren, green and red headlights to make it look like a detective vehicle, and a device that sprayed oil into the car's hot exhaust manifold to produce clouds of smoke that would deter pursuit.

Authorities had quickly traced the car to the auto sales and repair shop of Joe Bergl in Cicero, who now was to automobiles what Peter Von Frantzius had been to machine guns. Winkler was part owner of Bergl's operation—the one next door to Ralph Capone's Cotton Club. The car's discovery resulted in Bergl facing charges of murder before the fact, and it also put Winkler on the FBI griddle, since it was a Federal Reserve robbery.

Having already slammed the door on Miller because of Frank Nash's death, Winkler told Special Agent in Charge Purvis that if the feds wanted Miller, they should stake out the residence of one Bobbie Moore, who lived in the Sherone Apartments at 4423 Sheridan Road and was a close friend of Miller's girlfriend Vivian Mathis, whom Georgette called Viola. This supported the word of an unidentified informant shortly after the one-sided shootout in Kansas City, and the feds made their plans accordingly. Soon underworld rumors began to circulate that Miller was gunning for Winkler.

Winkler, trying hard to go straight (which in his case meant taking over Chicago's North Side operations without the usual gunplay), had meanwhile teamed up with County Commissioner Charles H. Weber as his front for a beer concession at the World's Fair. Without waiting for the tedious state-by-state ratification of Repeal, Congress had modified the Volstead Act to permit the legal sale of 3.2 beer in April 1933 simply by defining it as "non-intoxicating."

Georgette Winkler remembered one of her husband's happier days as the grand birthday party she staged for him on March 28, when she reserved the Chez Paree and Glen Pollack's Orchestra. It was a celebration privately arranged by her and attended by what she, at least, considered the cream of Chicago's society—high-hat politicians, plus select police officials, for by now Winkler was enjoying discreet police escorts. Another happy occasion was the wild night he spent personally loading beer and riding the trucks from the Weber Distributing Company at 1414 West Roscoe in a race to get the first legal brew to the city's hundredth-anniversary fair.

It may have been wishful thinking on her part, but Georgette Winkler imagined that her husband would soon be minimizing his ties with the downtown Syndicate, now ruled by Nitti, and not killing people. Life had been too harried for too long, the St. Valentine's Day Massacre was receding into history as the New York gang battles drew the spotlight away from "Capone's Chicago," and Winkler was tactfully helping the feds and the postal police identify certain mail robbers and cop killers, hinting at their best bets for locating the culprits. This was getting him labeled as an informer in underworld circles.

Also, Winkler's increasing independence, his favoring of "nice vice" (mainly gambling) that didn't bestir the cops, and the Nitti faction's outright lies about Winkler's physical and mental state following his car wreck in 1931 had convinced both Winkler and Georgette they could trust none of Capone's underlings. Ted Newberry's failed (and fatal) effort to waste Frank Nitti likewise reflected badly on his good friend Winkler, and only Winkler's improving image as new boss of the North Side staved off efforts by any of New York's emerging crime families to team up with the new boys in Chicago. They were held at bay (possibly with Winkler's help) when Chicago's increasingly friendly police arrested Lucky Luciano and Meyer Lansky along with local mob leaders Paul "the Waiter" Ricca and Rocco Fischetti outside the Congress Hotel on Michigan Avenue on April 19, 1932. The word circulating in the underworld and even finding its way into newspapers was that a New York-Chicago nightclub cartel was in the making, and the New Yorkers were especially excited by the prospects of Winkler's nearly finished Opera Club, which he had promised to Lebensberger.

Unfortunately for Winkler, his trusted man Lebensberger had been finding it hard to mind the store at the 225 Club when exposed to the same temptations that were being rejected by semi-reformed "Big Mike," as Winkler was becoming known, along with his aliases of Rand and Michaels. M. J. Michaels (the name he used on Lake Shore Drive) had meanwhile found a plastic surgeon who, besides altering his features, had performed some expert work on his fingertips to alter them by means of skin transplants that would change the pattern.

When Winkler, alias Michaels, learned that Lebensberger had been led astray by both Fred Goetz and the legendary "Boss" John J. McLaughlin in a stolen-bond deal he himself had carefully avoided, and that Lebensberger's indictment was imminent, he saw Lebensberger's fear at the prospect of prison. They spent the evening of October 5 together, and Winkler was able to convince him that the federal indictment might mean a trial, but that he could probably beat the rap with just a good lawyer, like Abe Marovitz, whose early mob clients did not prevent his rise to prominence as a federal judge. By the time he dropped him off at home, Lebensberger seemed in fine spirits and ready to take on the legal system.

So the news of his suicide the next morning was less than convincing. Even investigators were dubious. There were no conspicuous powder burns around the entrance wound in his head, and in some newspapers reports the death gun seemed magically to switch from the body's right hand to its left when relatives declared him left-handed.

The earlier murder of Ted Newberry by the mob had left Winkler more than a little uneasy, not only of the reviving Syndicate and its willingness to cooperate with the New York mob, but because he also was being sought for questioning. He would have gone to the police the same day, a Friday, but he already had been hassled by some unfriendly cops on dubious gun charges and vagrancy arrests and didn't feel like spending a three-day weekend (Monday was Chicago Day and city courts would be closed) in the lockup.

So he laid low in one of his several offices, this one in the Lincoln Park Arms at 2738 Pine Grove, where he anonymously operated the Sky High Club, and which was the reputable residence for disreputable folks like Art O'Leary, investigator for Leo Brothers's attorney Louis Piquett.

Winkler's worries only increased in the fall of 1933, and Georgette was picking up on the changes in his mood. Lebensberger's death weighed heavily on his mind, as did Newberry's murder, and the one-by-one disappearance of the new mob's "American" element. She and Winkler had been married by a judge in St. Louis, but out of respect for his mother's wishes they had recently remarried in a Catholic ceremony and had grown close to a Father Dwyer who did not let Winkler's line of business come between them.

Over the weekend, Winkler had mentioned the priest as someone they could trust, and then he gave Georgette shivers by describing his business involvements in greater detail than ever before. On Sunday she went to early Mass, and after returning to Winkler's suite at the Lincoln Park Arms, her husband called a trusted employee named Scotty to go over his business affairs in their presence. In retrospect, she realized Winkler had called on him to witness what he was telling her about his clubs and other holdings, none of which were in his name. For all the good it would do, Winkler was reading Georgette his will.

The atmosphere was tense on Monday morning, October 9, and Georgette tried to suppress her anxiety by driving in her own car to a hairdresser's in Cicero. She had told Marion Murphy, their black chauffeur and another man they trusted explicitly, that her husband would not be needing him that day, although she was curious why he had dressed in full business attire. Before she left around eleven, Benny Goldblatt, Winkler's usual bodyguard, had arrived in the car of a man she knew only as "Red." They were followed shortly by Ralph Pierce, a smiling Syndicate man whom she knew to be Nitti's personal spy, and another man called "Little Bobby." With Goldblatt there she thought Gus well enough protected, but so much was happening that while driving to Cicero she was filled with apprehension. In the beautician's chair she found the shampoo and rinse relaxing. She had been there possibly an hour when she received a telephone call from Benny Goldblatt. All he said was, "Hurry to the office."

What happened is not entirely clear. The men had engaged in some kind of discussion, and when that was winding down, Goldblatt left. Winkler already had asked to borrow Goldblatt's car to run some errands, for Winkler's machine was too well known to the police, and Goldblatt presumably went home to get it. Winkler himself was apprehensive enough that he asked Goldblatt to meet him at the corner of Pine Grove Avenue and Addison Street, half a block from the Lincoln Park Arms. Winkler said he intended to meet with his attorney, William Waugh, and Waugh later confirmed that they had a two o'clock appointment.

First, though, Winkler went to the Weber Beer Distributing Company on Roscoe, either driving or riding with another man who was never identified. He arrived at the plant about 1:30, and just as he reached the front door, six quick blasts from automatic shotguns knocked him flat on his face. Winkler's killers had been watching for him through the oval windows in the back doors of a green panel truck, which then drove west on Roscoe at a moderate speed, turned south on Greenview, and disappeared from the view of several neighborhood residents who had witnessed the shooting.

Inside the building was Weber's business partner Charles Conrad, who had heard the shots and reached the front door in time to see the panel truck make its turn onto Greenview. At his feet lay Winkler, whom he knew by the alias Rand, lying on the concrete and bleeding profusely from over seventy buckshot wounds in his back. His barely audible words to Conrad were, "Turn me over. I can't breath."

The first police to arrive at the scene were Officers Roy Coutre, Gus Bellack, and Stephen Languedera of the Town Hall Station, who rushed Winkler to the John B. Murphy Hospital at 620 West Belmont. There he managed to ask Dr. Salvador Huerta to summon a priest, and the Reverend James Fitzgerald reached Winkler in time to administer last rites. He attempted to recite the Lord's Prayer but got only as far as, "Our Father who art in heaven, hallowed be Thy name," before his voice became a whisper, he lost consciousness, and died.

Hospital personnel cutting away his outer clothing to get at the wounds found several religious medals and a cloth scapular. By the time Georgette Winkler reached the hospital, her husband's body was on its way to the Cook County Morgue.

This was front-page news, for by now Winkler was known to control a dozen or more clubs, casinos, and taverns in what previously had been Moran territory. He was still connected with the Syndicate but ruled the North Side with the kind of limited authority and independence enjoyed by the governor of a state. With the return of legal beer, and Repeal being ratified by Congress, he was almost a legitimate businessman, burdened only by the overhead of paying off the right police and public officials, and the annoying expense of opening and reopening his casinos after routine crackdowns.

The word circulating in the underworld and also mentioned in newspapers was that Winkler had been square dancing with federal authorities who wanted to know what he knew about stolen bonds and about his former friends soon to be declared interstate fugitives. Those connections had been through past involvements and third parties, such as Joe Bergl, the Cicero car armorer, and Doc Stacci of the O. P. Inn in Melrose Park. But after the Lang shooting, Nitti considered Winkler a personal threat, for some of the Syndicate's racketeering no doubt involved interstate activities.

In later FBI memos, Melvin Purvis speculated that Winkler was murdered to stop him from talking to the Justice Department and other federal agencies, which Nitti might soon have reason to fear. Another strike against Winkler was his loyalty to Capone, whose imprisonment was Nitti's ticket to the top of the Chicago branch of a criminal organization that finally had become national in scope. Strike three, probably from a pair of autoloading shotguns, retired Winkler as the sole surviving member of what his widow habitually referred to as the American Boys.

XXII

HOOVER'S "WAR ON CRIME"

JOHN DILLINGER, BABY FACE NELSON, Bonnie and Clyde, Pretty Boy Floyd, Machine Gun Kelly, Ma Barker, and the Barker-Karpis Gang symbolize the national crime wave of the 1930s. Especially when combined with the Great Depression, they were what sociologists call "people's bandits"—outlaws in the Jesse James tradition, driven to crime by circumstances, who "robbed banks, not people," made the police look foolish, became legends in their own time, and died with their boots on.

If that is not an entirely accurate image of the Thirties bank robber, the man who did the most to export it was J. Edgar Hoover. Of course, he called them rats, cowards, and human vermin, but that's what excitable lawmen of the era were expected to do. Say what you want, it took guts to rob a bank, risk getting shot, and generally thumb your nose—not at society, as Hoover always declared, but at authority, which was showing serious signs of collapse. It also was Hoover's job to turn public opinion against violent crime and criminals (while dismissing the "Mafia" as fiction). An outlaw like John Dillinger also needed to maintain good public relations. Both sides had their screw-ups.

Once President Franklin Roosevelt and Attorney General Homer Cummings reversed a national tradition of local law enforcement, they also unleashed a pit bull who began using the old Dyer inter-state car-theft act and the new Lindbergh kidnapping law to go pounding after any federal offender careless enough to get himself identified. The task was daunting. State "sovereignty" was a major issue in Congress and in the intellectual community, many U.S. senators and congressmen objecting to Cummings' anti-crime proposals that together with Roosevelt's economic reforms would (or might) give the U.S. President nearly dictatorial powers, while civil libertarians more specifically feared the creation of a national secret police.

The American public was being pulled in several different directions. Prohibition had almost totally corrupted local law enforcement and filled the prisons with friendly neighborhood bootleggers. Federal Prohibition agents not only were incompetent and corrupt but trigger-happy, having killed more than thirteen hundred Volstead lawbreakers (the "dry" count, which included every sparrow that fell) since 1920. On the other hand, it took the determined efforts and resources of the federal government just to lock up the country's Public Enemy Number One—for nothing sexier than unpaid taxes—and both citizens and the business community fancied that an "American Scotland Yard" was needed to clean up crime in American cities.

This went over poorly with local police, who were paid to do just that and were not *all* rotten apples. It also posed Constitutional problems for Cummings, who understood that without scrapping the Bill of Rights, his Justice Department agents could not legally catch crooks who did not in some way interfere with "interstate commerce."

As bad luck would have it, the country had been stunned on June 17, 1933, by the Kansas City Massacre in which Verne Miller and Pretty Boy Floyd killed four local lawmen and a federal agent in a botched attempt to rescue Frank Nash. That occurred while newspapers were still bannering the kidnapping of wealthy St. Paul brewer William A. Hamm Jr., which was followed two weeks later by the kidnapping of Oklahoma City oilman Charles F. Urschel, whose abductors demanded an unprecedented two-hundred-thousand-dollar ransom.

With three major crimes in a row, Cummings and Hoover had what they needed to jump-start their War on Crime. At first, it was, in the attorney general's words, "almost like a military engagement between the forces of law and order and the underworld army." After the Urschel kidnapping, it was "real warfare the armed under-world is waging upon organized society," and President Roosevelt obligingly urged him to transform the Justice Department's investi-gators into a "super-police force."

The idea of a super-police force worried cops as well as crooks and states' righters and civil libertarians. Desperate times called for desperate measures, nearly everyone agreed, and while some jour-nals of opinion approved of Mussolini's hammer blows against the Italian Camorra and Sicilian Mafia, others feared that Roosevelt's National Recovery Act was only a step or two short of Socialism, or National Socialism, or Communism, or something undemocratic. Not counting the Civil War, the country was as close as it would come to revolution, at least in print. Only the Supreme Court's bul-let through the head of the NRA Eagle showed that the U.S. system of checks and balances still was working.

As for the War on Crime, the opposing armies were not yet clearly defined. To the general public, criminals were criminals, whether they were gangsters (a generic term but most often linked to city bootlegging gangs), racketeers (who might shake down the business community or take over unions but also bombed and killed), bandits (organized or otherwise, who essentially were raid-ing parties of armed robbers), and kidnappers (who might be gang-sters or outlaws or individuals, depending on their choice of vic-tim). Some were glamorous and some were not.

And feds were feds, with no clear distinction between the Prohi-bition police under the Treasury Department, J. Edgar Hoover's Division of Investigation under the Justice Department, the Bureau of Narcotics headed by Harry Anslinger, the U.S. Postal Inspectors, and the Secret Service, which had the totally dissimilar jobs of pro-tecting the president and catching counterfeiters.

Without giving careful thought to the matter, Roosevelt created Cummings's super-police force in the spring of 1933 by signing an executive order that simply merged several federal agencies into a one as of August 10, which allowed two months to work out a few hundred details. This was the president's New Deal in crime control, and while it sounded as if his administration was finally mounting a full-scale crusade against crime, the turmoil it caused in Washington can only be imagined. Before the order could be implemented, a horrified Hoover convinced Cummings that transferring Prohibition enforcement from Treasury to Justice would be like combining an army of armed and dangerous high school dropouts with his small but elite group of bright young lawyers and trainees who carried briefcases instead of guns.

The Kansas City Massacre solved the gun problem, as Congress soon authorized Justice Department agents to carry firearms and make arrests. And at Hoover's request, the department's Bureau of Investigation was renamed the Division of Investigation. Then, to further distinguish his crimebusters from the Prohibition Unit's "hooch hounds," he cooked up one of the great folk tales of modern times.

The Urschel kidnapping case was wrapped up brilliantly, thanks to Urschel's memory for certain details (plus two Fort Worth detectives whom Machine Gun Kelly's wife, Kathryn, had tried to recruit but who took their information to the Justice Department instead). When Hoover's men tracked George Barnes, alias Kelly, to a Memphis rooming house on September 26, he supposedly threw up his hands and begged, "Don't shoot, G-men! Don't shoot."

Criminals had long referred to government agents as "the Gs," but according to FBI legend, the term was coined by Kelly, whose own version of his capture was much less interesting. In slightly differing accounts, he was going to or from the bathroom in his pajamas, and when confronted by heavily armed agents he only grinned dejectedly and said, "Okay, boys, I've been waiting for you all night."

Throughout Prohibition the focus of national attention had been on city bootlegging gangs which had (or were given) names, had organized to the extent that they had "members" and usually payrolls, battled over turf, and in a perverse way provided relatively safe and profitable "day jobs" for gunmen, burglars, robbers, and safecrackers. Capone was correct in warning that a serious clampdown on his Outfit would put thousands of common criminals out of work, and they would revert to street crime. Making Al Capone director of public safety would have been going too far, even if police and gangsters already had an unspoken agreement in certain areas of crime control. Or non-control, depending on the crime. And while J. Edgar Hoover would have loudly objected to any such arrangement, he did not want his G-men getting tangled up in organized crime. For several reasons.

Hoover's chief personal and professional adversary in Washington was Harry Anslinger, head of the Treasury Department's Bureau of Narcotics, who attributed all organized crime to the "Mafia." It was partly a matter of semantics. Hoover scoffed at the idea of nationally organized crime, or an American Mafia, by which Anslinger actually meant "crime families," which were not always Italian or Sicilian or necessarily into drug smuggling. In fact, some "families" objected to drug dealing, leading to underworld disputes.

The criminality Hoover failed to address—many believe deliberately—was racketeering in its much broader sense, which began to flourish in the 1930s without resort to bombs or public shootings, becoming nationally and effectively organized over the next thirty years. Anslinger simply didn't have a well-oiled public relations machine and a Communist Menace to keep him and his successors continually in the headlines. Hoover adamantly refused to acknowledge the very existence of organized crime until Senate hearings began to put him on the spot in the 1950s, complete with a New York State Police discovery in 1957 of a meeting of top mobsters from all over the country in the rural community of Apalachin.

Hoover had a dozen reasons for dodging any criminal investigations that would have required his FBI to collaborate with other federal law enforcement agencies, or even local police, who scornfully referred to the G-men as "briefcase cops." In many ways Hoover was as vain as Al Capone in his courtship of celebrities, some of whom were embarrassingly close to the racketeers he would have had to deal with. But that Hoover did not emerge until later. As director of the FBI, his increasing prominence had to come from battling Cummings's New Deal crime wave, even if he had to create it.

Following the First World War, bank and payroll robberies were practically daily events, not just in the Midwest, with its checkerboard road system that convenienced farmers and "motorized bandits" alike, but in most parts of the country. The criminal activity simply had not been officially designated a crime wave.

No one knows if Hoover read the comic strip *Dick Tracy*, which appeared in 1931, but once he had sold the Roosevelt administration on the role he wanted his G-men to play in the War Against Crime, they became federal versions of Tracy—at least in appearance, professionalism, and scientific methods. Partly to placate states' rights opposition to Cummings's War on Crime, he stressed that the FBI would confine itself to federal offenses only, leaving enforcement of state and local laws to state and local authorities. The local agencies would soon have access to FBI training, its state-of-the-art scientific crime lab (shamelessly copied from Goddard's lab in Chicago), a new centralized fingerprint and identification branch, and the systematic collection of national crime statistics (the *Uniform Crime Report*, based on data supplied by the International Association of Chiefs of Police).

Not many of these resources were yet it place, but Hoover already was viewed (skeptically by some) as Uncle Sam's top gang-buster, whose agents might be greenhorns and prone to mistakes, but the concept was new and the public bought it.

In the absence of reliable statistics, no one can say for sure, but, paradoxically, Prohibition did seem to reduce some kinds of crime by affording the underworld another and much safer source of revenue. The trouble was that armed robbery by the "motorized bandits" had been going into newspapers instead any central record-keeping agency. When gunmen held up a bank and escaped with five thousand or twenty-five thousand dollars, the event made headlines for a day or maybe two. Unless there was a shootout and a capture, local police usually had no idea (or often the wrong idea) of which robbers had committed the crime or what do to about them, beyond asking the victims for descriptions of the gunmen, who never left their names and addresses.

During the 1920s, Harvey Bailey and whoever was with him held up probably a hundred banks before he hooked up with Kelly and was convicted of the Urschel kidnapping in 1933. Eddie Bentz and his crew hit nearly that many banks, and the Newton Brothers from Texas were credited with some eighty bank jobs before the Rondout, Illinois, train robbery led to their capture by accident and conventional detective work in 1924. German expatriate "Baron" Lamm, whose gang robbed dozens of banks with military precision for most of the decade, was finally killed in a gun battle in 1928, also in Illinois, and also eluded national notoriety.

By comparison, Floyd, Kelly, Dillinger, Nelson, Bonnie and Clyde, and the Barker-Karpis Gang *were* the crime wave of the 1930s, even when they couldn't make ends meet. But from 1933 to 1935 they transformed Hoover's "G-men" into the most publicized crime-fighting force in America.

The chief architect of the FBI's image of professionalism and invincibility was a writer named Courtney Ryley Cooper, who published an early and laudatory magazine article on the bureau that caught Hoover's eye. Cooper became Hoover's unofficial public relations manager and knew how to downplay the bureau's blunders while promoting its achievements. When not publishing pieces "by J. Edgar Hoover, as told to Courtney Ryley Cooper," he was Hoover's ghostwriter and devoted special attention to the Barker-Karpis Gang. Not only were they genuinely big-time robbers and kidnappers and the last of the crime wave's notorious desperados, but they also were potentially ruinous to the FBI's carefully cultivated image.

On January 8, 1935, an army of agents tracked part of the gang to a courtyard apartment building at 3920 North Pine Grove in Chicago and laid siege to the place. They hadn't bothered to inform the police, who received hundreds of phone calls from terrified residents fearing that some kind of gang war had broken out. When the first city cops arrived, a G-man waving federal credentials managed to avert a bloodbath, and the police joined hundreds of neighborhood spectators who also didn't know what was going on or (given the average policeman's attitude toward the feds) which side to root for.

When the smoke had cleared—some of it from teargas shells fired into the wrong apartments—the FBI performed what damage control it could in the local press, which deplored the bureau's recklessness. Byron Bolton and two women surrendered after Russell Gibson had been killed trying to fight his way down a rear fire escape wearing a bulletproof vest. The armor couldn't stop a bullet from a powerful Winchester .351 autoloader, which penetrated both the vest and its wearer before (according to some accounts) flattening against the inside of the steel backplate.

Then the FBI mobilized for an equally extravagant (if less well-attended) raid eight days later on another of the gang's hideouts, at Lake Weir Florida, near Ocala. There, newspapers reported, agents spent over four hours pouring some fifteen hundred rounds into the two-story beachfront house. Forty-five minutes after the shooting had stopped, they sent a less-than-eager Negro handyman inside to see what was left. "They's all dead," he reported. At which point the agents rushed in to discover they'd killed only two people, and one of them was somebody's mother.

This required some quick thinking by J. Edgar Hoover—and Courtney Ryley Cooper. The frumpy older woman sometimes seen traveling with the Barker brothers, but whose full name and gang involvement were uncertain, quickly became "Ma" Barker, the criminal mastermind of the Barker-Karpis Gang. In Hoover's book, *Persons in Hiding*, ghostwriter Cooper[20] wrote:

> The eyes of Arizona Clark Barker . . . always fascinated me. They were queerly direct, penetrating, hot with some strangely smoldering flame, yet withal as hypnotically cold as the muzzle of a gun.

A reader might have wondered when Hoover could ever have looked Kate (or Arrie Clark) Barker, as she was known, squarely in the eye. Cooper, however, under Hoover's name, rolled right along in his delightfully lurid first-person account, reporting that in the heat of battle the conscientious Freddie had given his "Ma" a Thompson with a one-hundred-round drum, keeping a fifty-round Tommygun for himself. (Whether Ma even did any firing is open to question, for she died from a single shot to the head, possibly put there by son Freddie himself when he knew the end was near.)

The villainization of Ma Barker was dramatically interrupted on January 23 when the *Chicago American* devoted its front page to "solving" the St. Valentine's Day Massacre—citing Byron Bolton as the story's source, some six years after the fact—and causing J. Edgar Hoover to hit the fan. It was a self-incriminating account picked up by every major newspaper in the country and, if true, could derail the federal War on Crime that had featured Cummings and Hoover since 1933.

Bolton had been in federal custody for about three weeks when the massacre story broke, so the press jumped to the conclusion that the FBI had taken up that case, because of the magnitude of the crime. It had not; the murder of civilians, even gangsters, was not a federal offense. Even bandits who killed someone could become federal *robbery* fugitives only if the payroll was federally insured, and it would take a G-man with a very good memory to even recall that Bolton was a suspect at the time. But William Randolph Hearst's *American* reported as solid fact that "Bolton has given his story in a detailed formal statement to the U.S. Government [and] it is now in Washington being studied by high officials."

Hearst's *Chicago Herald and Examiner* likewise reported on January 24 that ". . . federal officials yesterday were said to be hopeful of pinning those seven murders on Al Capone, America's original Public Enemy No. 1. This, if successful, would take Capone from Alcatraz, where he is serving eleven years for income tax evasion, and head him toward the electric chair. . . ."

These accounts, especially the thought of surrendering Capone to local authorities for a murder trial, panicked the FBI's agents in Chicago, St. Paul, and Washington. Federal confusion increased when the Chicago police tried to interview Bolton only to learn that he could not be questioned by detectives there or anywhere because the feds already had shipped him out of town to be tried for kidnapping.

Bolton had not been mentioned in the early accounts of the massacre. And after that event he had made himself scarce for not only failing to spot Moran but also for leaving evidence at his North Clark Street lookout apartment that had sent Chicago detectives straight to the family farm between Thayer and Virden, Illinois. When he did resurface, his sponsor and protector, Fred Goetz, alias Shotgun George Zeigler, another massacre suspect, had hooked him up with the Barker-Karpis Gang, whose subsequent kidnappings had made Bolton a federal fugitive and a greater risk to the mob.

On March 9, 1934, less than two months after the Edward Bremer kidnapping, Goetz (formerly a Capone gunman then working with the Barkers) had been shotgunned to eternity coming out of the

Minerva Restaurant in Cicero, possibly because of his role in the massacre and presumably by Syndicate killers controlled by Frank Nitti, who was slamming the door on the outlaw community.

The *American*'s story of January 23, 1935, was quickly picked up by other papers and wire services, which reported that Bolton had been whisked to St. Paul, where readers assumed that he was spilling his guts about the wipeout of the Moran gang in 1929. This only sowed more confusion among his captors, and teletype, telegraph, and telephone messages started flying between Chicago, St. Paul, and Director Hoover. J. Edgar was demanding to know how and why a low-rent hoodlum in FBI custody was making the front page of every major paper with a self-incriminating account of a five-year-old bootlegging incident that predated the New Deal administration's War on Crime.

Unhappy bureau chiefs in those cities had to admit to their superiors in Washington that Bolton had been put through the wringer regarding every newsworthy crime *except* the massacre. So, with FBI phones ringing off their hooks, Hoover fell back on bluff and bluster and proclaimed the *American*'s story totally, absolutely, and positively false.

And that was all the Chicago office could tell the press. The War on Crime was turning into a war between rival law enforcement agencies.

It was bad enough that the FBI had been unwittingly dragged into a crime that was none of its business (or so Hoover would later insist), but the director was all the more incensed at the implication that the FBI was not sharing its massacre findings with local authorities. The embarrassing fact was that it didn't have any massacre findings; the Chicago FBI office hadn't even learned of the Bolton blockbuster until the *Chicago American*'s presses were ready to roll. And when Chicago cops quickly nabbed Claude Maddox, based on Bolton's published accusations, the refusal of the feds to release Bolton's confession—which it didn't have—forced the police to let him go.

The lame response from Chicago FBI chief D. M. Ladd was to blame Chicago police for not questioning Bolton at the time of his arrest. This only resulted in a counterattack by Detective Chief John

Sullivan, who said the feds had refused to allow police to quiz Bolton at detective headquarters; and by the time detectives agreed to question him at the federal offices in the Bankers Building, Bolton was already in St. Paul.

To newspaper editors around the country, this squabbling between the feds and the locals was puzzling and disturbing, mainly because they didn't know it also was ridiculous. There had been no confession, written or oral—at least not from Bolton, although he may have tried. The next day's accounts of the raid made it sound like federal agents had linked him to the massacre. There was no immediate follow-up, although a connection was made by some reporters, with no clear attribution.

When the big scoop came two weeks later in the Hearst newspapers, a careful reader might have spotted holes in the otherwise astounding story that turned hearsay into statements of fact. In the May 23 front-page account, after reporting that Bolton had made a "detailed formal statement to the U.S. Government," the next line read, "Meanwhile, however, he has also told it to Chicago friends and it is from them that the *Chicago American* learned the story."

Exactly how the *American* obtained its scoop of the century remains a mystery. It was a fairly garbled second- or even third-hand account that put Bolton himself in the garage with a Tommy-gun and three other machine-gunners, including Claude Maddox of the Circus Gang, who had an airtight alibi, and local racketeer Murray "the Camel" Humphries, who must have keeled over when he read the paper, for he wasn't even on the list of massacre suspects. (This presumes he was allowed newspapers in Leavenworth, where he was doing time for tax evasion.)

Naturally, other newspapers were frantically trying to pry loose information that the Justice Department seemed to have shared only with the Hearst papers. Meanwhile, Hoover was just as frantically trying to find out if his division directors had learned something from Bolton that he didn't know, or if someone had leaked information he didn't have, or if a leak had sprung from some U.S. Attorney who had talked to Bolton, or if the *American* had tapped the Chicago FBI office telephones—all the while adamantly declaring the story "bunk" without "a word of truth in it."

In an effort to preserve its "scoop," the *American* reported that the Chicago office had provided "left-handed" confirmation of the confession by its early statements denying Bolton had been questioned about the massacre—a possible loophole that could have meant he *volunteered* information. Various other papers, while picking at discrepancies in the published Bolton story, reminded readers that Justice Department officials typically had "nothing to say" in response to nearly any query about anything, leaving even its most insistent denials open to doubt.

The notorious "Dock" Barker, they learned many days later, had been quietly arrested on Surf Street the same night that the great fireworks display on Clarendon led to Bolton's capture for the same kidnapping. They also learned that about five weeks earlier, Helen Nelson was using family members to arrange her safe surrender to the G-men even as the same *Herald and Examiner* was translating a "show no mercy" instruction from Attorney General Cummings into:

'KILL WIDOW OF BABY-FACE!'
U.S. ORDERS GANG HUNTERS

Hoover instantly clamped a lid on Bolton (except for his attorney), then wondered if some lawyer had breached his wall of silence and denial. If enough pressure were brought to bear on the Justice Department's secretive ways, the confession could compel the image-conscious director to let state authorities argue that mass-murder charges would or should take precedence over kidnapping. This was a gray area in which possession might not be "nine-tenths of the law," especially if the Hearst newspapers turned public opinion against the new federalized crime control before the public understood how limited federal laws actually were.

The editor of the *American* was called down to the federal offices—a remarkable measure in itself—but refused, like a priest of his profession, to violate the sanctity of the journalistic confessional. Some newspapers, however, printed that Bolton suspected the Syndicate of providing federal agents with the tip that led to his arrest.

Response from Chicago police, the state's attorney's office, and other newspapers ran the gamut from excited acceptance of nearly every point to qualified disdain. But what worried Hoover most was speculation in many independent newspapers that any confirmation by the Justice Department could set the stage for murder trials of Capone as well as Fred Burke, who was lolling away his life sentence in a state with no death penalty.

This was an interesting time—for want of a better term—in the history of police and press relations, when each needed but distrusted the other. Reporters had to decide what was a tip, or a trick, or a leak to be taken seriously, then go with their best guess while harried editors were demanding copy for the next of several daily editions. The police dreaded reading what they had said after their carefully (or sometimes carelessly) chosen words had been crunched into the printed equivalent of sound bytes. Readers might not have known the intricacies of the process, but from long experience they knew better than to believe everything they read.

And for all his efforts to sound absolutely crystal-clear, Hoover was also a master of carefully crafted doubletalk, for the benefit of both the press and his superiors. On the day the *American* broke the massacre story, Hoover could not have accomplished much actual crime fighting, considering the amount of time he spent splitting hairs over the wording of dozens of memoranda issued from his Washington headquarters. In one memo to the St. Paul office he wrote:

> Mr. Carusi telephoned and stated that the press, in quoting my denial of Byron Bolton's connection with the above matter, seems to differ as to my conception of the same.
>
> I told him that while none of the press representatives had talked to me about it, Col. Gates had telephoned and I had absolutely denied that Byron Bolton made any statements or confessions relative to the above matter.

In a memo the next morning, also to St. Paul, Hoover wrote:

> Colonel Gates telephonically made inquiry concerning the truth of a statement carried by Universal Service to the effect that I said that I had not heard that Bolton confessed his part in the St. Valentine's Day Massacre. I stated that it was not correct; that the only comment I had made was

that Bolton said that he did not know anything about the St. Valentine's Day Massacre; and that the story appearing in the *Chicago American* concerning the matter was one hundred percent incorrect.

A translator might have distinguished between the two memos.

The telephone company was immediately called to test for any tapped lines in the Chicago office and presumably other FBI offices but none were found. A scheme thought up at the St. Paul office was to send fake messages by phone, coded to permit distinguishing the fakes, to detect any taps or leaks by that means.

While Hoover was coming up with ever craftier means of discovering how the press might be getting leads in advance of official press releases, and how to most convincingly deny Bolton's Big Story, other newspapers and wire services were alternately accepting or doubting the director's pronouncements. The *Chicago Tribune* and *The Chicago Daily News* tried to remain neutral and skeptical short of stupid, should it turn out their competition was on the right track after all. But Hoover had so many other newspapers currying favor, especially in Washington and New York, that after weeks turned into months without new revelations, Hoover's denials prevailed.

XXIV

THE CRIME NOBODY
WANTED SOLVED

AD THE PUBLIC OR HIS superiors known the aggravation the Bolton story was causing J. Edgar Hoover, his carefully culti-vated image as America's top law enforcement officer would have needed more repairing than his private public-relations machinery could have managed. Murder was viewed as a crime, period, especially mass murder, and to the legally uninformed that sounded like a job for the G-men. Few Americans or even the press understood the complex politicking and loopholing the New Deal Justice Department had needed to do to placate states'-rights advo-cates and local police even to create an FBI.

Time magazine's front cover glorified Hoover as the country's Number One crimefighter the same way it had portrayed Capone as the country's Number One criminal, and it would have been puz-zling to the average citizen if the government's top cop had dis-played no interest in solving the nation's greatest murder case. So, rather than confuse the country with a discourse on the difference between federal and state crimes, Hoover found it expedient simply to dismiss Bolton's confession as a total fabrication.

If Hoover was concerned at all about the killings, it was over the failure of his regional offices to put Bolton through the federal wringer first, if only for the sake of bragging rights. But even that would have meant turning the killers over to local authorities for prosecution. Personally, Hoover was far less interested in a six-year-old Chicago gang crime than he was in the attention the press was giving to a notorious mass murder that could derail his efforts to declare one last great victory in the War on Crime, especially when there were loose ends remaining.

The most important of those was kidnapper Alvin Karpis. His escape after a gun battle with Atlantic City police on January 20, 1935, just four days after Freddie and newly notorious Ma Barker had been killed in a hailstorm of G-bullets in Florida, the FBI was practically ignored (in Hoover's estimation) by other newspapers when the *Chicago American*'s St. Valentine's Day "scoop" appeared almost simultaneously. Hoover's flurry of memos and orders had agents in the St. Paul office scrambling to squeeze everything they could out of Bolton, even as Hoover was working day and night to flatly deny the massacre story. Bolton's FBI custodians were hampered by his relatively minor role in the Hamm and Bremer kidnappings and by his potential value as a prosecution witness, so they couldn't dangle him out a window to make him talk[21] or threaten him with life imprisonment.

Bolton knew this and no doubt was promised the minimum, short of total immunity, if he would just clear up a few questions. And that's just what he did, figuring that his account of what really happened in several major unsolved crimes would spare him a lot of federal grief in the kidnapping cases. Judging from the late date that Hoover relayed Bolton's information to Acting Attorney General Joseph B. Keenan, in the summer of 1936, after Karpis had been captured, Bolton's discussions of his criminal activities were not shared with local police agencies until or unless Hoover was ordered to do so.

Despite other services rendered (and to some extent welcomed), relations between the G-men and other authorities were never cozy, usually because federal agents weren't considered "real" cops, and the flow of information was almost always a one-way street, uphill to Washington, with Hoover giving little credit to police who had done the groundwork.[22]

When the *American* first broke the Bolton story on January 23, 1935, Hoover devoted so much effort to scotching it that he had not taken time to read his mail. Or perhaps he had forgotten what he had read. Or written, for on December 17, 1934, more than three weeks before the Bolton capture, Chicago FBI chief Melvin Purvis had forwarded to Hoover a letter from Gus Winkler's widow, Georgette, urgently requesting a secret meeting with Purvis "any time or place you may state, or be, but preferable somewhere out of Chicago." It included an appeal that he not tell anyone she was attempting to contact the FBI, and that "I know you will understand this request when you have talked to me."

Purvis immediately forwarded the letter to Hoover, who for some reason sent it to the FBI's new crime lab, which found "the typewriting could not be identified as resembling any specimens contained in the file of extortion notes and anonymous communications." Then he sent it to the Indianapolis office, and agents there were able to persuade Georgette that Purvis was so busy working up cases against all the outlaws and kidnappers in his region that he had to send them in his place.

Georgette was unaware that Purvis's starring role in the Dillinger shooting the previous summer had soured his relationship with Hoover, who by the year's end had assigned him to pointless projects that would take him out of the spotlight. She knew of Purvis through her husband and was not that fond of him when they did meet later. However, she found the Indianapolis agents sufficiently polished, polite, and professional that she started telling them about her stressful life with Gus.

She also gave them a manuscript running some 180 single-spaced pages which shed much light on the Chicago Syndicate and the major crimes Gus Winkler was either involved in or had knowledge of, including various bank and payroll robberies, kidnappings, the murder of Frankie Yale, and the St. Valentine's Day Massacre. It had been her intention to publish a book on her experiences, partly to expose Frank Nitti and take some measure of revenge against the reviving Chicago mob, but also as a warning to young women like herself who might think it exciting to take up with criminals.

Her unexciting writing style earned her a rejection slip from publisher Bobbs–Merrill, however, and she settled for a smaller Indiana house, which set the manuscript in type before reneging on the contract. Georgette provided the FBI agents with a page from the *Evansville Press* dated October 14, 1934, reporting that the unnamed publisher had even gone so far as to recall the type galleys of her prose. The only explanation given was that it was "too hot," presumably because it named Nitti, Campagna, and other active Chicago gangsters who were busily putting the "Capone" Syndicate back in order. The killing of Mayor Cermak in 1933 had ended that threat to Nitti, who found that he and the Kelly–Nash political machine which ruled Chicago for more than a decade thereafter were made for each other.

Since a number of the crimes described were of much interest to the newly empowered FBI, Georgette Winkler, who impressed the agents with her sincerity and remarkable fearlessness, became a major source of intelligence. She bristled at the term "informant," so that language was dropped. Eventually, she found a detective magazine willing to publish much of her manuscript in a five-part series during the winter of 1935-36, but as an article, it was so personal and uncorroborated that it was all but lost in the shuffle of the many new "true-crime" titles that had jumped on board the War on Crime bandwagon. Her own discussion of the St. Valentine's Day Massacre was relatively brief and woven in with other experiences, but she corrected much of the misinformation contained in the *Chicago American*'s Bolton "confession."

The paper itself had said only that its information came from Bolton's friends, and a good deal may have been lost in the translation, leading the FBI into much futile speculation as to the immediate source. It's even possible that the *American*'s scoop came as a surprise to Bolton himself and was relayed to the paper by unidentified Barker-Karpis Gang members or associates, or even a defense attorney attempting to derail the FBI's case against the Edward Bremer kidnappers.

Although Bolton was a valuable source of information, he was too small a catch to let the massacre investigation recapture the public's interest and interfere with a federal prosecution. So, while agents in St. Paul, Indianapolis, and Chicago were getting an earful from Georgette Winkler about her husband's life of crime and criminal associations, Bolton, in a new-found spirit of cooperation, was obliging the bureau with a much more elaborate account of events leading up to the massacre.

What he told agents varied considerably from the earlier newspaper report, and the record of his interrogation does not appear in the FBI's file on the massacre. However, Bolton's statements tallied closely with Georgette's accounts of the crime in her manuscript and in later conversations with G-men. In the summer of 1936, some unknown event at the Justice Department inspired Acting Attorney General Joseph Keenan to pry a boiled-down version of Bolton's massacre questioning out of Hoover.

The polite sparring began in August, involved the question of FBI jurisdiction, and finally yielded a more detailed three-page memorandum dated October 26 of that year from an unidentified agent using earlier files on the Hamm and Bremer kidnappings. A subtle blame game could be inferred from the efforts of various agents to attribute their lack of knowledge to the failure of other agents to include the information in reports on the Barker-Karpis kidnapping cases, which had nothing to do with the massacre. Thus, any failure could then be pinned on bureaucratic practices.

In the two most informative FBI memos, written in August and October, Bolton had said plenty, but none of that had been shared with the Chicago police. In the condensed versions it wasn't clear who had interrogated Bolton or when, except that the questioning probably took place in St. Paul soon after the *American*'s revelation. What later persuaded Chicago detectives that he was spilling the story as he knew it (and once Hoover shared it) was that he recalled using the name "James Martin" when he had bought one of the phony squad cars used in the massacre off the lot near the Lexington and Metropole Hotels—which was close enough to the "James Morton" reference that had sent the police on a wild goose chase to California at the time.

According to Bolton, the planning of the murders dated back to meetings in "October or November" of 1928 at a lodge owned by a man named George (probably Shotgun George Zeigler, who was called George Goetz by Georgette Winkler) at Cranberry Lake, six miles north of Couderay in northwest Wisconsin, near a hidden Capone estate. Those present were Capone himself, Gus

Winkler, Louis Campagna, Fred Burke, Goetz, and two eminent and crooked Chicago politicians, Daniel Seritella and William Pacelli. When one or the other wasn't serving as a ward alderman or member of the Illinois state legislature, Seritella had been Mayor Thompson's city sealer and the chief bribe conduit between the mob and city government.

The group had spent two or three weeks at the lodge, combining business with pleasure, a fact that could be confirmed (Bolton said) by its caretaker and the guides who took the men on hunting and fishing trips. His own job was to keep the working vacationers supplied with plenty of spaghetti.

The plan called for "Jimmy the Swede" Morand (sometimes spelled Moran) and one Jimmy McCrussen to reconnoiter the SMC garage from a flat across the street, because both knew Bugs Moran by sight and could track his comings and goings. This was probably the apartment at 2119 North Clark, which they vacated around the end of January. Bolton said he and Morand then took over the watch from a second apartment at 2127 North Clark. Maddox's Circus Café would be headquarters for the operation, but the actual shooters and drivers would harbor at the nearby residence of Rocco de Grazia awaiting the call from the lookouts.

The FBI probably left out many details, but as reported in its memos, the intention, Bolton implied, was mainly to kill Moran. No doubt this also meant killing anyone else who either resisted or might later be able to identify the shooters. But Moran's death would end his obstinacy toward the Syndicate, his threat to Capone personally, and his marriage of convenience with the equally dangerous Aiellos, who were battling Capone for control of the remodeled Sicilian Union. With no one clearly in line to replace the pugnacious Moran, and with the Aiellos still in hiding, Capone returned to Florida, leaving the project to Frank Nitti, who turned the details over to Frankie Rio.

Here the events become blurry. Nitti was more a businessman-gangster in the Torrio tradition, while Rio had been on the front lines, was personally loyal to Capone, and intended to be ready for anything. Hence, the pair of phony squad cars, one in back and one in front, and Bolton's observation that the men he saw get out of the car on North Clark Street were wearing topcoats rather than police uniforms. The uniformed men seen marching two "bootleggers" back out to their car had evidently slipped in through the back

doors, which would have had them surprising the garage's occupants all at once instead of bluffing their way into the front office and
then walking single file between several closely parked cars and
trucks. They would have disarmed the men, lined them up facing the
north wall, and opened the front door for the men with machine
guns concealed under their coats. After the shooting, they would
have walked out through the front door to create the appearance of
having made arrests, while the others left in the car at the rear.

According to Georgette Winkler, the uniformed men were Fred
Burke and Fred Goetz, and they fired the machine guns. The two
shotgun blasts into the bodies of May and Schwimmer may have
been the work of Goetz, who had come by his gangland alias of
Shotgun George Zeigler because of his practice of carrying such a
weapon, with barrels and buttstock shortened, in a golf bag—his
"twelve iron," as it were. Winkler, who was known for his driving
skills, probably stayed behind the wheel of the squad car in the
alley. Burke probably sped off more recklessly, heading south on
North Clark and passing the streetcar on the wrong side in a rush to
stash the Cadillac in the alley garage near the Circus Café.[23]

According to Georgette Winkler, Gus and Bob Carey holed up at the
Winkler house, where they soon learned from the afternoon newspapers that the man they had missed was their primary target, Bugs
Moran, whom the lookouts had mistaken for another visitor in a
heavy topcoat and hat. Without elaborating, she said the pair's principal topic was the "mistakes" that had been made. Killing seven
people firing-squad style may have been one of them, for the mass
murder was a gangland record, never before and never since
equaled—and had Moran arrived when expected, possibly with two
or three other ranking mob members who police believed were en
route, the death toll might have been ten or eleven.

Bolton's was the main blunder, not just in missing Moran but also
in leaving behind evidence that soon would link him to Capone.
That might have put him on the proverbial spot had he not fled the
state under the alias "O. B. Carter" and, through Goetz, hooked up
with the Barker-Karpis Gang—which would prove equally unwise
when their two kidnappings made him a federal fugitive. The FBI did
not comment on Bolton's initial blunder that spared Bugs Moran,

except to repeat his statement that the shooters, who did not know Moran by sight, had decided to take no chances, kill everyone, and let the coroner sort them out.

Had Moran been present, the Gusenberg brothers and Kachellek would have been a bonus, especially in the opinion of Jack McGurn, who (according to the newspaper series by ex-cop Bill Drury) was too well known to deploy on such a mission but obviously knew a plot was in the works, didn't know how long it would take word of it to reach Moran, and readied himself in advance. He no doubt welcomed the dispatching of Moran's most dangerous gunmen, who twice had failed in their attempts to kill him in 1928. Too bad about the optician and the mechanic, but nobody's perfect.

Included in Hoover's massacre summary was Bolton's claim that one of Chicago's star gangbusters, Detective Captain John Stege, also was on the Syndicate payroll, earning five thousand dollars a week. That was big bucks in 1929, and six years later Bolton had no reason to volunteer Stege's duplicity to federal agents who were pumping him for information purely to assuage Hoover's embarrassment over the *Chicago American*'s scoop.

If the accusation was true, and even if the money was more like payments than a payroll arrangement, Stege might have gotten wind of the impending meet through his own North Sider connections or even from someone at the telephone company. Moran's continuing worry about phone taps had repairmen regularly checking the lines, including a visit shortly before the massacre; so one way or another, word had to reach to killers that they could expect Moran himself that morning instead of some employees.

Moran was already suspicious of two strangers who appeared to be tailing Pete Gusenberg, and of a North Side hood who was suspected of spying for the South Siders. Nor was the garage the North Siders' headquarters, as claimed by many writers. The gang's favorite hangout at the time was the Marigold Hotel, 3750 North Broadway, where amenities included the Club Southern (or Wigwam) bar. The gang also had an office at 127 North Dearborn Street in the Loop.

For that matter, after the massacre dust had settled, the Syndicate was unusually warm in welcoming Ted Newberry as front man for Gus Winkler, who, according to his soon-to-be-widow, was being

groomed by Capone to take over Moran's North Side operations—
not Moran himself, as contemporary crime-writer Hal Andrews
later reported in a detective magazine exclusive that otherwise
depicted post-massacre developments with surprising accuracy.
Other stories describing a merging of the mobs appeared in the
weekly *Literary Digest* and *Chicago Herald and Examiner* in the
spring of 1930, but they were dead wrong about Capone's continuing control of the Syndicate that would forever bear his name and
on Moran's inclusion in it. And nobody picked up on Capone's
American Boys from St. Louis who had operated as his special-
assignment squad.

Hoover's efforts to immediately discredit Bolton's confession were
successful. Virtually every writer recounting the crime in books,
magazine articles, and newspaper features assumed that while the
increasingly celebrated director of the FBI might sometimes find it
necessary to withhold information or even bend the truth to polish
his agency's image, he would never outright lie. That took care of
the journalistic and literary communities.

Georgette Winkler's five-part series in the detective magazine
caused no ripples, nor did the brief but mainly factual account of
the massacre included in a ten-part newspaper series on
Chicago's "Gambling Murders" co-written for the *Herald-American*
(as the paper was then called) by cop-turned-columnist William
Drury in 1948. (Drury had been a detective assigned to raid gambling operations, so he and some fellow detectives must have
known this at the time, before he was turned out to pasture and
later murdered.)

But it wasn't considered history by the Justice Department six
years after the fact, to Hoover's continuing consternation. It seems
that the current Cook County state's attorney, Tom Courtney, had
read the papers as well as Hoover's denial of any Bolton confession, which the FBI had then felt obliged to obtain. Evidently,
Courtney's office already had Bolton down as a massacre suspect
and did not buy Hoover's denials that had satisfied the press at the
time. Either that, or state and local agencies had since learned

from experience that Hoover's statements were not to be taken at face value.

Many records from this period are missing, but evidently Courtney had gone over Hoover's head and asked his superiors for FBI documents relating to the massacre. In response to that, Hoover, on September 15, 1936, sent the following memorandum to Joseph Keenan, now officially the Assistant to the U.S. Attorney General:

> With reference to the request made of you some weeks ago by State's Attorney Courteney [sic] of Chicago for information in the possession of the FBI concerning the persons responsible for the St. Valentine's massacre in Chicago on February 14, 1929, you will recall that Byron Bolton had furnished us certain information relative to this matter. In discussing this matter with you, it was my understanding that you felt that this investigation should be conducted by the Bureau; that is to say, that we should proceed with the location of the various subjects who were involved in this massacre and when located and evidence gathered, then it would be time to determine the procedure to be taken relative to presenting it to State's Attorney Courteney.
>
> My purpose in bringing this again to your attention is due to the fact the federal statute penalizing unlawful flight to avoid prosecution was dated May 14, 1934, whereas the crime was committed, of course, on February 14, 1929. In memorandum received from departmental headquarters under date of June 25, 1934, the FBI was instructed that the Departmental interpretation was that this statute did not apply to past transactions but covers only actions which have been in violation of this law after it became effective. Consequently, I would appreciate being advised as to whether, in view of this interpretation, it is still believed desirable for the Bureau to proceed with an investigation of this matter. The Bureau has no objection to conducting this investigation, but my only doubt is as to our jurisdiction.
> John Edgar Hoover
> Director FBI
> Washington, DC

This was a classic Hoover memo—especially a memo to a superior—literate and scrupulously crafted to satisfy the sender's basic
query, raising only the issue of jurisdictional authority in words
carefully chosen to display a positive attitude and a willingness to
undertake the assignment if the assistant attorney general chose to
contradict the Justice Department memorandum of June 25, 1934.

Whether Hoover immediately grabbed the telephone and set
other wheels in motion is not indicated in FBI massacre records, but
a few days later he had in hand a seemingly unrelated memo from
one of his Washington assistants, E. A. Tamm, advising that Tamm
had just told another Justice Department official by telephone that
"we can see absolutely no federal violation in this situation; that
while Mr. Keenan was in the Criminal Division, we received a memorandum from him stating that no offense would come within the
provisions of the unlawful flight statute prior to the time of its
enactment. . . ."

The Tamm memo was dated September 19, 1936, and even if
Hoover had tried to get it to Keenan, as a little reminder of his
about-face on the subject, he would not have done so by waving it
under his nose or slipping it under his door. If Keenan saw the
memo at all, his response to Hoover almost a month later was not
the one the director desired.

Memorandum for Mr. J. Edgar Hoover
October 12, 1936
This will acknowledge the receipt of your memorandum of
September 15, 1936, with reference to the request of State's
Attorney of Chicago for information in the possession of
the Bureau concerning the persons responsible for the St
Valentine massacre in Chicago on February 14, 1929.
  It is noted that you call attention to the matter because
of the fact that the federal statute penalizing unlawful flight
to avoid prosecution was dated May 14, 1934, and was
approved May 18, whereas the crime in question was committed on February 14, 1929.
  In this connection you are advised that although as indicated in the memorandum under the date of June 23, 1934
addressed to you, the Department interpretation was that
the statute did not apply to past transactions, but covers
only actions which have been in violation of this law only

after it became effective, it may well be that in the circumstances presented in this case, the individuals responsible for perpetration of this crime might well have been in the state of Illinois and within its criminal jurisdiction on the date this statute was passed and may have moved from there sometime thereafter.

As a consequence, therefore, if they were still in the state of Illinois after that date, and as they are still fugitives from justice in that state, if they subsequently left it for the purpose of avoiding prosecution...they would be within the terms of the statute.

If such be the case, then there is no question but that the FBI would have investigative jurisdiction and you are so advised.

Joseph B. Keenan
Assistant to the Attorney General
Department of Justice
Washington, DC

Upon receipt of this memo, Hoover probably muttered the FBI equivalent of "Damn!" However, being "advised" was not quite the same as being instructed or ordered, just as totally ignoring a memorandum from a Justice Department superior was not the kind of patient and expert bureaucratic maneuvering that had made Hoover the national symbol of law and order. So he wrote to E. J. Connelley at the FBI office in Cleveland, Ohio, enclosing a memorandum summarizing Bolton's statements concerning the massacre but not mentioning either Keenan's "advisory" memo or State's Attorney Courtney, the original troublemaker:

To Mr E. J. Connelley, FBI Cleveland
October 27, 1926
Dear Mr. Connelley,
I am attaching hereto a copy of a memorandum prepared in the Bureau under the date of October 26, 1936 which summarizes the information contained in the Bureau files concerning the identity of the perpetrators of the St. Valentine's Day massacre. I desire that at the earliest possible date you personally call upon Commissioner Allman of the

Chicago Police Dept and furnish a copy of the memorandum to him, explaining that this is all of the information
developed during the Bureau's investigation into the facts
surrounding the perpetration of the St Valentine's Day massacre.

Please advise me fully of the results of your interview
with Commissioner Allman.

John Edgar Hoover
Director FBI
Washington DC

Why Hoover sent the letter and memo to Connelley in Cleveland
isn't known, unless it had something to do with the resignation of
Melvin Purvis, who had been Special Agent in Charge of the Chicago
FBI office. Purvis had been "reassigned" the previous year after the
John Dillinger and Pretty Boy Floyd cases had made him a national
celebrity, the one living G-man to earn personal headlines instead of
Hoover, who sent him on a series of "inspection tours" until he quit
the bureau in frustration.

When there was no satisfactory response from Cleveland's Connelley, Hoover sent him another letter repeating his request for
details of his meeting with Commissioner Allman "as soon as you
are able to arrange this conference." Which suggests that Connelley,
in Cleveland, was having problems even getting an appointment
with Allman in Chicago.

And that was that. In its New Year's Eve 1936 edition, *The Chicago
Daily News* carried a short article headlined, CONVICT BARES STORY
OF VALENTINE DAY MASSACRE, in which it reported that "A new and
revised version of the Clark Street carnage of St. Valentine's Day
seven years ago is in the hands of Chicago police officials. Police
officials, however, maintained a close-mouthed silence and decline
to discuss the report. . . ."

The newspaper mentioned Bolton as a federal prisoner following
two kidnapping convictions, but it did not mention the FBI, so the
story probably was leaked by someone in the Chicago Police
Department. The paper stated only that "This information was
recently turned over to Police Commissioner James P. Allman," but
that "police officials asserted they could not discuss it." The *Daily*

News added, for the benefit of discerning readers, "Chief of Detectives John L. Sullivan, in refusing to deny or verify the reported statement, said, 'If it were a case of any other caliber I might be disposed to discuss it. I will not discuss this case under any consideration, however.'"

So, between Georgette Winkler's manuscript written in 1934, Bolton's belated "confession" to the FBI the following year, and one installment of Bill Drury's newspaper series in 1948, the St. Valentine's Massacre was unofficially solved.

Not until certain FBI materials became available years later could it be seen how J. Edgar Hoover had successfully avoided pursuing the case by finally giving the Chicago police a legally worthless summary of Bolton's statements, seven years after the fact.

And even at that late date, the Chicago police and State's Attorney Courtney must have read Bolton's account of the massacre planning session at the lodge on Cranberry Lake in Wisconsin and noted with dismay that two of those present—besides Capone and other full-fledged gangsters—were one of Chicago's most durable aldermen, William Pacelli, already twice the state's delegate to the Republican National Convention, and Daniel Seritella, city sealer under Mayor Thompson, crony of Chicago's most illustriously corrupt police Captain Tubbo Gilbert, and whose tenure as Illinois state senator from 1931 to 1943 also include a trip to the Republican National Convention in 1936. These two powerful West Side politicians operated for years as the Chicago mob's connections with both city and state government.

By this time, Courtney himself was protecting local gambling action and turning a blind eye to any "polite" racketeering that did not involve bombs or gunfire.

It would have required no formal meeting of Chicago's police and public officials to decline any investigative assistance from the FBI, whose director had his own agenda and dreaded the prospect of tangling with the city's and Cook County's well-oiled Kelly–Nash political machine. The latter was working quite efficiently with a well-managed organized-crime syndicate whose very existence would not be acknowledged by J. Edgar Hoover until the Senate investigations of the 1950s.

When the Kelly–Nash machine grew feeble from old age and Mayor Richard J. Daley took the helm, he governed in a style that, like Hoover's, did not acknowledge a mob that had cleaned up its act enough to render it nearly invisible. Even the body count had diminished, except for the occasional parking-lot shooting or a body ripening in a car trunk. Following Daley's election in 1955, long-time Alderman "Paddy" Bauler earned himself an enduring place in local history by dancing on a table in his combination tavern and ward office, declaring, "Chicago ain't ready for reform!"

Maybe not, but the Outfit's leaders had since relocated to the western suburbs, where most of them lived in expensive homes and mansions in the style of latter-day Godfathers, leaving the Levee district and the various "bloody" wards to become or revert to urban slums.

As for the Big Fellow, whose brain wasted away at Alcatraz before his release in 1939 and death in 1947, his name is still synonymous with the Chicago Syndicate. Scarface Al Capone learned the hard way that Crime Does Not Pay—but it can be a shortcut to immortality.

POST MORTEM

This book owes much to the memoirs of Georgette Winkeler (as she spelled it), the widow of one of the massacre participants, who described her unhappy experiences as the wife of a career criminal in the hope of publishing the story as an object lesson for other misguided young women. That was her stated intention. It may also have served some deeper need to atone for her fifteen years of complicity in remaining loyal and devoted to such a man.

Confession may be good for the soul, but hers is better for the historian. It revealed a changing of the guard in Chicago's underworld in 1930, provided insider information on several major unsolved crimes, and introduced what she called the "American Boys." These included her husband Gus, Robert Carey (alias Conroy and Bob "Gimpy" Newberry), Ray Nugent, Frederick R. Burke, and Byron "Monty" Bolton, who had worked together in St. Louis but whose names and faces were unfamiliar to Chicago police. They were also unfamiliar to crime reporters and have all but eluded their roles in the murder of Frankie Yale and the St. Valentine's Day Massacre.

✍ ✍ ✍

Jack McGurn remains the massacre's mastermind, at least to most crime buffs, and the precautions he took to distance himself from the event suggest he expected as much. Unfortunately for him, his notoriety as "the professional killer who killed professional killers" (to quote historian Mark Levell) had diminished his usefulness to the Syndicate by the time Bugs Moran was targeted. Given to flashy outfits (especially light-blue suits) and a Capone loyalist during the massacre's aftermath, he found himself a celebrity hitman without an employer or protector once Capone was in prison, making Chicago safe for the World's Fair. Under Nitti he was put out to pasture in the western suburbs while trying to beat the one conviction that the feds, as a courtesy to local authorities, thought they could make stick.

His travels to Florida with Louise Rolfe led to charges of co-conspiracy in violation of the Mann Act, originally enacted in 1910 to break up interstate prostitution rings but dusted off in later years mainly to harass celebrities who offended racial sensibilities (as in the case of a black prizefighter and his white "paramour"—a favorite FBI expression of the time). Jack had since married Louise but not before he had been sentenced to two years and she to four months. The happy couple then made legal history, in a small way, by appealing their case to the U.S. Supreme Court, where their sentences were reversed. The Court held that the law, as written, could not be used to convict a woman of white-slaving herself and vacated her conviction. This eliminated McGurn's partner in the crime, and because the law does not recognize a one-person conspiracy, his conviction also had to be reversed.

Having meanwhile fallen on relatively hard times, McGurn wanted back in the Nitti-operated Syndicate, and died trying. The fact that he was ceremoniously killed in a bowling alley at 805 North Milwaukee on the seventh anniversary of the St. Valentine's Day Massacre (as the newspapers played it, although the shooters arrived shortly after midnight, making it technically February 15) led to speculation that he had threatened to blow the whistle on the massacre if not reinstated. This seemed to be supported by the fact that a comic Valentine was waiting for him at the bowling alley, not dropped on his body by the departing killers, as commonly reported. (At the risk of ruining a perfectly good story, it should be mentioned that at least three similar cards had been left at the same bowling alley for other minor hoodlum customers who had no connection with the massacre.)

Many years later, FBI wiretaps would record elder mobster Murray Humphries sentimentally recalling the murder of McGurn by his ostensible friend, Claude Maddox, and someone whose name is blacked out, presumably because he was still living at the time. Ex-cop Bill Drury says the second shooter was McGurn's former driver, Tony Accardo, who later came under bureau wiretap surveillance. Louise Rolfe made her last appearance in connection with a local tourist attraction called Capone's Chicago in the early 1990s, then a few years later died of natural causes, maintaining to the end that McGurn had never left their hotel room that fateful morning.

According to Bolton, the murders were contemplated as early as October or November 1928, and that Capone left Nitti in charge. Nitti's agenda for the Syndicate differed considerably from the Roaring Twenties that produced an increasingly flamboyant Capone, and he palmed the operation off on Frankie Rio, who was not at the planning session and who in turn left the details to Fred Goetz, allowing plenty of room for confusion—and the reckless decision to kill everybody in the garage. Possibly to distance himself from the massacre, Bolton told the FBI that the second team—James "Jimmy the Swede" Morand and Jimmy McCrussen—were the lookouts who actually called the executioners, missing Moran in the process.

Irene Goetz, as she was known to Georgette Winkler, confused the story further by later stating that she had heard one of the killers was *Ted* Newberry, unless she was confusing him with Carey, alias Conroy, alias *Robert* Newberry. If Irene had the correct Newberry, he, more than Capone, would have had good reason to leave no witnesses.

Capone's biographers understandably devote their efforts to researching his life from childbirth on, and with the benefit of hindsight (not to mention previous biographies) involve him in the murders of Colosimo in 1920, O'Banion in 1924, Weiss and McSwiggin in 1926, Yale in 1928, and the St. Valentine's Day Massacre in

1929, followed by his two imprisonments and eventual death. Such cradle-to-grave coverage creates the impression that Capone's name was familiar to Chicagoans throughout the Twenties, when in fact the first notice he acquired was after 1926, as a Cicero mobster suspected of killing the county prosecutor.

Actually, Chicagoland was so well stocked with newsworthy gangsters during the Prohibition years that Capone did not stand out from the crowd, except in police and political circles, until former Mayor Big Bill Thompson had been reelected in 1927 (ending Dever's reform administration) to conduct the greatest show on earth.

Capone's personal notoriety coincided more with the release of the massive *Illinois Crime Survey* in 1929 (which noted his virtual anonymity before the shooting of Johnny Torrio four years earlier) and his historic conviction that same year on a weapons charge in Pennsylvania (after the Atlantic City "national gangster convention," convened largely because of the massacre), followed by his picture on the cover of *Time* magazine for March 24, 1930, and Fred Pasley's biography, which was the first devoted to any individual gangster. Finally targeted by the U.S. Government's tax police, he won elevation that same year to Public Enemy Number One—the country's first, in a brilliant grandstand play by the Chicago Crime Commission.

As if to make up for their oversight, the journalistic and literary communities thereafter made Capone's name synonymous with Chicago crime. After his trip to the Atlanta penitentiary, Capone was among the first arrivals at Alcatraz, and little written about "the Rock" since then fails to name Capone as its most celebrated inmate, almost as though the new federal prison had been built specially for him. Before his release in 1939 *Look* magazine published a two-part feature fretting that he would rematerialize as a national crime czar, unaware that by this time he was financially and mentally broken, barely able to handle a fishing pole, much less the Chicago mob.

Many Americans today would only vaguely remember Frank "the Enforcer" Nitti, who quietly turned the Syndicate back into a streamlined model (as originally envisioned by Torrio) during the middle Thirties, or know about the "Untouchables" had it not been for Eliot Ness's co-author Oscar Fraley and the subsequent long-running television series, which had to feature Nitti instead of Scarface Al because of a lawsuit filed by the Capone family.

Nitti, incidentally, is the only big-time gangster to have committed suicide. After a comfortably short prison term on tax charges, he returned to lead the mob as successor to Capone for more than a decade before blundering into more tax troubles and an indictment for a movie-industry shakedown. Trainmen in the railroad yards near Nitti's home in the southwest suburb of Riverside said they saw a man walking unsteadily, apparently drunk, along their tracks on the afternoon of March 19, 1943, and to their amazement he pulled a nickel-plated revolver from his pocket and shot himself in the head. Three times. The first two bullets went through his hat and might have caused someone else to believe in divine intervention. But the despairing Nitti found his head with a third shot that did the job.

Nitti's understudy, Paul "the Waiter" Ricca, assumed control, which over the next thirty or so years was handed down more or less peacefully to a succession of mob bosses and underbosses specializing in different aspects of locally organized crime. When killings were required, the bodies usually turned up in car trunks, sometimes in the long-term parking area at O'Hare International Airport.

A spectacular exception was Sam Giancana, murdered in the basement kitchen of his expensive ranch-style home in Oak Park in 1975 with a silenced .22 pistol, a far cry from the old Tommygun. He had been recruited originally from the youthful 42 Gang by Jack McGurn and had been nabbed by police "on general principles" in the wake of the massacre but not considered a suspect.

A contemporary who survived Giancana as a mob boss was Tony Accardo, another recruit from the 42s who became McGurn's driver and who *was* suspected of involvement in the massacre. Accardo lived out his last years in a lavish *Godfather*-style home also in River Forest, where he died of surprisingly natural causes in 1992 at age eighty-six, having spent only one night in jail.

Maddox, whose Circus Café had been the launching pad for the massacre, was an American Boy mainly by virtue of his St. Louis origins, and his effectiveness in union racketeering spared him Gus Winkler's fate when Nitti began housecleaning in the early Thirties. That, plus his partnership in a quasi-legal gambling equipment firm, allowed him to rise high in the mob before his death in 1958.

With Fred Burke in prison, Bob Carey dead, and Ray Nugent vanished and presumed dead, Gus Winkler's murder[24] on October 9, 1933, eliminated the last of the American Boys. Georgette returned from his funeral in St. Louis to find their Lake Shore Drive apartment looted, and Syndicate men loyal to Nitti made it clear that she would not be receiving any share of her late husband's North Side holdings. When an old mobster friend she called "Schnozzle" tried to collect a cash debt she knew about, he was killed, and other supposedly close friends turned cold, hinting that any claims she tried to make on the Chez Paree or her husband's other operations would mean the same for her. Nearly broke and in despair, she made a phone call to Bonnie White, Fred Burke's legal wife who lived a few blocks away, to say good-bye—that she was going on a long trip.

It sounded like too long a trip, and Bonnie called a mutual friend in the Winkler apartment building. The woman, a Mrs. Sherman, went to Georgette's door, smelled the strong odor of gas, and called the fire department. Georgette was resuscitated on the way to a hospital, later joined a sister in Louisville, and after some further recuperation began writing her manuscript.

The women who surrendered with Byron Bolton at 3920 North Clarendon referred to him as "Andy," whom the FBI identified first as "O. B. 'Monty' Carter" and then as Bolton. Once that much was released to the press, followed two weeks later by the *American*'s mystery "scoop," Chicago newspapers jumped to the conclusion that the FBI was investigating the massacre. From their own morgue files and city detectives they knew about the shipment of guns from a Cicero apartment occupied by Winkler, Burke, and Ralph Capone to Bolton, and the finding of the empty trunk fitted for two Thompsons at the family farm near Thayer a month after the North Clark Street murders.

By this time they were so accustomed to the FBI's nondisclosure policy they wrongly assumed the bureau was interested in Bolton's role as a massacre lookout. So, for a day or two, reporters filled in many gaps, attributing their information to anonymous detectives and to unnamed "federal authorities" who, it would turn out, wanted only bank robbers and kidnappers—until Bolton's massacre confession sent J. Edgar Hoover into fits of denial.

When Fred Goetz was killed on March 21, 1934, police initially believed his slaying was the work of Syndicate men mopping up after the massacre, and that might have been the case, for his tongue had been loosening by booze or drugs or both. But according to underworld accounts, his death was payback by the Barker-Karpis Gang for his gross mismanagement of ransom money he was supposed to transmute into usable cash through gamblers in Reno. In his pocket the cops found a thousand-dollar bill that he apparently carried around as a souvenir of one crime or another.

Bugs Moran remained out of sight and out of range for better than a year after the massacre, or maybe longer. Newspapers reported him holed up in Windsor, Detroit, St. Paul, and southern Wisconsin, where he owned a summer home on Lake Como, only a hundred or so yards down a beachfront road from Hobart Hermanson's Lake Como Inn, which four years later would be Baby Face Nelson's last stop before his fatal gun battle with Hoover's G-men on the outskirts of Barrington, Illinois.

Despite newspaper and magazine reports of a great "gang merger" in 1930, an unforgiving Moran found himself busted in Waukegan for vagrancy and gun-toting a few days before his former ally Joe Aiello—who *had* thrown in the towel and was trying only to escape Chicago with his life—became a victim of machine-gun overkill on October 23. For the next few years Moran rattled around southern Wisconsin and Lake and McHenry Counties in Illinois but failed at reviving anything like his old North Side gang, although he dabbled in bootleg beer and slot machines in the Chain O' Lakes area northwest of Chicago.

In researching her excellent Dean O'Banion biography, *Guns and Roses*, Canadian author Rose Keefe talked to a former booze truck driver for the North Siders who had left the business prior to the massacre but encountered Moran three years later in a Waukegan tavern. He had never bought the idea that Moran would ask his "board of directors" to unload crates of whiskey, and while Moran did not mention what trickery had been used, he made the cryptic remark that he had just returned from "the coast," where he had taken care of Bob Carey. That name meant nothing to either the driver or to the author, but it belonged to one of the original American Boys whom New York police had (perhaps carelessly) listed as an alcohol-inspired suicide in 1932. How Moran would have known or later learned that Carey was one of the massacre gunmen is another mass-murder mystery.

At the time of the massacre, Moran had a seven-year-old-son, who recalls mainly the commotion it caused. He remembers his father mentioning a telephone call from an informant and that it, too, was the caller's last. He also remembers his father's sudden and enduring animosity toward Ted Newberry, who received too warm a welcome from his Syndicate foes soon after the massacre, leaving Rose Keefe to wonder if he might have played some role in the suspected treachery.

In any case, Moran's life of crime continued spiraling downward. For a time he robbed Syndicate handbooks as a member of the minor-league Bookie Gang, then resorted to ordinary burglaries and armed robberies. One of these finally landed him in the Ohio State Prison in 1946, and upon his release he was still looking at federal time for an earlier bank job in Ansonia, Ohio. That meant Leavenworth, where he died of lung cancer in 1957, never revealing what had led to the impromptu meeting of his top gang members whose deaths ended the Twenties with a roar.

CHRONOLOGY

1900-1967

An Overview of Chicago's Vice, Crime, and Corruption Providing the Context for the St. Valentine's Day Massacre

S hying away from any form of municipal government that might cramp their personal styles, Chicagoans vested political power in elected city commissioners called aldermen, who were loyal to the wishes or tolerance of their district's constituents. The result was a bizarre kind of democratic process so independently managed by precinct captains and ward committeemen that famous reformers could coexist with notorious vice lords, enjoy much popular support, and not get in one another's way.

YEARS BEFORE PROHIBITION

1900

February 1 Despite 8-below-zero weather, the palatial Everleigh Club opens at 2131 South Dearborn Street by Kentucky-born sisters Ada and Minna Everleigh, adding a crown jewel to the proletarian brothels clustered in a several-block red-light district known as the Levee for its Chicago River docking facilities. The boundaries of the Levee are Archer Avenue on the north, 22nd Street on the south, North Clark Street on the west, and Wabash Avenue on the east. In the district are 119 brothels housing nearly 700 prostitutes. The South Side Levee is slowly replacing Chicago's old red-light district around Custom House Place in the south end of downtown.

William T. Stead, a London editor and anti-vice crusader, publishes *If Christ Came to Chicago*, exposing the older district, located between Van Buren and 12th Streets and from State to Pacific Streets.

February 14 In an farcical celebration of St. Valentine's Day, First Ward Alderman "Bathhouse John" Coughlin, wearing his green dress suit, leads the grand march at the annual masked ball given by the First Ward Democratic Club at the Seventh Regiment Armory on South Michigan Avenue. Alderman Michael "Hinky Dink" Kenna and a colorful assortment of politicians and office holders are honored guests.

1907

Gambling chief Mont Tennes launches his wire service over the Western Union system to provide bookie joints with instant race results from tracks across the country and Mexico.

July Explosions mark the beginning of the bombing war of 1907. Bombs explode at Mont Tennes's home, his gambling houses, and the homes of his lieutenants. Tennes controls gambling on Chicago's North Side, James O'Leary runs gambling on the South Side, and Tom McGinnis

controls gambling in the Loop. The O'Leary faction operates the steamship *City of Traverse* on Lake Michigan as a floating casino.

The bombings are the result of Tennes's attempts to take over downtown gambling. Huge profits are made daily by the hundreds of gambling parlors and bookie joints across the city, while Police Chief George Shippy insists, "There is no gambling worthy of the name in existence here at the present time."

1908

February 14 Thousands celebrate at the annual First Ward Ball, sponsored by Aldermen Hinky Dink Kenna and Bathhouse John Coughlin in the castle-like Coliseum on South Wabash Avenue. Guests, besides fearless fun-seekers, include political jobholders, madams, pimps, saloon owners, bartenders, touts, hustlers, prostitutes, and crooks who prosper in the Levee's red-light district. Hundreds of policemen keep order outside. As many as 15,000 persons attend, some coming from as far as San Francisco.

1909

Thirty-one-year-old Johnny Torrio from Brooklyn begins managing Chicago's South Side brothels that belong to his uncle, vice lord "Big Jim" Colosimo, whose cabaret on South Wabash becomes a city landmark.

February 14 The Federated Council of Churches and citizens groups succeed in suppressing the notorious First Ward Ball. Sponsors Kenna and Coughlin sarcastically protest the end of their uproarious "Ball" by staging an alcohol-free "First Ward Concert."

October 18 Evangelist and reformer Gipsy Smith leads a band of 12,000 reform-minded men and women in a protest march through the Levee and 22nd Street red-light districts.

1910

January 31 The Church Federation, composed of clergymen representing 600 congregations in Chicago, unanimously passes a resolution asking for the appointment of a municipal vice commission.

February 9 Gambling chief Mont Tennes continues to operate his racing news-wire service in direct competition with the Payne News Service. The two services provide bookie joints with up-to-the-minute race information.

June 12 Mayor Fred A. Busse strips Assistant Police Chief Herman Schuettler of power over Chicago's vice and gambling. In January 1909 Busse had assigned Schuettler, one of his few honest police officers, to "get" gambling boss Mont Tennes; Busse's action leaves enforcement to the district police captains, most serving on "recommendation" of ward aldermen and committeemen.

Wide-open gambling is soon found throughout the city.

July 1 The Chicago City Council appropriates $5,000 for the work of the newly formed Municipal Vice Commission which releases its first report in 1911, entitled "The Social Evil in Chicago."

1911

April Democrat Carter H. Harrison, Jr. succeeds Republican Fred A. Busse as mayor of Chicago and appoints John McWeeney as police chief. Word swiftly spreads that police have been instructed to confine their efforts to crimes against persons and property, and gamblers from other parts of the country swarm to Chicago.

July 11 *The Chicago Daily Socialist* reports that notorious brothel-keeper Mike "de Pike" Heitler has opened a new vice district on Carpenter Street. The paper states that Heitler has paid the police $5,000 to monopolize the district and extract a monthly tribute of $40 to $50 from each brothel-keeper.

September The Civil Service Commission, while investigating bribery charges against police officials, discovers a vice trust headed by First Ward Alderman Hinky Dink Kenna, who controls gambling from Madison Street south to 63rd Street; James "Hot Stove Jimmy" Quinn (so named because he would "steal anything but a hot stove), who controls gambling from the Chicago River north to Wilson Avenue; and B. J. "Barney" Grogan, who controls gambling on the West Side. The investigation is hampered by bombs and bribery.

October 12 Mayor Harrison orders police to crack down on vice along Michigan Avenue from 12th to 31st Streets.

October 25 Bowing to further press and public pressure, Mayor Harrison personally orders police to close the now-famous Everleigh Club ending its 11-year-run.

1912

August After a six-month European vacation, Minna and Ada Everleigh return to Chicago, purchase a home on the West Side, and seek to reopen the Everleigh Club. Ike Bloom, longtime brothel operator and link to First Ward aldermen, asks the sisters to contribute $40,000 to a fund to pay off politicians so that the Levee brothels can reopen. Bloom claims to be acting on instructions from Police Chief McWeeney, and the sisters wisely refuse.

September 25 Five "dive" owners are indicted, including A. E. Harris, First Ward Democratic precinct committeeman and "right bower" of Alderman Hinky Dink Kenna. State's Attorney John Eucell Wilson Wayman took the action based on evidence gathered by a Committee

of Fifteen. The legal action is the second victory of the committee in its drive to rid the Levee district of underage prostitutes.

September 29 Ten thousand civic, welfare, and anti-vice crusaders march through the Loop demanding a "clean Chicago."

October 2 Police raid and temporarily close the Levee red-light district around 22nd Street and Michigan Avenue.

October 4 State's Attorney Wayman obtains warrants to close 135 "dives" and brothels in the Levee.

October 29 Social activist Kate Adams reports that 200 Levee "vice resorts" are back in operation as part of a powerful vice trust whose members are Big Jim Colosimo, with Johnny Torrio, Andy Craig, and Sam Hare; Ike Bloom and Solly Friedman; Jakie Adler and Harry Hopkins; "Jew Kid" Grabiner; Harry Cusick [sic] and Jack Cusick (alias Jake Guzik); and "Dago" Frank Lewis.

November 21 Mayor Harrison orders Captain Michael Ryan, commander of the 22nd Street District, to again close the Levee; it soon re-opens.

1913

March 13 Mayor Harrison appoints Metellius L. C. Funkhouser as second deputy commissioner of police to investigate corruption. Later he will release controversial reports describing ten police districts as being "wide open."

April 17 Former State's Attorney Wayman shoots himself twice in the chest. He is found still alive in his bedroom and tells friends that the gun went off accidentally. He dies the following day.

October 24 Police Chief McWeeney resigns to protest the increasing vice-control powers given to Second Deputy Commissioner Funkhouser. Mayor Harrison names James Gleason as chief.

1914

April Levee hoodlums stab and kill an investigator assigned to Funkhouser's staff.

July 16 Fred Amart and Joseph Medill, special investigators from Inspector William Dannenberg's morals squad, raid the Turf saloon and brothel on 22nd Street despite a crowd of hecklers that includes gunman Roxy Venilo. Johnny Torrio, manager of Big Jim Colosimo's vice syndicate, had talked Venilo into leaving Montana and coming to Chicago as a mob enforcer.

Near Michigan Avenue, the investigators encounter 22nd Street District detectives John Sloop and Stanley Birns. In a gun battle, Birns is killed, Sloop is critically wounded, and Investigators Merrill and Amart are shot in the legs. Venilo is also wounded but escapes in an auto owned by brothel-keeper Maurice

Van Bever, a future associate of Brooklyn's Alphonse Capone.

July 21 The *Chicago Tribune* reports that two years after the first closing of the Levee district, three organized vice rings are still operating in the old South Side vice area. The most powerful is controlled by Colosimo, Torrio, and Van Bever; a second by Julius and Charlie Maibaum; and a third by independents, including Joe Grabiner, Harry Cusick (Jake Guzik's brother), Judy Williams, John Jordan, and the Rothchilds.

July 23 State's attorney's investigators arrest vice lords Jakie Adler and Maurice Van Bever for plotting to kill raiders operating under morals squad Chief Dannenberg. By the end of 1914, the raiders will close the Levee district again.

October 13 The city council's crime commission learns that Mont Tennes controls 71 handbooks in the city.

1915

April William Hale Thompson is elected to his first term as mayor by the biggest plurality ever registered for a Republican in Chicago, defeating Municipal Court Judge Harry Olson, a reform candidate in the Republican primary, and County Clerk Robert Sweitzer, a Democrat, in the regular election.

April 26 Mayor-elect Thompson appoints Captain Charles Healy as police chief to replace Chief James Gleason.

May 15 Republican Bill Thompson is inaugurated as mayor of Chicago; Democrat Maclay Hoyne remains state's attorney.

1916

January 14 The *Chicago Tribune* discloses that prostitutes from the closed Levee red-light district have moved to residential areas throughout Chicago and such suburbs as Cicero, Burnham, and Stickney. This is the precursor of the Torrio–Capone gambling, vice, and future bootlegging Syndicate.

August Chicago's Civil Service Commission reports that slot machines made by the Mills Manufacturing Company are operating unmolested in certain police districts, with profits divided among various politicians.

August 30 *The Chicago Daily News* publishes a list of handbooks belonging to king of bookmakers Mont Tennes, all of which are operating without police interference. The *News* asks: "Does Tennes control the police department?"

October An investigation by U.S. South District Court Judge Kenesaw Mountain Landis finds corruption and gambling flourishing in most police districts, including those captained by Morgan Collins and William Russell, both of whom will later become police commissioners.

October 13 State's Attorney Hoyne arrests Police Chief Healy on charges of malfeasance. Ten days later Healy, William Luthardt, and Charles T. Essig, all officials of the Sportsman's Club of America, are indicted for accepting graft from major gambling figures.

1917

January 11 Mayor Thompson accepts the resignation of indicted Police Chief Healy and appoints Herman Schuettler as police superintendent.

October State's Attorney Hoyne publishes a list of 75 brothels ("vice resorts") on Chicago's South and West Sides.

October 15 South Side vice lord Big Jim Colosimo and Johnny Torrio from Brooklyn purchase the Speedway Inn in Chicago's far-south suburban area and employ Jew Kid Grabiner as manager. The Speedway will be become one of the first roadhouses to attain notoriety during the coming Prohibition years.

December Congress approves a liquor-prohibition amendment to the Constitution and sends it to the state legislatures for ratification.

1918

With the death of Police Superintendent Herman Schuettler, Mayor Thompson appoints First Deputy John Alcock as acting head of the police department.

November 25 Mayor Thompson appoints John J. Garrity, former colonel in the Second Illinois Regiment, Chicago chief of police.

PROHIBITION YEARS

1919

January 1 The Chicago Association of Commerce responds to the city's increasing crime and vice problems by establishing the Chicago Crime Commission, the first in the U.S., headed by Edwin West Simms, former U.S. District Attorney and secretary of the 1910 Vice Commission of Chicago. (The crime commission's charter confines it to harmless investigative work until the late 1920s, when several CAC members anonymously organize an extra-legal action arm that becomes known as the "Secret Six.")

January 29 Nebraska becomes the 36th state (the required minimum) to ratify the 18th (Prohibition) Amendment, to be implemented jointly within one year by federal, state, and local statutory laws.

April 1 Mayor Thompson narrowly wins a second term as Chicago's mayor over Democratic County Clerk Robert M. Sweitzer, 259,000 votes to 238,206, thanks to strong support from the South Side's "Bronzeville" (black) community. Hinky Dink Kenna is easily re-elected First Ward alderman.

Spring Manhattan Brewing Company owner Charles Schaffner sells his brewery at 3901 South Emerald Avenue to South Side gang leader Johnny Torrio and brewer Joseph Stenson. Later, bootleggers Dean O'Banion, Hymie Weiss, and Maxie Eisner buy in as co-owners.

July 27-31 A race riot, sparked by a drowning, leaves 36 dead before National Guard troops are called in.

October 28 The National Prohibition Enforcement Act (Volstead Act), passed over President Woodrow Wilson's veto, defines as "alcoholic" any beverage containing more than 0.5% alcohol by volume. The law does not apply to consumers, home stockpiles of pre-Prohibition liquor, or "medicinal" spirits prescribed by physicians.

Late 1919 Colosimo vice manager Johnny Torrio hires 20-year-old Alphonse Capone, on the run from police in Brooklyn (where he had worked at Frankie Yale's Harvard Inn and received his trademark facial scars), to serve as bodyguard and all-around-man at the Four Deuces, a combination saloon, brothel, gambling parlor, and office at 2222 South Wabash Avenue.

1920

January 17 The Volstead Act becomes federal law, ironically the same day Al Capone turns 21, in most places the previously legal drinking age.

February 3 Maurice "Mossy" Enright, hoodlum and pioneer in labor union racketeering, dies from several shotgun blasts fired by men in a Chalmers sedan in front of his home at 1110 West Garfield Boulevard. The killing is the result of the fight over control of the Street Cleaners Union, and the chief suspect is "Sunny" Jim Cosmano, presumably working for union racketeer Timothy "Big Tim" Murphy. This is the first "important" murder of the 1920s.

April 20 Big Jim Colosimo marries youthful Dale Winter, singer and stage attraction at his South Wabash Café, in West Baden, Indiana. He had recently divorced his wife of many years, Victoria Moresco, who helped finance his vice operations and had been a madam at one of his most profitable brothels in the Levee.

May 11 Colosimo is shot to death in the lobby of his famous café. Police suspect Brooklyn's Frankie Yale, who is in Chicago that day "visiting" Torrio, who assumes command of Colosimo's prostitution and gambling rackets. According to the Chicago Crime Commission, this shooting is the fourth gangland slaying of 1920 and the 26th since 1919. Many years later newspaperman and playwright Charles MacArthur will report that Capone admitted the crime.

May 14 The hearse carrying the flower-bedecked coffin of "Lord of the Levee" Colosimo, passes along South Side streets followed by carloads of aldermen, judges, and public officials. Five thousand citizens line the sidewalks to marvel at the funeral procession, led by First Ward Aldermen Hinky Dink Kenna, Bathhouse John Coughlin and a thousand members of the First Ward Democratic Club. Two 20-piece bands accompany the mourners to Colosimo's place of burial at Oakwood Cemetery.

September 28 Eight Chicago White Sox players are indicted for bribery in federal court in Chicago as part of a conspiracy to "fix" the 1919 World Series, after which the team is often called the "Black Sox." New York's famous gambler and underworld financier Arnold "the Brain" Rothstein is suspected of masterminding the plot.

November 2 Circuit Court Chief Judge Robert Emmet Crowe is elected state's attorney by a 20,000-vote plurality over his Democratic opponent Michael J. Igoe. Len Small is elected governor. Both Crowe and Small are the handpicked candidates of the state's powerful Republican Party faction headed by Chicago's Mayor Thompson and political bossman Fred Ludin.

Warren G. Harding is elected president of the United States.

November 10 Mayor Thompson fires his own appointee, Police Commissioner John J. Garrity, for failing to "clean up" the police department, replacing him with 36-year-old Charles C. Fitzmorris, former newspaper office boy and fast-rising political figure.

1921

January 27 Under the alias of "Al Brown," Al Capone is charged in Criminal Court with keeping slot machines and operating a whorehouse.

February 7 A bomb explodes during a political meeting for Anthony D'Andrea at 854 South Blue Island Avenue, seriously wounding five persons. D'Andrea, head of the Unione Siciliana, is running as a non-partisan candidate against John "Johnny de Pow" Powers for alderman of the 19th Ward.

February 21 Powers wins the "Bloody 19th" Ward aldermanic seat over Anthony D'Andrea by a narrow margin of 435 votes.

February 22 North Side Gang boss Dean O'Banion is accused of shooting blowhard drunk John Duffy of Philadelphia after an encounter in front of the Four Deuces. Duffy's body is later found in a snowdrift beside the road from Chicago to Joliet.

February 24 State's Attorney Robert Crowe, in a major crackdown on gambling, indicts Mont Tennes as the boss of the national racing handbook syndicate. The case goes to trial on March 27, 1922, but charges are nol-prossed for lack of evidence.

March 8 Longtime Municipal Court bailiff Paul Labriola, associate of gangsters and bootleggers, is fatally shot near his home at 843 West Congress Street, and gambler Harry Raimondi is killed in his cigar store at 910 Garibaldi Place. Labriola and Raimondi were active supporters of 19th Ward Alderman John Powers. Police suspect both murders were committed by the the Genna gang, which had supported losing candidate D'Andrea. Two months later the murder of D'Andrea allows Mike Merlo to become Unione Siciliana president.

April 14 "Al Brown" pleads guilty to slot-machine and brothel charges and is fined $150 plus $110 in court costs.

July 20 Governor Small is indicted by the Sangamon County Grand Jury on charges of embezzlement and other crimes allegedly committed when he was state treasurer.

August 3 Kenesaw Mountain Landis, major league baseball czar, bans the eight White Sox players charged with "fixing" the 1919 World Series. They are acquitted August 21 in a Federal District Court, but the story goes into sporting history as the "Black Sox Scandal."

September 25 Police Chief Charles Fitzmorris publicly deplores the discovery that half of his force is regularly involved in the illegal sale or transportation of liquor.

October *The Chicago Daily News* reveals that the Big Bill Thompson–Fred Lundin city hall political alliance is "shaking down" organized vice on the West Side.

October 29 Six squads raid Chicago gambling parlors on orders of State's Attorney Robert Crowe in a struggle with Mayor Thompson for control of the Republican Party in Cook County.

1922

March A salary dispute between contractors and workers in the building trades results in a bombing war.

April 11 Anton Cermak, a rising Democratic leader, wins the nomination for president of the County Board of Commissioners. Cermak's success is partly due to the political power he acquired as secretary of the United Societies, a local organization of saloonkeepers, beer brewers, and alcohol distillers which opposed Illinois's prohibition laws.

May 21 The Chicago City Council votes against any expenditures to enforce the Prohibition Law.

June 24 After months of legal battling, Governor Small is acquitted of charges filed against him as state treasurer.

August Using the authority of his office to fight prostitution in Chicago, Coroner Herman Bundesen orders a quarantine, with placards placed on brothels where venereal disease is found.

August 30 "Alfred Caponi" crashes his car into another at Randolph and Wabash Streets in downtown Chicago and is charged with drunken driving, assault with an automobile, and carrying a concealed weapon. The charges are later dropped.

November 7 Anton Cermak, former chief bailiff of the Municipal Court, is elected president of the County Board of Commissioners and remains in that office until he is elected mayor of Chicago on April 7, 1931.

1923

January Newspapers uncover a city-wide bootlegging cartel managed by Johnny Torrio.

February Vice investigators report that Chicago prostitution profits amount to $135 million a year, part of which goes to the police.

March Police Chief Charles Fitzmorris stations officers in front of 134 brothels.

April 3 Circuit Court Judge William E. Dever, a Democrat with a reputation for honesty, is elected mayor of Chicago by a plurality of 100,000 votes in a three-way race against Socialist William A. Cunnea and Republican Arthur C. Lueder after incumbent Mayor Thompson withdraws from the primary because of scandals in his administration.

Mayor Dever takes the power over prostitution and gambling away from the ward politicians and gives it to the police captains, who usually owe their jobs to the ward politicians and therefore show no inclination to enforce the laws. He replaces Police Chief Fitzmorris with Morgan A. Collins who immediately raids Torrio's Four Deuces vice emporium at 2222 South Wabash Avenue.

Spring Torrio and Capone dodge Mayor Dever's reform campaign by moving their operations to surrounding suburbs, establishing new headquarters at the Anton and Hawthorne Hotels in Cicero.

May 4 Disgusted with reckless enforcement of the Volstead Act, the New York legislature repeals its state prohibition law.

August 2 President Warren G. Harding dies in office. Vice President Calvin Coolidge succeeds to the presidency.

August 29 Prohibition agents visit the old Sieben Brewery on North Larrabee Street, charge operator George Frank with violation of the Prohibition law, and revoke the brewery's permit to make "near beer." The brewery soon resumes operation under the management of Johnny Torrio and Dean O'Banion.

September 5 Al Capone is arrested in Chicago for carrying a concealed weapon, but the case is thrown out by Municipal Court Judge O'Connell.

September 7 Jeremiah "Jerry" O'Connor, bootlegger for Spike O'Donnell's gang, is killed with a sawed-off shotgun in Joseph Kepka's saloon at 5358 South Lincoln Avenue, probably by the rival Saltis–McErlane Gang, setting off the first South Side Beer War.

September 12 Citing the O'Connor murder and the killing of two more bootleggers in the South Side Beer War, Mayor Dever orders the closing of any illegal breweries and the seizure of any beer from breweries licensed for "near beer."

September 17 Two more O'Donnell gang bootleggers are killed; Mayor Dever blisters Police Chief Collins and suspends District Commander Thomas Wolfe, whom he replaces with tough and respected Lieutenant William "Old Shoes" Schoemaker. The Beer War killings continue and include at least two police officers.

December 17 Johnny Torrio pleads guilty in federal court to violation of the Volstead Act and is fined $2,500.

1924

The press estimates there are 15 breweries and 20,000 retail outlets for the sale of beer, wine, and liquor in the city. Competition for the profits continues to fuel the beer wars.

April 1 Chicago police deputized by Circuit Court Judge Edmund K. Jarecki invade Cicero to suppress election-day violence, killing Al Capone's older brother Salvatore ("Frank") in a gun battle at 22nd Street and Cicero Avenue. All Capone-supported candidates are elected.

May 8 Independent bootlegger and hijacker Joe "Ragtime" Howard roughs up Torrio bookkeeper Jake Guzik at Heinie Jacob's tavern, 2300 South Wabash, and is shot to death by Capone.

May 10 J. Edgar Hoover becomes acting director of the U.S. Justice Department's Bureau of Investigation and is appointed director eight months later. The agency will become a division in the 1930s and be renamed the Federal Bureau of Investigation in 1935.

May 19 A special squad arrests Johnny Torrio and other top bootleggers at the Sieben Brewery, where Chicago police officers are found to be guarding a beer-loading operation. Chief Morgan Collins immediately turns Torrio over to federal authorities before friendly circuit court judges can secure his release on writs of habeas corpus.

June 30 A federal grand jury indicts four members of President Warren G. Harding's cabinet and several major business officials for bribery and conspiracy to defraud the United States in what becomes known as the Teapot Dome Scandal.

November 3 Al Capone convenes a meeting of gangsters at the Ship, his notorious gambling joint on 22nd Street in Cicero. Attending the meeting are North Side Gang leader Dean O'Banion, Frank Nitti, Frank Maritote, Hymie Weiss, Frankie Rio, and Vincent Drucci. Capone had promised a part of the gambling profits from the Ship to O'Banion, who refuses to forgive a $30,000 debt owed by Angelo Genna, leading to a revival of inter-gang warfare.

November 4 Claude Maddox escapes injury in union-related gun battle that kills gangster Anthony Kissane and mortally wounds John McCay.

State's Attorney Robert Crowe is re-elected to a second term.

November 8 Mike Merlo, respected president of the Unione Siciliana who had helped keep the peace between rival gangs, dies of cancer, and the "Battle of Chicago" begins.

November 10 Dean Charles O'Banion, politically prominent and the best-known gangster of the day, is "handshake-murdered" in his North State Street flower shop by three gunmen led by Brooklyn's Frankie Yale, who was in town for Mike Merlo's funeral. Hymie Weiss accedes to North Sider leadership vowing revenge that plunges the city into bloody gang wars culminating in the St. Valentine's Day Massacre.

November 24 Calvin Coolidge is re-elected U.S. president in a race against Democrat John E. Davis of West Virginia.

1925

January 12 Five gunmen in a dark sedan fire pistols and shotguns at Al Capone's car at 55th and State Streets, wounding his chauffeur, Sylvester Barton. Capone is not in the car but soon orders an armored Cadillac.

January 18 As a result of the Sieben Brewery raid, South Side gang boss Johnny Torrio—now called the chief of Chicago's underworld by the *Chicago Tribune*—is convicted a second time of violating the Volstead Act, fined $5000, and sentenced to nine months imprisonment, which he will serve in the safer confines of Waukegan's Lake County Jail.

January 24 Torrio, out on bond following his Volstead conviction, is seriously wounded by North Side gunmen as he and his wife arrive at their Clyde Avenue apartment.

February 14 County Board President Anton Cermak promotes passage of a bond issue for $4 million to build a new county jail at 2600 South California Avenue, replacing the old jail, popularly known as the "Bridewell," on Chicago's Near North Side. Cermak and his associates own land in the vicinity of the proposed facility.

March 7 Cicero newspaper editor Arthur St. John is beaten up for conducting a publicity war against the Syndicate's takeover of the city.

April Police Chief Morgan Collins continues his vice raids, forcing old-time Levee bosses to relocate their operations in Chicago's south suburbs.

April 10 Chicago police arrest Al Capone on a concealed-weapon charge that is later dropped.

May 16 Berwyn Congregational minister Henry C. Hoover, representing the West Suburban Ministers and Citizens Association, leads a "citizens raid" on a Syndicate gambling den at 4818 West 22nd Street in Cicero, across the street from Capone's headquarters at the Hawthorne Hotel. The raiders are driven off by hoodlums with brass knuckles and blackjacks.

May 26 Four gunmen using sawed-off shotguns kill gang leader Angelo Genna, who had succeeded Mike Merlo as head of the Unione Siciliana.

June 13 Chicago police shoot and kill gangster Michael "Mike" Genna after a high-speed car ends at 59th Street and South Western Avenue. Officers Charles Walsh and Harold Olson die, and Officer Michael Conway is badly wounded. Capone gangsters John Scalise and Albert Anselmi are captured and charged with murder. A large defense fund is raised through intimidation and murder.

Summer Federal Prohibition agents raid a schooner docked at the north end of Belmont Harbor that serves as a drinking spot for Mayor Thompson's Fish Fan's Club, an organization of Republican Party workers.

July 8 Gangster Anthony "Tony the Gent" Genna is killed and his three surviving brothers, Sam, Pete, and James, go into hiding.

August 21 A series of daylight robberies of handbooks begins with the robbery of the largest race book in the Loop, at 120 South Clark Street. Nearly 30 bookmakers, sheet writers, clerks, and customers are lined up against the wall. The robbers collect $15,000 to $25,000, but operators Mont Tennes and Jack Lynch file no police report.

September 25 The Thompson submachine gun is introduced to Chicago by Saltis–McErlane gangsters in a failed attempt to kill Edward "Spike" O'Donnell at the corner of 63rd Street and South Western Avenue. O'Donnell hits the sidewalk and the bullets riddle a large Walgreens drug store.

October After his release from jail in Waukegan, Johnny Torrio turns Syndicate affairs over to Al Capone, vacations in Europe, and settles in White Plaines, New York, as gangster emeritus. He continues to dabble in bootlegging and reportedly chairs a post-massacre organized crime convention in Atlantic City.

October 4 The Saltis–McErlane Gang fires a Thompson submachine gun into the Ragen Athletic Club at 5145 South Halsted Street, Chicago, headquarters of the Ralph Sheldon Gang. Charles Kelly is killed and Thomas Hart is mortally wounded. Kelly is the first recorded victim of gangland machine-gun fire.

November 10 Samuzzo "Samoots" Amatuna, successor to the slain Angelo Genna as head of the Unione Siciliana, is shot by two men in Isidore Paul's barbershop at 804 West Roosevelt Road. He dies three days later.

December 26 In the Adonis Social Club, an Italian mob hangout in Brooklyn, unidentified gunmen kill Irish "White Hand" gang boss Richard "Peg-Leg" Lonergan, Aaron Harms, and Cornelius "Needles" Ferry and wound James Hart. Chicago visitor Al Capone is among those arrested and released.

1926

February 9 The Saltis–McErlane Gang fires a machine gun into Martin "Buff" Costello's saloon at 4127 South Halsted Street, wounding William Wilson and John "Mitters" Foley.

February 15 Capone gangsters Charlie Carr and Charles Fischetti order three machine guns from hardware and sporting goods dealer Alex Korecek on 18th Street in the Valley neighborhood south of the Loop.

February 27 Vice President Charles Dawes, on behalf of the Chicago Better Government Association, asks the U.S. Senate for a federal investigation of crime conditions in Chicago. He cites the attendance of State's Attorney Robert Crowe at a banquet in the Morrison Hotel given by notorious bootleggers.

April 1 The Chicago Crime Commission notes that 27 gangland killings have been recorded since January 1, with no murder convictions in any of the cases.

April 17 Capone machine-gunners riddle Pearl Hruby's beauty shop at 2208 South Austin Boulevard in Cicero, wounding Pearl's gangster boyfriend, James "Fur" Sammons.

April 27 The killings of Assistant State's Attorney William McSwiggin and two members of Klondike O'Donnell's West Side bootlegging gang in front of a Cicero speakeasy create a scandal and national uproar over the use of machine guns by Chicago gangsters. These murders bring to 30 the total killed in the booze war between January and April 1926.

In the days following the McSwiggin killing, police raid more than 30 vice and gambling houses operated by the Torrio–Capone mob and other gangs in Cicero, Burnham, Stickney, Chicago Heights, Melrose Park, and other suburbs. Several coroner and grand jury investigations yield no indictments.

September 20 Several automobiles filled with North Siders led by Hymie Weiss, O'Banion's successor, pour machine-gun, shotgun, and pistol fire into the Hawthorne Hotel on 22nd Street, Capone's headquarters on Cicero's main thoroughfare. A Chicago newspaper editorial headline cries, THIS IS WAR!

October 11 Hymie Weiss and Patrick "Paddy" Murray are killed and three others wounded in front of the Chicago's Holy Name Cathedral by machine-gun and shotgun fire from an apartment window next to Dean O'Banion's North State Street flower shop. Vincent Drucci assumes leadership of the North Siders.

October 21 Al Capone holds a peace conference with Chicago gang leaders in the Morrison Hotel in downtown Chicago. Thirty gangsters, including representatives from the North Side Gang, attend and agree to a truce, which lasts only a short time.

December 28 George E. Q. Johnson is nominated to replace Edwin Olson as U.S. District Attorney for the North District of Illinois. Johnson will later become Al Capone's nemesis.

1927

March 14 Vincent Drucci fails in his attempt to kill Al Capone in Hot Springs, Arkansas.

March 16 Chicago gamblers Frank Wright, Joseph Bloom, and Rueben Cohen are machine-gunned to death in Detroit, probably by Fred "Killer" Burke on behalf of Detroit's Purple Gang.

April 4 North Side Gang leader Vincent Drucci is shot and killed by Detective Daniel Healy during a struggle in the back seat of a detective bureau squad car at Wacker Drive and North Clark Street. Leadership of the gang passes to George "Bugs" Moran.

April 5 Republican former Mayor Bill Thompson is returned to office, defeating incumbent Democrat William Dever, 512,740 votes to 429,668. Fifteen hundred revelers try to crowd onto a schooner docked in Belmont Harbor to celebrate Thompson's victory, causing it to sink. The press estimates that Al Capone contributed up to $260,000 to Thompson's campaign.

April 13 Thompson begins his third and final term as mayor of Chicago by replacing Police Chief Collins with Michael Hughes. He pays off political debts to Al Capone by giving the office of city sealer (and graft conduit) to Daniel A. Seritella, a well-known and politically connected associate of the crime syndicate.

Capone returns to the Metropole Hotel at Michigan and 23rd Street while his future headquarters in the Lexington Hotel, one block north at 22nd Street, is refurbished to his liking.

May 15 Thousands of greeters, including almost every Italian official in city, county, state, and federal government in the Chicago area and thousands of others, gather along the lakefront in Grant Park to see a squadron of seaplanes on a world tour to promote Italy. Police discreetly ask Capone to assist with crowd control, and he is one of the first to greet the flight commander.

Summer A falling-out develops between Capone and Brooklyn's Frankie Yale over liquor shipments, dog track revenues, and leadership of Chicago's Unione Siciliana. Yale supports Joe Aiello over Capone candidates, and the Aiello clan affiliates with the North Siders, now headed by Bugs Moran. Aiello offers a $50,000 bounty to anyone who kills Capone. Four out-of-town hoodlums respond and are killed, as are four local shooters. Machine Gun Jack McGurn is the Usual Suspect.

August 2 *The Chicago Daily News* reports a revival of prostitution in the Levee district with no interference from Police Chief Hughes. Notorious vice lord Dennis Cooney reportedly entertains police officials, vice officers, and district patrolmen at his Hotel Rex, 2138 South State Street, a thinly disguised whorehouse which has operated with impunity for more than 17 years regardless of political parties and reform movements.

November 9 North Side Gang enforcers Frank and Pete Gusenberg seriously wound Capone enforcer Machine Gun Jack McGurn in the McCormick Hotel's cigarstore phone booth at Rush Street and Chicago Avenue. McGurn survives serious wounds.

November 10 Aiello brothers Robert and Frank are killed in Springfield, Illinois, as a result of the feud between Al Capone and Joe Aiello for control of the Unione Siciliana.

November 22 Chicago police engage in a running gun battle with several gangsters near the home of Tony Lombardo, Capone-supported president of the Unione Siciliana, at 4442 West Washington Boulevard.

Police discover a machine-gun nest across the street.

Police arrest Al Capone for vagrancy and disorderly conduct; the charges are dropped by Judge William E. Helander.

The year ends with over 100 bombings recorded in the city.

1928

U.S. Attorney George E. Q. Johnson hires a young Eliot Ness as a federal Prohibition agent on the recommendation of Ness's brother-in-law, Alexander Jamie, also a Prohibition agent.

January 4 Capone gangsters riddle the Aiello Bros. Bakery at 473 West Division.

February 5 Al Capone and his brother Ralph are arrested in New Orleans on "suspicion" and released. Continuing his policy of avoiding Chicago during the gang war with Aiello and Moran, Capone stays on the move between various cities and his Miami estate.

March 21 Labor racketeer Joseph "Diamond Joe" Esposito, an influential leader in the Italian community and a powerful Republican politician, is slain near his home at 800 South Oakley Boulevard. Esposito had operated the Bella Napoli Café, holding lavish dinners attended by politicians, elected officials, and police commanders.

April 10 In the Republican primary, State's Attorney Robert Crowe loses his bid for a third term to Judge John A. Swanson by a margin of almost two to one. Black lawyer and political candidate Octavius C. Granady is machine-gunned to death in a wild day of sluggings, shootings, ballot-box stuffing, kidnappings, and bombings that earn it the title "Pineapple Primary." A dejected Mayor Thompson leaves for his home in Wisconsin, where he remains for the next few months.

April 22 Benjamin "Jew Ben" Newmark, former chief investigator for State's Attorney Robert Crowe, is fatally shot by a bullet fired through his bedroom window at 7316 South Merrill Avenue. When Newmark headed the state's attorney's investigations division, Crowe had referred to him and his officers as "Ali Baba and his forty thieves."

June 26 Gangster and racketeer Big Tim Murphy is machine-gunned to death in front of his home at 2525 West Morse Avenue, attracting attention to the racketeering wars.

July 1 Brooklyn crime boss Frankie Yale becomes New York's first machine-gun murder victim. In the abandoned sedan used by the killers, New York City police find a Thompson which had been purchased from gun seller Peter Von Frantzius in Chicago.

July 19 Dominick Aiello, uncle of gang leader Joe Aiello, is killed in front of his store at 928 Milton Street.

August 1 Mayor Thompson appoints Captain William F. Russell as police commissioner, replacing Michael Hughes.

August 14 *The Front Page*, a play by Chicago newspapermen Ben Hecht and Charles MacArthur, opens in New York City. Although a fictional comedy, the play tells the story of cops, gangsters, politics, corruption, and the cutthroat newspaper business in Chicago during the Roaring Twenties.

September 7 Unione Siciliana head "Tony" Lombardo and bodyguard are shot and killed by North Siders allied with the Aiello brothers before hundreds of passersby near Madison Avenue and Dearborn Street in downtown Chicago.

October 18 U.S. Treasury officials give the Special Intelligence Unit of the Internal Revenue Service permission to open a case on Al Capone for possible income tax violations.

November 6 Republicans John A. Swanson and Dr. Herman Bundesen are elected to the offices of state's attorney and coroner, respectively, easily defeating their Democratic opponents. Cook County Board President Anton Cermak loses in his bid for the U.S.

Senate, and Mayor Thompson is no longer considered a viable political power in Chicago.

Herbert Hoover is elected U.S. president over "very wet" and Catholic Al Smith.

December 5 Twenty-three Sicilian gangsters from New York, Chicago, Buffalo, Tampa, Detroit, St. Louis, and Newark are arrested by local police at a meeting in the Statler Hotel in Cleveland. Newspapers describe the event as the first meeting of the "Grand Council" of the Mafia. One item on the meeting's agenda is the war over leadership of the Chicago chapter of the Unione Siciliana.

December 8 Agents of the U.S. Treasury Department issue a report, which covers the period from the enactment of the Prohibition Law to November 1928, showing 75,307 arrests and 58,813 convictions in connection with the illegal liquor trade.

1929

The Illinois Crime Survey is released. Three years in the making, the document is a statistical and narrative review of the criminal justice systems in Illinois and Chicago. The final section, entitled "Organized Crime in Chicago," is written by John Landesco, research director of the American Institute of Criminal Law and Criminology. He reports

that as early as 1912 and even before, the business of vice in Chicago was moving into the hands of rings designed to protect their members by directing the zeal of reformers against their independent and unsyndicated rivals.

No report will ever again provide such a clear and factual account of organized crime in Chicago during its most turbulent years, and it will be largely ignored except by future scholars and historians.

January 8 Unione Siciliana head Pasqualino "Patsy" Lolordo is shot to death in his home at 1921 West North Avenue in a continuation of the War of Sicilian Succession between Capone and Moran–Aiello gangs.

February 14 The country and much of the world is shocked by the St. Valentine's Day Massacre of six Moran gangsters and their optician pal Dr. Reinhart Schwimmer.

February 15 Cook County State's Attorney John A. Swanson summons County Sheriff John Traeger and Chicago Police Commissioner William Russell with their deputies and captains to a meeting at which he "lays down the law" for a drastic cleanup of Cook County. Swanson places Assistant State's Attorneys David Stansbury, Harry Ditchburne, and Walker Butler in charge of the massacre investigation.

Major Frederick D. Silloway, head of federal Prohibition agents in

Chicago, makes national headlines by announcing that real Chicago police officers had committed the massacre. Silloway is soon transferred out of Chicago and later fired.

February 18 A local newspaper reports that a few hours after the massacre Bugs Moran checked into Evanston's St. Francis Hospital under an assumed name and has since gone into deep hiding.

February 19 Captain Schoemaker says he believes the massacre was committed by gunmen working for Al Capone to avenge the killing of Unione Siciliana boss Tony Lombardo on September 7, 1928.

February 20 James B. Cunningham, president of the Illinois Manufacturing Association, holds a meeting in the Union League Club to discuss crime conditions in Chicago. Afterward, State's Attorney Swanson, members of the Chicago Association of Commerce, and Police Commissioner Russell announce a $100,000 reward for the arrest and conviction of the St. Valentine's Day killers.

February 21 The Chicago Fire Department responds to a garage fire at the rear of 1722 North Wood Street where they discover a burning, dismantled Cadillac outfitted to look like a detective squad car. Evidence leads police to the recently closed Circus Café on North Avenue that had been operated by Capone allies Claude Maddox and Tony Capezio.

February 24 Referring to the massacre, Assistant State's Attorney Stansbury reports, "I can name 50 motives for this crime, but no one stands out as being important enough to be called the probable cause of these murders."

February 25 Stansbury reports he now believes the massacre killers are former members of the St. Louis Egan's Rats gang operating out of Maddox's Circus Café. Chicago Police Lieutenant William Cusack agrees that evidence points to the St. Louis men and the North Avenue gunmen (Maddox's gang) as the killers.

February 27 An explosion wrecks a Peerless touring car at First Avenue and Harvard Street in Maywood. Chicago police believe it to be a second phony detective car used in the alley behind the massacre garage.

Chicago police arrest Jack McGurn, their principal suspect in the massacre, and Louise Rolfe, his "blond alibi," at the Stevens Hotel, where state's attorney's investigators also have a suite.

February 28 With McGurn's arrest, Assistant State's Attorney David Stansbury announces, "The crime has been solved. There is no question about it. Two witnesses have positively identified the prisoner [McGurn] as being one of the killers. The motive for the killing is also known. We know the names of the five other slayers, and we will have them in custody soon."

March 4 Herbert C. Hoover is inaugurated as U.S. president. Later, he meets with a committee led by Frank Loesch of the Chicago Crime Commission to map out a campaign against Al Capone.

March 20 Capone appears before the federal grand jury in Chicago for questioning about bootlegging and other criminal activities in Chicago Heights.

March 30 Assistant State's Attorney Stansbury and Commissioner Russell send a message to every police agency in the United States naming Fred Burke as one of the two men who posed as policemen in the massacre, and Byron Bolton as one of the lookouts.

April 2 The state's attorney's office announces that Stansbury is turning over the massacre investigation to Assistant State's Attorneys Walker Butler and Harry Ditchburne.

April 12 Coroner Herman Bundesen holds a session of his ongoing coroner's inquest at which Major Calvin Goddard describes his testing of bullets and cartridges recovered from the massacre scene and reports that the guns used were two Thompson submachine guns and a 12-gauge shotgun. Bundesen recommends establishing a modern crime-detection laboratory in Chicago.

April 19 Bundesen reconvenes his coroner's inquest at which witness Peter Von Frantzius, operator of a gun shop at 608 West Diversey Parkway, testifies that he has sold "probably 50" machine guns to various persons, many of whom cannot be identified.

May 4 The Chicago Crime Commission accuses State's Attorney Swanson of excessive use of felony waivers—a legal process that allows the state to reduce a grand jury indictment from a felony charge to a lesser crime.

May 8 The bodies of John Scalise, Albert Anselmi, and Joe "Hop Toad" Guinta are found by police on a side road near Hammond, Indiana. Underworld rumors range from their conspiring against Capone to a peace offering from Capone for the massacre.

May 13-15 East Coast and Midwest mob chieftains meet at the President Hotel in Atlantic City, New Jersey, to find ways to arbitrate disputes short of mass murder, which is considered bad for business. The national bootlegging network has provided the foundation for a nationally organized crime syndicate.

May 16 Leaving the Atlantic City crime conference, Al Capone and his bodyguard Frankie Rio arrive in Philadelphia and submit to a prearranged arrest for carrying concealed weapons.

May 17 Capone and Rio plead guilty in expectation of three-month jail terms but instead receive the maximum of one year in the Holmesburg County Prison. Chicagoans are amazed at Philadelphia's swift justice, which makes national headlines.

July 31 Ex-convict and police character James "Bozo" Shupe is shot and killed in a gun battle that mortally wounds former court bailiff Thomas McNichols at Madison Avenue and Aberdeen Street. Shupe had purchased machine guns from dealers Frank Thompson and Peter Von Frantzius, including one that Major Goddard will later determine was used in the massacre. Shupe's death ends the possibility of calling him as a witness who might have implicated gunmen working for Capone.

Summer The massacre investigation results in no new leads or arrests.

October 6 After an eight-month search, Claude Maddox is captured by Oak Park police near his home in that western suburb, but he is released after establishing that he was in police court at 11th and State Streets at the time of the massacre.

October 8 Ralph Capone is arrested at the Chicago Stadium by IRS Special Investigations Unit agent Clarence Converse and a deputy U.S. marshal for a preliminary hearing on tax charges.

October 29 After years of unprecedented growth, the stock market fal-ters and on this day crashes in what becomes known as "Black Tuesday," the first major event of America's Great Depression.

December 2 Massacre charges against Machine Gun Jack McGurn are dismissed for lack of evidence.

December 14 St. Joseph, Michigan, police officer Charles Skelly is shot and killed by a motorist leaving the scene of a minor auto accident. The killer escapes, but police identify him as Fred Burke, their one solid suspect in the St. Valentine's Day Massacre.

December 23 After testing by Calvin Goddard establishes that two machine guns seized at Burke's home were used in the massacre, Assistant State's Attorney Harry Ditchburne and newly hired State's Attorney's Chief Investigator Pat Roche indict Burke and issue a murder warrant.

1930

January 17 New York City Police Commissioner Whalen announces that, based on more tests by Major Goddard, one of the machine guns used in the massacre was also used to kill gang leader Frankie Yale in Brooklyn on July 1, 1928.

February 8 Colonel Robert Isham Randolph announces the formation of the Secret Six, which becomes a privately funded, extralegal action arm of the Chicago Association of

Commerce headed by Alexander G. Jamie, who takes a leave of absence from his work as chief special agent of the Chicago's Prohibition Unit.

March 17 Al Capone and bodyguard Frankie Rio complete their one-year prison sentences in Pennsylvania.

April 24 The Chicago Crime Commission issues its first "Public Enemies" list, with Al Capone as Public Enemy Number One.

May 29 State's attorney's prosecutors indict Edward J. Kelly, chief engineer of the Metropolitan Sanitary District, in their continuing investigation of graft and corruption. The indictment is later dismissed.

June 1 Joe Bertsche, Sam Peller, and Michael Quirk, three Capone-affiliated gangsters are killed and two others wounded by machine-gun fire while dining at a waterfront hotel in Fox Lake, Illinois. Newspapers report the Fox Lake Massacre as a resumption of warfare between Capone and Moran, but evidence eventually points to Verne Miller, an independent gangster and outlaw avenging a murdered friend.

June 9 A lone gunman shoots and kills *Chicago Tribune* police reporter Alfred "Jake" Lingle in the pedestrian underpass at Randolph Street and Michigan Avenue. Police Commissioner Russell says, "His work brought him into contact with the highest and the lowest, and to my personal knowledge he was trusted by everyone who knew him. He led a clean and honorable life and was deserving of all the confidence placed in him."

June 12 Federal prohibition agents led by Alexander Jamie and Eliot Ness raid a Capone brewery at 2108 South Wabash Avenue where they seize 50,000 gallons of beer, 150,000 gallons of mash, and two trucks.

Mid-June The public outcry over the shooting of Jake Lingle and the city council's announced intention to investigate police corruption leads Mayor Thompson to fire Commissioner William Russell. Before the mayor can take action, the commissioner returns himself to the rank of captain in command of the Kensington District and also returns Deputy Commissioner John Stege to the rank of captain in command of the Irving Park District. Upon Russell's resignation, Deputy Commissioner John Alcock becomes acting police commissioner.

June 30 Machine-gun salesman Frank V. Thompson is shot in the chest but refuses to reveal who shot him or why.

August 1 Moran–Aiello gangster Jack Zuta is cut down by machine-gun fire on the dance floor of a summer resort near Delafield, Wisconsin, where he had been hiding.

August 14 On a tip that Bugs Moran had established a local headquarters there, St. Paul police find three bodies by a road near Wildwood Amusement Park and mistakenly identify one of them as Moran.

August 23 In the continuing federal attack on Al Capone, agents close his dog tracks seize many of his stills.

September 16 Municipal Court Judge John H. Lyle signs 26 vagrancy warrants against the men named public enemies by the Chicago Crime Commission. Lyle will shortly announce his candidacy for mayor.

September 25 Federal agents seize Harry and Sam Guzik, brothers of Jake Guzik, for income tax evasion.

September 30 Capone is arrested in connection with the August 1 slaying of mobster Jack Zuta.

Jake Guzik is arrested by federal agents and charged with income tax evasion.

October 23 Joe Aiello is killed in the crossfire from two machine-gun nests outside 205 Kolmar Avenue, the apartment building where he had been in hiding.

October 31 While working up their case against Al Capone, Internal Revenue agents arrest Frank Nitti on similar charges of income tax evasion.

December 20 In a pre-agreed deal between the U.S. District Attorney's office and defense lawyers, Nitti pleads guilty to tax law violations and is sentenced to Leavenworth and fined $10,000.

December 26 Municipal Court Judge John H. Lyle, a foe of Chicago gangsters and exponent of good government, announces his candidacy for mayor of Chicago. Lyle is running on the Republican ticket against Mayor William Thompson and City Alderman Arthur F. Albert. On the Democratic side is County Board President Anton Cermak. Lyle had been Cermak's principal rival when they both served on the city council during their aldermanic days.

1931

January 8 State's Attorney's Chief Investigator Pat Roche names Leo Brothers as the slayer of *Chicago Tribune* reporter Jake Lingle.

January 19 After nearly two years of study, the National Commission on Law Enforcement and Observance, appointed by President Herbert Hoover in response to a national concern about crime and disorder, returns a report. Headed by U.S. Attorney General George Wickersham and popularly called the Wickersham Commission, it recommends sweeping changes in law enforcement, revision but not repeal of Prohibition, and is seen by both wets and drys as a great equivocation. It, too, is filed away for future scholars to cite in their papers.

February 15 Judge John Lyle publicly denounces the rule over Chicago by Mayor Thompson and Al Capone.

February 24 Mayor Thompson defeats Judge Lyle and Alderman Albert in the Republican primary. Cermak defeats John B. Voney in the Democratic mayoral primary.

February 25 Chicago police arrest Al Capone for vagrancy. He is released on bond and the charge is dropped on April 3, 1931. Imaginative use of vagrancy laws against wealthy gangsters, instituted by Judge Lyle, faces legal challenges in court.

March 26 Fred Burke is captured near Green City, Missouri, and turned over to Michigan authorities for trial in the murder of Officer Skelly. Other states with outstanding warrants defer to Michigan, and no serious effort is made to extradite him as chief suspect in the St. Valentine's Day Massacre.

March 31 The federal grand jury in Chicago returns a secret indictment charging Al Capone with evading income taxes for 1924.

April 2 St. Louis gangster Leo Brothers is convicted in Cook County Criminal Court of murdering *Chicago Tribune* newspaperman Jake Lingle and receives 14 years. Lingle has since been found to be more gangster than martyr, to the *Tribune*'s embarrassment. (At least one juror later complains he was intimidated into finding Brothers guilty.)

April 7 Democratic boss and County Board President Anton Cermak is elected the 35th mayor of Chicago, defeating Republican incumbent Thompson by 194,267 votes. Cermak, born in Czechoslovakia, becomes Chicago's first foreign-born mayor, and his victory is a political milestone that opens the long era of Democratic domination of city government.

June 5 The federal grand jury in Chicago indicts Al Capone on 22 counts of tax evasion for the years 1925 through 1929.

June 30 Machine Gun Jack McGurn is sentenced for two years for violating the Mann Act, a conviction he and Louise Rolfe successfully appeal to the U.S. Supreme Court.

July 29 Chicago police and newspapers, still unaware that Frank Nitti is directing the Syndicate, expect the return of Johnny Torrio from New York, or a battle between old Levee boss Dennis Cooney and Capone's bodyguard Frankie Rio for control of the Chicago Syndicate.

August 1 The Chicago Crime Commission issues a second list of Public Enemies which still does not include Frank Nitti.

August 6 Gus Winkler is injured in an auto accident near St. Joseph, Michigan. Although Winkler now controls North Side gambling for the Syndicate, he makes news when he is wrongly identified as a participant in a million-dollar bank robbery. Al Capone puts up Winkler's bond, and Winkler, who knows the robbers, buys back the loot and returns it to the Secret Six to free himself of charges.

August 17 Rumors circulate that Ray Nugent has been "bumped off." His body is never found.

September 9 Al Capone, accompanied by his son, Albert "Sonny" Capone, attends a Cubs-White Sox benefit game at Comiskey Park. Seated in the front row with Capone is Illinois state Senator (later U.S. Congressman) Roland Libonati. Cubs catcher Gabby Hartnett is memorialized that day in a newspaper photo signing a ball for Sonny.

October Since the Wall Street Crash in 1929, 500 banks have closed.

October 1 Mayor Cermak appoints Captain James P. Allman as police commissioner, with the tacit understanding that the city's policy toward gambling will be again be determined by political leaders (ward committeemen and aldermen) rather than district captains, so there is little change in enforcement practices.

October 18 A federal jury finds Al Capone guilty on five charges of income tax evasion and failure to file tax returns on income derived from his bootlegging, gambling, and vice empire.

October 24 Federal district Judge James Wilkerson sentences Capone to 11 years in the Atlanta penitentiary, assessing fines of $50,000 and court costs of $30,000.

November 3 Al Capone's brother Ralph "Bottles" Capone begins a three-year sentence for income tax evasion.

November 17 Coroner Herman Bundesen closes his inquest into the massacre with the comment, "All who were under suspicion are now dead save one, and he (Fred Burke) has received a life penitentiary sentence." The final report reads, "The killings were by persons unknown."

1932

March 24 Frank Nitti is released from Leavenworth and returns as head of the Syndicate.

April 19 Chicago police arrest New York mob leaders Charles "Lucky" Luciano and Meyer Lansky outside the Congress Hotel, along with Chicago Syndicate leaders Rocco Fischetti and Paul "the Waiter" Ricca, an early event in the history of nationally organized crime.

October 25 Colonel Randolph, head of the Secret Six, charges that State's Attorney Swanson's campaign for reelection has been heavily financed by Cook County saloon-keepers and endorses his opponent, Thomas J. Courtney.

November 8 Swanson loses to Courtney, who later appoints notoriously corrupt Captain Daniel "Tubbo" Gilbert as his chief investigator.

Democrat Franklin Delano Roosevelt is elected U.S. president in a landslide defeat of Republican Herbert Hoover.

December 6 Congress passes a resolution to repeal the 18th Amendment.

December 19 Detective Harry Lang and police officers Harry Miller, Chris Callahan, and Michael Shannon raid the Chicago Syndicate's Loop headquarters at 221 North LaSalle Street. Frank Nitti is shot by Lang and seriously wounded.

1933

January 7 Former Moran gang mobster Edward "Ted" Newberry, now front man for Gus Winkler's North Side gambling operations, is found shot to death outside Chesterton, Indiana. Newberry, loyal to Winkler and increasingly at odds with the Syndicate, is suspected of paying $5,000 to Sergeant Lang to kill Nitti during the December 19 raid.

February Both the U.S. Senate and House of Representatives vote to submit to the state legislatures a 21st Amendment that would repeal the 18th Amendment.

February 15 Mayor Anton Cermak is mortally wounded by Giuseppe Zangara while riding with President-elect Franklin Roosevelt in Miami.

March 4 Franklin D. Roosevelt takes office as president of the United States.

March 9 In a one-day trial in Miami, Giuseppe Zangara is convicted of murdering Mayor Cermak.

March 14 Frank J. Corr is elected acting mayor of Chicago by vote of the city council.

March 20 Giuseppe Zangara is executed in Florida.

March 23 President Franklin D. Roosevelt signs the Cullen-Harrison Bill allowing the manufacture of and sale of 3.2% beer and light wines in states without their own prohibition laws.

April 6 Cook County Grand Jury indicts Chicago Police Detective Harry Lang on charges that he assaulted and intended to kill mob chief Frank Nitti after other officers fail to back up Lang's story of self-defense.

April 7 At 12:01 A.M. trucks leave their yards and begin deliveries of 3.2% beer to retail establishments.

April 13 In the city council, 24th Ward Alderman Jacob Arvey nominates and the council elects Edward Joseph Kelly to fill the unexpired term of deceased Mayor Cermak.

April 19 The Chicago Association of Commerce disbands the Secret Six following charges of vigilantism and other illegal practices.

May 27 Chicago's Century of Progress World's Fair opens on the Lake Front, raising hopes of city boosters that it will improve Chicago's gangster image. Its five-and-a-half-month run proves so popular that the exposition is extended, reopening in May 1934.

August 10 The scandal-ridden Prohibition Bureau is transferred from the Treasury Department to the Justice Department despite the misgivings of Division of Investigation Director J. Edgar Hoover.

October 9 Gus "Big Mike" Winkler is killed by shotgun blasts outside the Charles H. Weber Beer Distributing Company, 1414 West Roscoe Avenue. Police suspect the killers were sent by gang leader Frank Nitti in his campaign to take over the Capone mob. Charles Weber, a member of the Cook County Board of Commissioners, is vacationing in Florida on the day of the murder.

December 5 Utah becomes the 36th state to ratify the 21st Amendment, repealing the 18th Amendment and ending National Prohibition.

YEARS AFTER PROHIBITION

1934

August 22 Al Capone and 52 other prisoners are transferred from the federal penitentiary in Atlanta to Alcatraz in San Francisco Bay.

1935

January 23 The *Chicago American* publishes a front-page "scoop" reporting that Byron Bolton, who had been captured in a federal raid in Chicago earlier in the month, admits to being one of the St. Valentine's Day Massacre machine-gunners. FBI Director Hoover denies there is any truth to the story, the press believes him, and the story fizzles.

1936

February 15 Machine Gun Jack McGurn is shot to death in a bowling alley at 805 North Milwaukee Avenue, presumably on orders of Frank Nitti.

March 3 Anthony DeMora, who had sworn to avenge the killing of his half-brother Jack McGurn, is shot and killed at a poolroom in Little Italy.

1939

November 16 Al Capone is released from federal custody. Now in failing health, he retires to his Palm Island home in Miami.

1940

July 10 Fred Burke, serving a life sentence in a Michigan penitentiary for the murder of a St. Joseph's, Michigan, police officer, dies of natural causes. Burke was the only person named by the blue-ribbon Cook County coroner's jury as one of the St. Valentine's Day Massacre killers.

1943

March 19 Frank Nitti, Al Capone's successor, commits suicide on the day indictments are returned in New York in a movie extortion case.

1944

March 19 Three-time Chicago Mayor William Hale Thompson dies. He leaves no will, but his estate is worth about $150,000 and safe deposit boxes in his name are found to contain cash, stocks, and gold certificates worth over $2 million.

1945

September 24 John A. Swanson, the Cook County State's Attorney whose office investigated the massacre, dies on his farm at Gage's Lake in Lake County, Illinois.

1957

February 25 Bugs Moran, the intended target of the St. Valentine's Day Massacre, dies of lung cancer in Leavenworth Penitentiary while serving time for bank robbery.

1958

June 21 John Edward "Screwy" Moore, better known as Claude Maddox, dies of a heart ailment in his home at 3536 South Harlem Avenue in Berwyn.

1967

The building at 2122 North Clark Street, site of the St. Valentine's Day Massacre and later used for antique furniture storage, is torn down and eventually becomes a tree-filled side yard adjoining a retirement home.

Notes

1. Capone seems to have been the first to refer to his criminal organization as an "Outfit."

2. The Unione Siciliana had been founded in Illinois in 1895 and provided modest insurance, burial benefits, and other social services to Sicilian immigrants, who could also turn to it for help in settling personal feuds, Black Hand extortion attempts, and ordinary dealings with civil authorities. During Prohibition, however, its leadership encouraged small household stills that made "alky-cooking" a highly profitable cottage industry in Sicilian and Italian neighborhoods that were largely ignored by the "white" police and press except when violence spilled out of their respective ghettos.

3. Despite the unsanitary image this term now evokes, a bathtub with its high faucets was, in most cases, simply a convenient place to hold a bottle while diluting alcohol with tap water and adding juniper extract for flavoring.

4. Rio Burke, who had married Dominic in the Twenties, lived another 70 years, the last of them in a retirement community on

Chicago's North Side where she enjoyed entertaining local crime historians with tales of her Chicago adventures until the time of her death
in the late 1990s.

5. After his release, supported by many letters from Illinois politicians describing him as a really swell fellow, Jimmy Murray never
strayed far from the criminal community. In the early Thirties he operated the Rainbo Barbecue restaurant on the northwest corner of
Harlem and North Avenue (across the street from the Chicago city limits), with an upstairs bunking area used by John Dillinger, Baby Face
Nelson, and other outlaws of the day. He also owned a bungalow in the
Illinois village of Wauconda which served as a hideout. It was in a
house he owned on Walnut Street in suburban Wilmette that the mortally wounded Nelson died after his gun battle with federal agents at
Barrington, Illinois, on November 23, 1934. Murray helped move Nelson's body to the roadside next to St. Paul's Cemetery in Niles Center
(now Skokie), where it was found the next day.

6. A dice game devised in Chicago and played on the felt-covered
surface of a barrel-shaped contraption that a "26 girl" could wheel
from table to table in cabarets, and which barely skirted city gambling laws by paying off in chits or chips that could be exchanged for
drinks.

7. "Winkeler" was Gus's birth name, tombstone name, and the
spelling used in his wife's manuscript and most FBI documents later.
However, in newspapers stories the first e was dropped, making it
plain Winkler—a mistake he didn't bother correcting since he usually went by Rand or Michaels or some other alias. The same
spelling confusion applies to many Italian names, which tend to dif-
fer on birth, baptismal, and death certificates, as well as on tomb-
stones and in news stories. Even Dean Charles O'Banion often
appears as Dion O'Bannion—his baptismal first name plus an extra
n in his last name. Friends called him "Deanie." The goofier nick-
names that became attached to other gangsters were often (according to Capone biographer John Kobler) the late-night inventions of
Chicago Tribune reporter Jim Doherty and *Chicago Daily News*
rewrite man Clem Lane, who gave their subjects such monikers as
"Greasy Thumb," "Schemer," and "Screwy." That practice probably
accounts for Murray Humphries becoming "the Hump" in some stories, which led to "the Camel" in others. His friends, in tribute to his
hair, called him Curly.

8. Some press accounts mention one Sergeant Clarence Sweeney, but how he entered the picture is anyone's guess. His role in the massacre supposedly includes conversations with Pete Gusenberg, both at the garage and later in the hospital, where Officer James Mikes had been assigned to Gusenberg's bedside by Sergeant Loftus and where he had heard the victim's last words. However, Sweeney's name is conspicuously absent from any police reports, which describe the killings in detail and the visit to the hospital by Sergeant Loftus and Officer Mikes. By the second day Sweeney had insinuated himself into the case enough to convince some newsmen and latter-day writers that he, rather than Loftus, had heard much of what Loftus reported.

9. In a personal interview by one of the co-authors some 50 years later, Dr. Tacker, retired and living in San Antonio, Texas, recalled his experience vividly, still wondering what bearing it had on the massacre, which took place about an hour later. After reading about the getaway car driver with a missing tooth, and weighing his good-citizen options, he decided to report the incident to police, who asked him to look at some mug shots. He didn't recognize his patient, but that's not what appeared in the newspapers. Some reported Captain Egan announcing that the dentist had picked out the photo of a "notorious killer," and "We happen to know ourselves that he was in the car that left the North Clark Street garage."

Before that appeared in print, Tacker had returned home to his apartment in the Sheridan-Surf Hotel at 425 Surf Street, near Clark, about 1 P.M., and described his interesting squad room experience to his wife of nine months, who was soon expecting their first child. A week later the phony squad car had exploded in the garage near the Circus Café, and that same evening about seven, while he was walking down nearby Hampden Court, Tacker was jumped by two men who knocked him senseless. The next thing he knew, at least two hours later, he was lying on the back floorboard of a large touring car, gagged, hurriedly blindfolded, and bound hand and foot. He guessed that the drive lasted all night, and once or twice the men who had grabbed him stopped at roadside cafés, presumably for coffee—and possibly to make phone calls. Although trussed up and bloody from head blows, Tacker could tell that his pockets had been emptied and his clothes were in disarray. This, he thought, was not a good sign.

When the dentist didn't return from his usual evening walk, his wife called friends and relatives, fearing that he'd had an accident. But

Tacker didn't turn up in a local hospital, the morgue, a friend's place, or even a tavern, so a cousin went to the Sheffield Avenue police station at 4:30 in the morning to report that Tacker had disappeared and his family now feared he'd been kidnapped. The cops started making the standard inquiries and also turned up nothing.

About sunrise on Saturday, February 23, Tacker could tell that the car was entering a large city, but he had no idea which one until his abductors, without explanation, cut the ropes from his hands and feet and pushed him out into a gutter. He removed the gag and blindfold and crawled onto the sidewalk, trying to clear his head. There were tall buildings nearby, and the first clue to his location was a large painted sign on side of one of them advertising *The Detroit Free Press*.

He managed to get to his feet and was limping in that direction when he encountered a policeman at the corner looking at him with great curiosity. The officer must have wondered if the disheveled man had spent one hell of a night on the town, or if he was incoherently babbling the truth. The next thing Tacker remembered with any clarity was being surrounded by cops in a Detroit police station, trying to answer questions. All he could tell them was that his abductors were "big men" (to a man who stood just five-five and weighed maybe 120 pounds, most men seemed big), and that he thought the car was a Peerless. Police first aid consisted of some basic bandaging of Tacker's head wounds and a lot of coffee.

Detroit had already called Chicago to check on missing dentists. That was confirmed, and an alert police reporter reached the Tacker residence even before the Chicago cops. The door was answered by Mrs. Tacker's aunt, a Mrs. Gavin, who said her niece was under the care of a nurse and couldn't talk to the press. The reporter told her that Dr. Tacker had been found by the Detroit police and was safe. Mrs. Gavin ran to the bedroom, and from there he heard the young wife cry out, "Thank God! Thank God! I thought he would be killed!"

Tacker had been thinking the same thing, especially after discovering that all identifying labels had been cut or torn from his clothing. He spoke to his wife on the phone and was anxious to get home by bus or any other means, but the Detroit police said no. They told him that the minute he showed up in Chicago he'd be arrested and, if not charged with masterminding the massacre, at least held as a material witness or just locked up until they could decide on some grounds on which to hold him. For the Chicago cops were still on a rampage, nabbing anyone they could for any reason they could think of—except the headline hoods they were looking for. In the two weeks following the North Clark Street slaughter, police had rounded up more than 200 people, probably none of whom knew any more about the North Clark Street slaughter than what they had read in the newspapers.

Detroit police assigned two detectives to drive Tacker back to Chicago, confirm his story, and fend off any attempts to take him into custody—which may not have been necessary after all. With Tacker's safe return, Captain Egan backpeddled and said that the dentist, alas, had been mistaken, that the man he'd identified from the mug shots had been in jail the day of the massacre. At least one reporter took that to mean that Egan was trying to get Tacker off the hook as a potentially incriminating (and soon dead) witness.

The whole episode did not make sense. If the man Tacker pointed out in the mug-shot book was in fact the notorious Fred "Killer" Burke, why would Burke be going to a dentist near the garage an hour before the massacre? (Probably by coincidence, one of the Gusenbergs had called his wife that morning and asked her to cancel a dental appointment.) And why was Tacker still alive, if his attackers had gone to the trouble of making him as hard to identify as possible? The dentist never figured that out, although it's possible one of the late-night coffee stops had included a phone call to someone in Chicago who countermanded the "one-way ride" order, possibly on the grounds that they didn't need any dead dentists (like their dead optician) to keep the cops in an uproar. Why Tacker was taken to Detroit is another mystery, unless it had something to do with gangsters dumping odd bodies out of state, in Michigan or Indiana, as a favor to their friends on the Chicago police force.

10. Corruption was so rampant in the Chicago Police Department that the new crime lab was established at the Northwestern University Law School. It began operations in July 1929, first in a empty office at 469 West Superior Street and later moving to larger quarters at 222 East Superior. Its initial project was an investigation of the massacre, and one of Goddard's early discoveries was that some of the slugs from the victims matched those taken from the body of New York's Frankie Yale, confirming to the satisfaction of New York police that at least one of the guns was used in both cases.

The two massacre guns were discovered at Burke's house in Michigan in December 1929, and the case was described in the first issue of the *American Journal of Police Science*, published by the Northwestern

University Press for January-February 1930. Four-week classes in the forensic sciences began in April and May 1931, and Goddard was less than pleased when one graduate turned out to be a Department of Justice agent who had enrolled for the purpose of taking his knowledge of techniques and specially designed equipment back to Washington at the behest of J. Edgar Hoover. Eighteen months later Hoover announced, with much fanfare, the opening of what was billed as the nation's first crime laboratory, without a word of credit to the lab at Northwestern. Fred Inbau joined the laboratory staff in 1932 as a law student, became Goddard's replacement, and was its director at the time it was purchased by the City of Chicago in late 1938 for $25,000. He remained at the school as a law professor into the 1990s.

11. Edward O'Hare popularized the mechanical rabbit used in dog racing, reputedly provided evidence that helped convict Al Capone of tax evasion, and was murdered in 1938. Chicago's O'Hare International Airport is named for his son "Butch," who was a highly decorated naval aviator at the time of his death in combat early in World War II.

12. In 1982 the late Al Capone was "retried" in Chicago before a legal judge and jury on the fiftieth anniversary of his conviction, using present-day rules of evidence. He was found not guilty.

13. Probably one owned by Willie Harrison, a friend of Burke and Winkler from St. Louis, who later hooked up with the Barker-Karpis Gang. Some kind of trouble led to his being shot by Dock Barker, Russell Gibson, and Byron Bolton, who left his body in a burning barn near Ontarioville, Illinois.

14. Author Dennis Hoffman writes in his booklet *Scarface Al and the Crime Crusaders* that the original Secret Six were Julius Rosenwald, chairman of the board of Sears, Roebuck and Company; Frank Loesch, president of the Chicago Crime Commission; Samuel Insull, traction and utilities magnate; Edward E. Gore; George A. Paddock, Evanston stockbroker; and Col. Robert Isham Randolph, whose connection with the group was not kept secret.

15. Contrary to nearly every reference to "Public Enemies," the FBI did not create and never used a Public Enemies list. The idea was conceived by the Chicago Crime Commission after the term *gangster* had become so overused and misused that it was little more than a cliché loosely applied to criminals ranging from bootleggers to bandits. The Public Enemy campaign was welcomed by the press as a novel

approach that rang with righteousness and conjured up an image of menace instead of glamour, which Capone was starting to acquire. However, when a national Public Enemies list was proposed to the Justice Department, the idea was flatly rejected by J. Edgar Hoover, who ingenuously reasoned that status-conscious lawbreakers would seek top billing to demonstrate their criminal accomplishments.

However, this didn't stop other cities and states from creating their own Public Enemy lists, or discourage newspapers from labeling the FBI's fugitive bank robbers and kidnappers as Public Enemies. Hoover didn't mind benefiting from such technically inaccurate publicity, but the bureau carefully avoided using that expression in its press releases and rare news conferences. Finally, in 1950, the director capitulated to the extent of creating the FBI's "Ten Most Wanted" list. The few writers who know their Public Enemy history would probably agree that Hoover turned down the Chicago Crime Commission's offer because he didn't think of it himself.

16. In a seventh-anniversary article for the February issue of *Startling Detective Stories*, a writer who seemed to have had access to Chicago detective files correctly named Winkler, Burke, Goetz and Bolton as members of the murder crew. For what it's worth, he also implied that one of killers was bank robber Harvey Bailey himself, who had claimed he was having drinks with Burke at the time of the massacre, and at whose relatives' farm in Missouri Burke had gone into hiding.

In his coauthored newspaper series, entitled "Untold Secrets of Chicago's Gambling Murders" in 1948, former Lieutenant Bill Drury, writing in the *Chicago Herald and Examiner*, names Burke, Winkler, Nugent, Goetz, and Homer "Moose" Wilson (also known as "Big Homer") as the gunmen, probably on the basis of Wilson's prior bank-robbing record with Burke and Winkler, and who may have been in Chicago at the time. However, Drury agrees with Georgette Winkler that Jack McGurn was "too hot at the time to be called into action."

17. This was New York's first, biggest, and most entertaining gun battle of the era and has been cited by earlier writers as an example of how difficult it was to ignore a ringing telephone (police had yet to add this to their communications repertoire in hostage situations). It seems that some enterprising reporter located the number for the apartment, called it, and "Two-Gun" stopped shooting to answer the phone. This in itself surprised the newsman, who could only think to

ask Crowley what he was doing. The flustered Crowley explained that he was too busy to talk just then, and hung up.

18. Some 20 years after Ray Nugent's disappearance, his fifty-one-year-old wife, Julia, filed documents in the Probate Court of Cincinnati to have him declared legally dead, hoping to collect about $1,500 in bonus and pension funds owed her and her two children by the government, based on Nugent's military service during World War I.

19. Kelly seems to have acquired his interesting nickname only after a Thompson seized from one of the other Urschel kidnappers was traced to a Fort Worth pawnshop whose owner said it had been purchased by a woman he identified as Kathryn Kelly. Every newspaper account after that called him "Machine Gun" Kelly. In *Persons in Hiding*, Hoover, or his ghostwriter Courtney Ryley Cooper, took it from there:

> "[S]he rode into the country with him [George] while he practised to become an expert, finally reaching the point where he could knock a row of walnuts from the top of a fence and at a good distance. Meanwhile, Kathryn garnered the empty cartridges, to be kept for such times as she could hand them to friends, remarking: "Here's a souvenir I brought you. It's a cartridge fired by George's machine gun—Machine Gun Kelly, you know.'"

20. In 1940 Cooper hanged himself in a New York hotel room, driven to suicide by some falling out with J. Edgar Hoover, according to his widow. Cooper had provided *American* magazine with an interminable series of "as told to" articles heaping praise on Hoover and the FBI, and after condemning tourist courts as "Camps of Crime," he was running short of ideas. He foolishly wound up the series with "as told to" articles by Harry Anslinger, Hoover's nemesis in the Narcotics Bureau who had spent most of the 1930s trying to sell the public on "nationally organized crime" and the "Mafia," which Hoover insisted did not exist. He may have had other problems, but that would have been enough to make Courtney Ryley Cooper *persona non grata* at Hoover's FBI.

A similar fate possibly befell Chicago's Special Agent in Charge Melvin Purvis, who Georgette Winkler first contacted in an effort to share her story. The publicity Purvis received in the Dillinger case angered Hoover sufficiently that he not only made life so miserable for Purvis that he resigned from the bureau in 1935, but thereafter made sure that Purvis could find no work in law enforcement, or even as a

consultant on crime movies. ("The director would like you to recon-
sider . . ." was the word passed from the bureau to prospective employers, and that was enough.) Purvis eventually found less-than-fulfilling
work as titular head of the "Melvin Purvis Junior G-Man" club for Kel-
logg's Corn Flakes, to the disgust of Hoover, who never mentioned
Purvis by name in his version of the Dillinger case that appeared in *Persons in Hiding*, ghosted by Cooper, and even deleted him from the FBI's
map of the Biograph Theatre that showed the locations of agents in the
trap set for Dillinger the night of July 22, 1934. When Purvis died of a
gunshot wound at his home in North Carolina in 1960, the FBI treated
it as a suicide, despite evidence that it was accidental.

21. While most G-men were indeed young lawyers and accountants
with no police experience, Hoover recruited a few beefy ex-cops as
point men for riskier operations and for interrogating stubborn suspects. Chicago's "Boss" McLaughlin privately raised hell at being
threatened with defenestration, as did Jack Perkins, friend of Baby
Face Nelson and John Dillinger. Perkins later withdrew his complaint
when he was acquitted of an Indiana bank robbery. That form of questioning ended after the death of James Probasco, a small, wiry 70-year-
old fellow in whose house Dillinger had undergone plastic surgery, was
ruled a suicide when he plunged 19 floors from a back window of the
FBI's offices in the Bankers Building.

Special Agent in Charge Melvin Purvis, who was in Washington at the
time, expressed sadness over the loss of "Little Jimmy Probasco," who
"in the middle of a routine inquiry . . . rose from his chair, and before
anyone could bar his way, rushed to the window and thrust himself
through." Art O'Leary (investigator for Louis Piquett, Dillinger's attorney) overheard agents discussing this privately during his own interrogation, saying that Inspector Sam Cowley was dangling a frantic
Probasco out the window by the ankles and didn't mean to lose his grip.

22. Aware of the animosity that many local and state cops felt
toward his agents, Hoover made occasional efforts to throw the police
a bone. The most significant early gesture was Hoover's support for a
pact made between several midwestern states which pooled their
reward money for the dead-or-alive capture of John Dillinger and other
outlaws during the War on Crime period. The bureau (especially if it
lacked jurisdiction in a particular crime) generously printed up and
distributed state-issued wanted posters with state police information
on the front and a nationwide list of FBI offices on the back.

After the killing of John Dillinger on July 22, 1934, Hoover found himself the unexpected recipient of a casting of one of the outlaw's death masks, made by a dental company ostensibly to demonstrate the usefulness of a rubbery compound that could be poured into tire tracks and other temporary surfaces. After discerning no ulterior motives (and probably duplicating the material for FBI use), the bureau made a mold and offered castings to any agency requesting one—and to get more mileage out of Dillinger, it came with a leftover FBI "I.O." (Identification Order).

The stunt generated so many requests for death-mask castings that Hoover soon ran out of original I.O.s, which inspired a reprint that differed mainly in changing the Washington address of the FBI from the Hurley-Wright Building to the new Justice Department headquarters, as scheduled the same summer. Eventually Hoover's casting department pleaded with him to remove the masks from the market. (Melvin Purvis's book *American Agent* indicates only one edition, but a review of some printings shows minor flaws indicating that Purvis supplied the publisher with both earlier and later I.O.s of the Dillinger photo, the only obvious difference being the FBI address on the reverse. The book lists Hoover by name once—in a list of Justice Department officials.)

23. In his 1971 biography *Capone*, the first published after Fred Pasley's in 1930, John Kobler accepts the standard hijacked-liquor story but in a last-minute footnote names the gunmen as Burke, Winkler, Zeigler (Goetz), Nugent, and Maddox. This was based on second-hand information from Alvin Karpis, recalling a conversation with Nugent, who had told him that the Capone Syndicate regularly employed this group at a collective salary of $2,000 a week plus an occasional bonus, and that the planning was done by Zeigler. In his autobiography, *On the Rock*, Karpis says he was told part of this by fellow Alcatraz inmate Al Capone.

24. The underworld grapevine eventually yielded the names of Winkler's killers to be his supposed friends Fred Goetz and Tony Capezio.

BIBLIOGRAPHY

This book is largely the product of the personal memoirs and cooperative interrogations of Georgette Winkeler (who later married Walter Marsh of Louisville, Kentucky) and the paraphrased information obtained from the Federal Bureau of Investigation, in which Byron Bolton corrected many of the mistakes that appeared in the "scoop" published in the *Chicago American* on May 23, 1935; records of the patrol division of the Chicago Police Department; and much of the coroner's jury inquest held in 1929. Other sources are books, booklets and newspapers too numerous to mention, although special attention was given to Robert J. Schoenberg's *Mr. Capone* (William Morrow, 1992); Richard C. Lindberg's *To Serve and Collect* (Praeger, 1991); Ovid Demaris's *Captive City* (Lyle Stuart, 1969); Alson J. Smith's *Syndicate City* (Regnery, 1954); Curt Johnson's *Wicked City* (December Press, 1994); Richard Gid Powers's *G-men* (Southern Illinois University, 1983); Virgil W. Peterson's *Barbarians in our Midst* (Little, Brown, 1952); Bob Skilnik's *The History of Beer and Brewing in Chicago* (Pogo, 1999); *The Illinois Crime Survey* (Illinois Association for Criminal Justice, 1929); and William Helmer's *The Gun that Made the Twenties Roar* (Macmillan, 1969) and *Public Enemies* (Facts on File/Checkmark).

INDEX